ADVANCES IN COMPUTER VISION AND IMAGE PROCESSING

Volume 3 • 1988

TIME-VARYING IMAGERY ANALYSIS

ADVANCES IN COMPUTER VISION AND IMAGE PROCESSING

A Research Annual

TIME-VARYING IMAGERY ANALYSIS

Editor: THOMAS S. HUANG
Coordinated Science Laboratory
University of Illinois

VOLUME 3 • 1988

 JAI PRESS INC.

Greenwich, Connecticut   *London, England*

CONTENTS

LIST OF CONTRIBUTORS

S. Bartlett

Department of Electrical Engineering
and Computer Science
University of Michigan

Su-shing Chen

Department of Computer Science
University of North Carolina

D. Cyganski

Department of Electrical Engineering
Worcester Polytechnic Institute

J. P. Gambotto

MATRA
France

S. Gunasekaran

Department of Electrical and Computer
Engineering
Worcester Polytechnic Institute

Ramesh Jain

Department of Electrical Engineering
and Computer Science
University of Michigan

Yann LeGuilloux

SAGEM
France

N. O'Brien

Department of Electrical Engineering
and Computer Science
University of Michigan

J. A. Orr

Department of Electrical Engineering
Worcester Polytechnic Institute

Michael Penna

Department of Computer Science
IUPUI

T. Y. Young

Department of Electrical and Computer
    Engineering
University of Miami
Coral Gables

PREFACE

The goal of this series is to present in-depth treatment of topics of current interest in computer vision and image processing. The terms computer vision and image processing are used in their broad sense to include image coding, enhancement, restoration, and understanding, as well as the analysis of three-dimensional (3D) time-varying scenes. Computer vision and image processing have important applications in diverse areas, such as robotics, industrial automation, medical diagnosis, and defense-related problems. These applications draw concepts and techniques from many different disciplines, including multidimensional signal processing, pattern recognition, and artificial intelligence. We aim to have each volume of this series concentrate on a special topic or several closely related topics.

Although in this series we publish mainly invited papers, suitable unsolicited contributions may also be published after careful reviewing. Potential contributors are advised to contact the Editor before submitting their manuscripts.

The topic of this volume is time-varying imagery analysis. Specifically, the emphasis is on the detection and tracking of moving objects and the estimation of their motion parameters. Motion analysis has become an active research area recently. It has a broad spectrum of applications including the monitoring of dynamic industrial processes, the navigation of autonomous vehicles, and the analysis of heart-wall motion for detecting abnormalities.

Most work in motion analysis deals with a single rigid object, and use the techniques of either point correspondences or optical flow. In contrast, the chapters in this volume explore new grounds. Chapters 1 and 2 treat the problem of segmenting and tracking multiple moving objects. Chapters 3 and 4 describe methods of motion estimation that are based on regions rather than point correspondences. Chapter 5 presents an elegant mapping that is likely to prove useful in not only motion analysis but also many other areas of computer vision. Finally, Chapter 6 discusses the motion of deformable objects.

Thomas S. Huang
Series Editor

Chapter 1

SEGMENTATION AND INTERPRETATION OF INFRARED IMAGE SEQUENCES

J. P. Gambotto

OUTLINE

Advances in Computer Vision and Image Processing, Vol. 3, pages 1–38.
Copyright © 1988 JAI Press Inc.
ISBN: 0-89232-635-2

ABSTRACT

This chapter addresses the problem of tracking several targets simultaneously in an infrared (IR) image sequence. Some important aspects of motion perception by the human visual system are first discussed, and we analyze the influence of several factors on the correspondence process. Then, two approaches for tracking several targets simultaneously in an image sequence are presented. Both approaches are based on a prior segmentation of the images into elementary regions, but the motion analysis is performed in two different ways. Experimental results are also presented.

1. INTRODUCTION

In the past years, several attempts to develop techniques for the detection and classification of targets have been reported [5, 6, 7, 9, 23, 28]. In many applications where only low-resolution and noisy images are available, the information content of a single image is usually very poor. Also, the detection performance of a human observer viewing a static scene is not always higher than the performance of an automatic system. The detection capability of an autonomous system can be greatly increased by the analysis of scene changes between two consecutive frames. Moreover, some of the required performances of an intelligent tracker are only achieved by analyzing the spatio–temporal changes in the image sequence; some of these performances are: the ability to track several targets simultaneously, the automatic acquisition of new targets in the field of view, and the reacquisition of targets occluded for a short period of time.

This chapter addresses the problem of tracking several targets simultaneously in an infrared (IR) image sequence. IR image sequences usually have a low resolution, are noisy and, in some applications, the frame rate can be very low. Thus, it seems to be important to understand what kind of information can be used by a tracking system under such constraints. Section 2 of this chapter discusses some important aspects of motion perception by the human visual system and analyzes the influence of several factors on the correspondence process; these factors are: the temporal continuity of the image sequence, the choice between low-level or high-level primitives, and the different classes of transformations that occur in the image plane.

Two approaches for tracking several targets simultaneously in an image sequence are presented in sections 3 and 4. Both approaches are based on the segmentation of each frame of the image sequence into a set of elementary regions. However, the motion analysis is performed in two different ways. In the first approach (section 3), the correspondence relationship between successive frames is established before computing the motion, whereas in the second approach (section 4), the computation of motion and the correspondence analysis are performed simultaneously.

In the first approach, a correspondence relationship is established between the regions detected in the current frame and a model of these regions. This analysis uses the area, the position of the centroid and the gray level of the detected regions. A one-to-one mapping between the tokens in the current frame and the model is obtained by minimizing a global cost function. The model contains the regions of the previous frame and several other regions that have disappeared for some time. Then, these regions are merged on the basis of similar motions to build objects. In parallel with the symbolic analysis, a background registration procedure provides information on the motion of the camera.

The second approach is based on computing the intersections between overlapping regions belonging to two consecutive images. An algorithm recursively detects each motion component in the image plane, and forms potential correspondences between regions. Then, several inferences of specific motion situations and shape transformations are made to determine the correct correspondence and interpret the motion.

2. MOTION PERCEPTION AND THE CORRESPONDENCE PROCESS

Motion is perhaps one of the simplest informations on the world around us that is available to all biological vision systems. The detection of changes and the recognition of moving objects are vital to all species. However, the display of a sequence of still pictures can also produce a perception of motion. Currently this technique is widely used for generating motion pictures and television images. Generally, two consecutive images in the sequence are very similar because the time interval between frames is small enough. Thus, the displacement of an object in the scene is perceived as a smooth movement of this object.

2.1   The Correspondence Problem

Consider two consecutive images in the sequence and assume that each image contain N objects. There are $N!$ possible associations between the two sets of objects but, for each object, only one association is correct. To find the solution, it is useful to make some assumptions about the structure in the dynamic scene. Researchers [18, 32] have suggested that the human visual system uses the rigidity assumption to recover the motion and structure of the objects. This assumption imposes particular constraints on the relative motion of object points. Likewise, the image points of a deformable object will be subject to specific constraints. Therefore, the number of matches that need to be considered to find the correspondence can be significantly reduced [2, 3].

The rules that are used in the human vision to establish a correspondence relationship have been investigated by psychologists [8, 18, 34]. Typical psychological experiments use very simple stimuli such as flashing dots or lines. It appears that proximity is a very important factor in perceiving motion. If the elements in two consecutive images are dots, each dot in the current image will be matched with its nearest neighbor in the previous image. Ullman's experiments [33] suggest that when the elements are line segments, the correspondence depends not only on the interline distance, but on their relative length and orientation.

The clues that are used by an observer viewing a real image sequence are not yet fully understood. However, recent psychophysical studies [27] indicate that the human visual system detects the correspondence between objects having low spatial frequencies faster than it detects line or point correspondences. In the following, we analyze the situation where the images contain several regions. To simplify the analysis, we will first assume that the motion is restricted to a plane perpendicular to the optical axis of the camera.

When each image contains a single object (as in Figure 2.1) only one association is possible. The transformation is a translation in Figure 2.1a and a deformation of the object in Figure 2.1b. However, these drawings can lead to different interpretations; the transformation in Figure 2.1a can be seen as the result of the motion of the camera, whereas another interpretation for Figure 2.1b is that the object in image n leaves the field of view and another object appears in image $n + 1$.

When there are several objects in the scene the rules tend to be very complex. However, it is interesting to consider three particular situations;

1.   one object is moving with respect to the others,
2.   all the objects have a common motion,
3.   each object has its own motion.

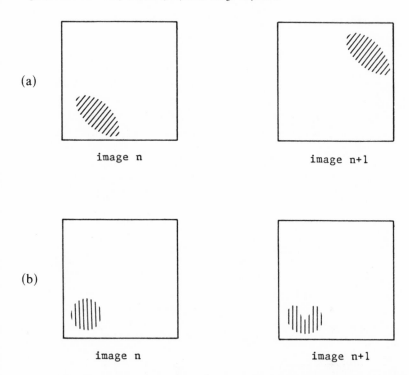

Figure 2.1. Correspondence when two consecutive images contain one object. In each scene only one match is possible, leading to a translation in (a) and a deformation in (b).

These three different situations are sketched in Figure 2.2. In Figure 2.2a and 2.2b the correspondence relationship can be easily established; the knowledge of the position of each object and their relative positions are sufficient. However, in Figure 2.2c, the relationship between the objects is not clear. In this case, too many changes occur between the two images, and a correspondence cannot be established on the basis of the position itself.

Actually, these simple examples represent typical motion situations. Several authors [11, 18, 27] have used similar dynamic configurations of objects to study the perceived kinematic relations. The experiments have revealed that the absolute motion of each element in the configuration is usually not seen as such. More precisely, the perceived motion seems to be decomposed into two components: the first one is the common motion of the whole configuration, and the second one is the relative motion of each element within the configuration.

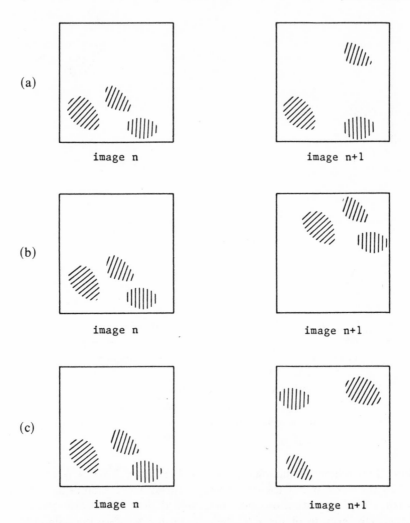

Figure 2.2. Correspondences when the two images contain several objects. Three motion situations are shown: (a) One object is moving, (b) all the objects have the same motion, and (c) each object has its own motion.

These findings suggest that the interpretation performed by the visual system is not based on local measurements of motion, but on a more global estimation of the spatio-temporal characteristics of the visual field. Moreover, the perception of relative and global motions seems to be very important for the interpretation of three-dimensional (3D) structures. Using shadow projections of unfamiliar objects rotating in depth, Wallach and O'Connell [35] have demonstrated that the visual system can interpret the

3D structure and motion from these two-dimensional displays. It is suggested that the global motion is used to recover 3D translations, and that the relative motions between the different parts of the objects are used to infer rigid motion and to recover the 3D structure.

2.2 Various Factors Influencing the Correspondence Process

2.2.1 Tokens and Primitives

Matching can be performed at several levels of the processing algorithm. At a low level, the correspondence is established between tokens such as points, edge fragments or homogeneous regions. At a higher level, the correspondence can be established between the segmented objects. The use of complex objects can simplify the correspondence process, but at the expense of a large amount of computation. On the other hand, the detection of simple tokens requires less computation.

In our work, matching is performed between homogeneous regions. The use of regions has several advantages. First, a direct relation usually exists between the temperature of the object in the scene, and the gray levels in the IR image. A second advantage is that the motion of a connected region in the image can, in principle, be recovered exactly. Problems similar to the aperture problem [33] are only encountered when the region is partially occluded.

Regional descriptors have been used by several authors for tracking objects in image sequences. Radig [26] describes the image using a facet model and then uses a graph representation to organize elementary regions into relational structures; motion analysis is then performed by a graph matching algorithm. Kories and Zimmerman [20] have recently described a blob-detection operator to track objects in several frames. These authors argued that the stability of regional descriptors is very high compared to other descriptors.

The choice of the primitives is also very important and depends mainly on the information content of the image sequence. The use of low-level primitives such as position, size and average gray level of the region is appropriate for processing low-resolution and noisy images. In (most) examples presented in Figures 2.1 and 2.2, the correspondence can be established on the basis of the position alone. In these examples there is a dichotomy between two groups of objects (moving objects and still objects) that is easily detected. Conversely, when each object has its own motion, the dichotomy does not exist and higher-level primitives such as shape, texture or color must be used to find the correspondence. In addition, it is worthwhile to note that low-level primitives such as size and average gray level, are less sensitive to noise and to the instabilities of the segmentation algorithm.

2.2.2 Temporal Continuity

Another important parameter for the analysis of an image sequence is temporal continuity. When the frame rate is high enough, very few changes occur between two consecutive images. This situation is depicted in Figure 2.3a. In this example, the positions of the object do not change very much, and therefore the motion can be computed locally. Two different approaches have been proposed for determining the local motion. In the optical flow approach [29] the velocity is computed at every location in the image. The general assumption is that the intensity varies smoothly over the image plane. Thus, this approach will be highly sensitive to noise. The second approach is to detect the changes between two consecutive images in the sequence. Many researchers have used image subtraction methods to detect and locate these changes [15, 16, 37]. This approach usually requires that corresponding tokens overlap.

When the frame rate is low, corresponding objects do not necessarily overlap (see Figure 2.3b) and a correspondence should be established before the computation of motion begins. Therefore, the two previously mentioned approaches may not always work and it is often necessary to segment the image and extract the tokens before the correspondence can be established.

2.2.3 Local-Versus-Global Correspondence

From a mathematical viewpoint the correspondence analysis is to construct a mapping from the set of tokens in the image n to the set of tokens in the image $n + 1$. In the general case, the complexity of this problem is very high because the number of objects, common to these two images, is unknown.

Two different schemes can be used for establishing a correspondence between the sets of tokens in successive frames. In the local correspondence

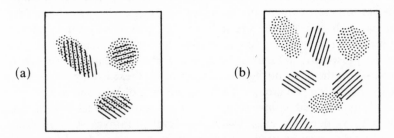

Figure 2.3. Changes that can be observed when the frame rate is high (a) and when the frame rate is low (b). Hatched objects are in the current frame and dotted objects are in the previous frame.

image n   image n+1

Figure 2.4. A complex scene: the number of objects common to the two frames is unknown. A high-level primitive (shape) is used to establish the correspondence.

scheme, a token is detected in the current frame and searched for in the previous frame. Conversely, a global correspondence scheme will minimize a single mapping-cost function between the two sets of tokens.

The same distinction between these two types of correspondence schemes can be drawn at a lower level. For instance, the optical-flow approach is basically a local scheme. On the contrary, the cross-correlation methods [1, 22] and the dynamic programming technique developed for the analysis of horizontal motion by LeGuilloux [21] are global correspondence schemes.

Clearly, a local correspondence scheme will rely solely on the attributes of each token, whereas a global correspondence will also rely on intertoken relations (e.g., relative distance, adjacency relationship, ...). Thus, a global correspondence scheme seems appropriate when only few changes occur between frames. Conversely, when large changes in the positions of the tokens occur from one frame to the next, each one-to-one pairing must be evaluated separately. This fact is illustrated in Figure 2.4; the two frames have only 2 objects in common (3 objects disappeared and 4 new objects appeared in frame $n + 1$), but the correspondence is easily found using shape informations.

3. TRACKING SEVERAL OBJECTS FROM FRAME TO FRAME

In this section, we describe an algorithm [12] that can track several moving objects in an image sequence. This approach is based on establishing a correspondence between the segmented regions in the current frame and a model of the regions that represents the past. An outline of this algorithm is given below, and the remainder of this section is devoted to a detailed description of the algorithm. This algorithm (Figure 3.1) consists of the following steps:

- segmentation of each frame into a set of connected regions,
- correspondence analysis between the current frame and a model of the regions that is updated at each new frame,
- aggregation of moving regions on the basis of similar motions and several other inferences,
- background registration from frame to frame, which provides informations on the motion of the camera,
- building a model of the objects in the scene.

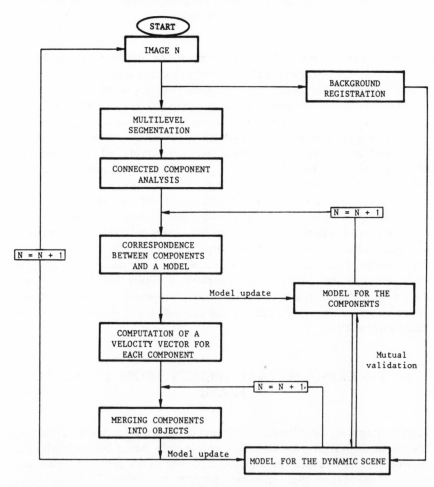

Figure 3.1.   Flow chart for the multitarget tracking algorithm.

3.1   Image Segmentation

Several segmentation algorithms for IR images have been described in the literature. Techniques using a combination of gray levels, gradient and texture [23], based on a statistical information criterion [9], or region growing techniques [7] have been developed to discriminate the target from the background clutter. A cooperative research between several laboratories have been reported [30]. It presents a comparison and an evaluation of several algorithms using a common data base.

Here, two different techniques have been used. The first technique is the histogram based multilevel segmentation algorithm proposed in [12]. This recursive algorithm performs a hierarchical clustering on the gray level histogram $H(i)$: at each iteration the two neighboring levels $H(i)$ and $H(i+1)$, which minimize the function

$$|H(i+1) - H(i)|/[H(i+1) + H(i)]$$

are merged into a single level with value $[H(i+1) + H(i)]/2$.

This procedure is repeated until a given number of gray levels L is reached. An example is shown in Figure 3.2. Next, the modified histogram is used as a lookup table to modify the original image. The transformed image Tn is composed of regions having a constant intensity in the range 1 to L.

The second technique was proposed by Keskes [19]. It consists in convolving the image by two low-pass filters of different sizes, and then to substract the results. The difference image is then thresholded to obtain a binary image Tn.

In the next step, a connected component analysis is performed, and several features are computed for each region.

3.2   Correspondence between Regions

In IR images, the intensity distribution over an object usually does not change rapidly with respect to the frame rate. Thus, matching regions can be performed independently for each gray level of the transformed image Tn.

An additional hypothesis will be used to simplify the correspondence problem. We assume that the area of a given region does not change drastically from one frame to the next. Then, only a limited set of all possible matches need to be tested. Practically, we will not try to pair regions with overly different areas.

3.2.1   A Correspondence Algorithm

Let us consider two sets of regions ordered according to decreasing areas:

$$A = (a1, a2, \ldots, ak) \qquad B = (b1, b2, \ldots, bl). \qquad (3.1)$$

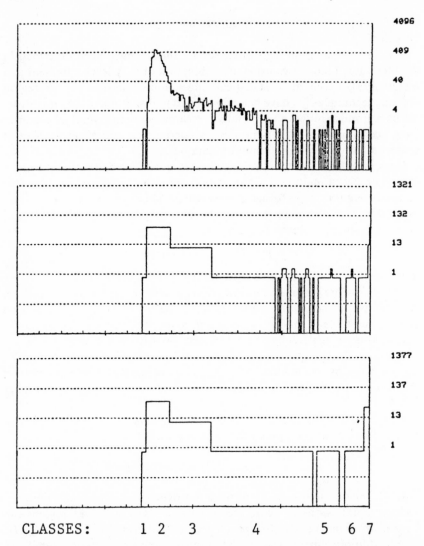

CLASSES :   1 2   3   4   5   6 7

Figure 3.2. Segmentation of the histogram using a clustering algorithm: (a) histogram, (b) intermediate segmentation, and (c) final segmentation.

The correspondence between sets A and B is established by a recursive algorithm that tests the global similarity between 2 subsets $A' \subset A$ and $B' \subset B$. Let m be a constant such that $m \leqslant \min(k, l)$, the subsets A' and B' are also ordered sets and contain m elements:

$$A' = (a'1, a'2, \ldots, a'm) \qquad B' = (b'1, b'2, \ldots, b'm). \qquad (3.2)$$

The global similarity between subsets A' and B' is measured by a cost function:

$$C(A', B') = \sum c(ai, bj), \tag{3.3}$$

where $c(ai, bj)$ is the cost of the elementary association between region ai and region bj.

The elementary cost $c(ai, bj)$ is here defined as a function of the distance $d(ai, bj)$ between the centroids of ai and bj, and the absolute value of the difference between the areas $w(ai)$ and $w(bj)$ of the two regions. The following function was chosen:

$$c(ai, bj) = d(ai, bj) + |w(ai) - w(bj)|. \tag{3.4}$$

We assume that the set B contains the regions in the current image and the set A contains the regions in the previous image. The correspondence algorithm is as follows:

ALGORITHM 1
Correspondence between the 2 sets A and B. While A and B are not empty do the following:
① $n(A) = \min(CARD(A), m)$; $n(B) = \min(CARD(B), m)$
  Store the $n(A)$ first elements of A in A'
  Store the $n(B)$ first elements of B in B'.
② Minimize the global cost function $C(A', B')$.
③ Look for the one-to-one pairing (ap, bq) with the 'minimum cost $c(ap, bq)$
  Assign ap to bq
  Remove ap from the set A
  Remove bq from the set B.
Creation of new regions. For each $b \in B$ do the following:
④ Assign a new label to b.

The size m of the sets A' and B' must be chosen according to the number of regions in the image. This size will be small enough in order to allow fast processing. The underlying hypothesis is that the objects have different sizes that vary slowly over time. If this assumption is not valid m should be increased.

3.2.2 An Adaptive Model for the Components

A global correspondence analysis is appropriate for matching two images that share common features. However, when the analysis is performed on the whole image sequence several problems arise: first, if an object is occluded or if it leaves the field of view, it disappears from the image and can possibly reappear in a subsequent frame; second, unknown objects can appear in the field of view, or because of a 3D rotation or a partial occlusion, the aspect of a known object can change completely. Clearly, the occurrences of such cases are not taken into account by the procedure described in the former section.

Algorithm 1 creates new labels for the regions that appear for the first time in the image n (step ④ of the algorithm). To take into account the objects that have disappeared, it is necessary to replace the set A that represents the information in the previous frame by a model representing the past information in the sequence. Hence, the correspondence will now be established between the regions in the current image and a model of the regions.

The current state of the model is defined by a set of regions A, and a feature vector $fi = (ci, wi, pi)$ is associated with each region ai. The parameters ci, wi and pi are, respectively, the centroid, the area and the probability of existence of the region ai.

In practice, if a region is present in the current frame, its probability will be equal to one, whereas the probability of a region that has disappeared for some time from the image will take a lower value.

The current frame is matched to the model using Algorithm 1; however, the similarity function is modified to include the probability pi. We have:

$$c(ai, bj) = F(pi) \quad \{d(ai, bj) + |wi - wj|\}, \tag{3.5}$$

where $F(p)$ is a decreasing function of p and $F(1) = 1$.

An adaptive algorithm is used to update the model. Whenever a new region is found, its feature vector is added to the model. If the region already exists its feature vector is replaced by the current feature vector and its probability is set to one. If a region is not found in the current frame, its probability pi is decreased by a constant α and, when pi reaches zero, the region is removed from the model.

ALGORITHM 2
For each region ai, do the following:
If $ai \in A$ then
    If ai is assigned in the current frame then

                Replace the values of wi and ci by the
                current values and set $pi = 1$

    Else

                Set $pi = pi - \alpha$

                If $pi \leq 0$ remove ai and fi from A

Else
Add the label *ai* and the feature vector *fi* to the model *A*; set $pi = 1$.

3.2.3 Discussion of the Matching Algorithm

Some important features of this matching algorithm will now be described.

It is worthwhile to analyze two different situations: first, when $CARD(B) < CARD(A)$, each region in the current image is matched to a region in the model and no new region is added to the model. On the other hand, if $CARD(B) > CARD(A)$, new labels will be added to the model, usually in the last steps when all the existing labels have been already assigned.

Another important property is that the algorithm first processes the large regions and, next, the small ones. Consequently, new labels can be assigned only to the smaller regions.

The algorithm looks for a maximum number of matches between the current image and the model. This rule seems to be appropriate when the frame rate is high with respect to all the physical time constants in the scene. In this case, an object will enter or leave the field of view progressively. Hence the sizes of the regions do not change very much, and the new regions entering the field of view will first appear very small. Unfortunately, the continuity assumption is not always satisfied. A counterexample is given by the splitting of a given region into smaller regions that can occur at any frame rate.

Conversely, when the frame rate is low, the algorithm will probably fail to correctly label the large regions that can possibly appear in the field of view. To avoid matching errors we will use a constraint on the local correspondence. A correspondence is now established if the distance between the regions *ap* and *bq* is less than a threshold *Do*. Therefore, the step ③ of the Algorithm 1 is replaced by the following:

③′ Look for the one-to-one pairing (*ap*, *bq*) with the minimal cost $c(ap, bq)$
If $(d(ap, bq)) < Do$ then
    Assign *ap* to *bq*
    Remove *ap* from *A*
    Remove *bq* from *B*
Else
    Assign a new label to *bq*
    Remove *bq* from *B*.

3.2.4 Results

The correspondence algorithm was applied to several low-resolution image sequences that have been collected with an IR camera and represent ground targets in tactical situations. The rate of the digitized images is only 3 images/sec, and the size of the image is 64×64 pixels.

All the sequences were segmented using the histogram based multilevel segmentation algorithm. Then, the correspondence algorithm was applied to track the regions in each level of the transformed image sequence. The value of the parameter m was equal to 3, and the value of α was 0.1. According to Algorithm 2, this means that a given region will remain in the model during ten frame intervals after it disappears from the image.

In the first subsequence (see Figure 3.3) a single vehicle is approaching the camera while changing its direction. At the segmentation stage, two thresholds have been obtained. The silhouette of the vehicle (regions 1 and 5) and several background objects (regions 2 and 3) were segmented using the first threshold value. The hot spots on the vehicle were detected using the second threshold. Therefore, the correspondence algorithm was used twice to obtain the tracking result shown in Figure 3.3.

A second subsequence is shown in Figure 3.4. Two vehicles and several background objects were segmented using only one threshold. The first vehicle (regions 6, 2 and 10) leaves the field of view after some frames. The second vehicle (regions 1 and 4) is also tracked successfully during this short sequence. We remark that several regions are tracked though they disappear from time to time. This performance is achieved by the use of a model for the regions.

The algorithm was applied to other sequences and good results have been obtained even when the aspect of some object changes rapidly. This algorithm is robust to shape changes because the correspondence is based only on the positions and areas of the regions. In addition, tracking can be performed with a moving camera, and it was shown [12] that the correspondence is established even if there is a large displacement between the two frames. However, a critical situation for this algorithm is the sudden appearance of large objects in the field of view, and also, to some extent, the splitting and merging of regions.

3.3   Aggregation of Moving Regions

In many applications, the goal is to recognize and track one or several moving targets in the image sequence. Usually, an object is first detected in one image and tracked in the succeeding images. However, these two different tasks can also be performed concurrently. Generally, some a priori knowledge about the objects and the camera is needed at the recognition stage. It appears that the motion information that is extracted at the tracking stage can be also very useful to recognize objects.

In our scheme, the image of a vehicle is often split into several regions during the segmentation process. To recover a vehicle from its several parts,

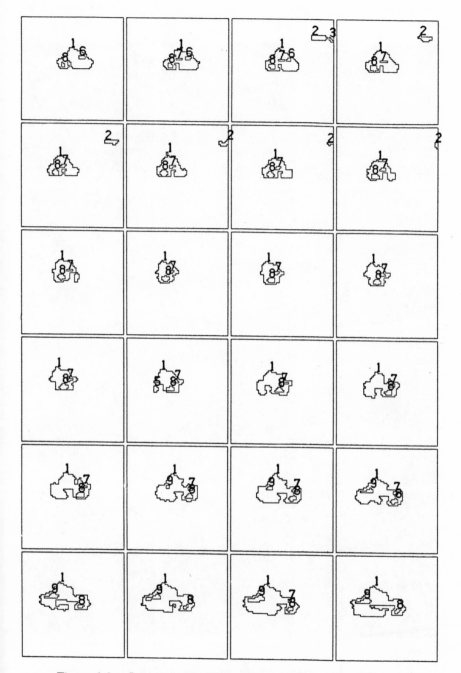

Figure 3.3. Segmented image sequence and correspondences.

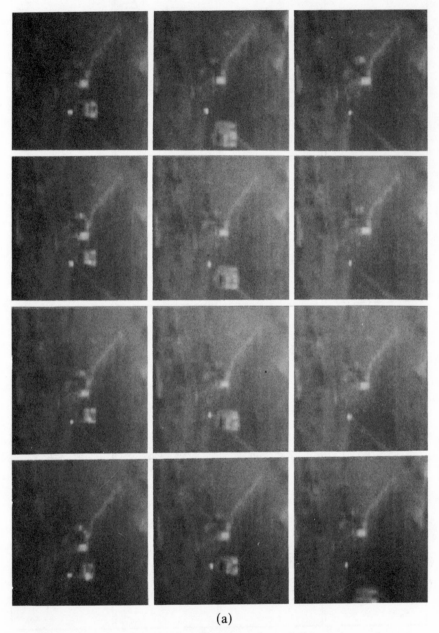

(a)

Figure 3.4. (a) Original image sequence, and (b) correspondences.

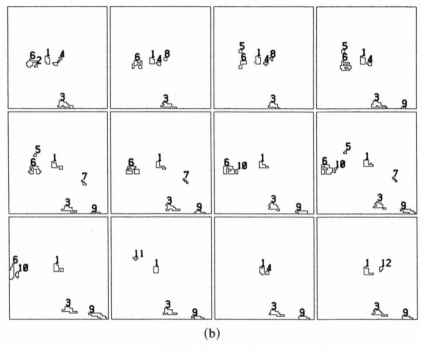

(b)

Figure 3.4. (cont.)

it is interesting to analyze the relative motions between the different regions in the image. Based on scene-specific knowledge, several inferences will be made.

If two neighboring regions have the same velocity for some time, we infer that they are parts of a single object. The unlikely alternative is that two different objects have the same velocity, and thus, behave like a rigid object. In the sequence shown in Figure 3.5, a moving vehicle is split from time to time into two or three regions. For each frame f, the distance $RD(f)$ between the centroids of the regions 3 and 8 was computed; the incremental distance $\Delta RD(f) = |RD(f) - RD(1)|$ between the first and the current frame is plotted in Figure 3.5b. These values are very low (some are less than one pixel) indicating that the two regions are parts of the same object. Although the segmented regions are corrupted by noise, the velocities estimated from the centroid positions are very stable. In practice, the application of this inference is based on a comparison between the incremental velocity and the velocity of the object using a preset threshold.

When a vehicle undergoes rotation or is approaching the camera, it is not always possible to use the above-mentioned inference. Other inferences

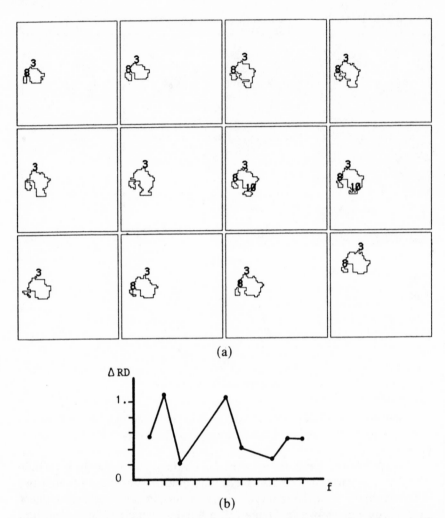

(a)

(b)

Figure 3.5. (a) Isolated vehicle composed of several regions, and (b) changes in the estimated distance between regions 3 and 8 with respect to the first image. The values are in fractions of pixels.

based on relational or topological properties of neighboring regions are used. Let us consider the sequence shown in Figure 3.3; a large region (the outline of the vehicle) and several smaller regions (hot spots) are tracked. An initial assumption is that each region is the projection on the image plane of an object; this assumption would imply that the smaller regions move in the foreground of the larger object. This interpretation is improbable because, during the motion, the small regions remain always inside the largest one. A more likely inference is that all the regions are parts of the same object.

3.4 Background Registration

Background registration is performed by a cross-correlation between a reference window in frame $n + 1$ and a search area in frame n. The maximum of this function gives the optimum displacement (u^*, v^*) between the two images. The normalized correlation was shown to yield the best result.

This displacement information can be very useful when the motion of the camera is unknown. First, it helps to discriminate moving objects from background objects, and the trajectories of moving objects on the image plane can be recovered. Second, the expected motion of a given object can be used to infer several events occurring in the scene. For instance, it is possible to predict whether a known object will enter (or leave) the field of view, or to predict occlusions on the basis of the expected velocity of each object [10].

There are two motion situations that allow the use of a simple correlation between consecutive images. First, when the ground-based camera is panning. Second, when the motion of the camera is perpendicular to its optical axis. However, even for these simple motion situations several difficulties must be overcome to develop a reliable registration procedure. The first difficulty comes from the low signal-to-noise ratio that is typical of a background IR image. A second problem is the choice of the size and position of the window. The window should be large enough to have a reliable estimation of the correlation function, but it must not overlap areas where the moving objects are located. A first solution that has been investigated is to select a window in the upper part of the image, near the horizon. Because the image of a vehicle is usually small in this area, its motion will not disturb the background registration algorithm. An alternative solution is to perform the registration over several rectangular windows. The number of windows is chosen a priori, but the algorithm uses the constraint that the windows must not overlap the segmented targets to compute their positions and sizes in each frame.

Figure 3.6 shows an example of background registration. About 20 images have been registered to a 1-pixel accuracy using a fixed window of size 3×45. Similar results are obtained using the second algorithm.

Another difficulty may come from subpixel motions. Suppose that the camera is panning from left to right at a slow constant velocity. If the displacement of the background in the image is less than half a pixel, this motion will not be detected by the registration algorithm. The accumulation of these small errors will lead, after some time intervals, to a large drift in the recorded position of the object. This problem is usually not encountered

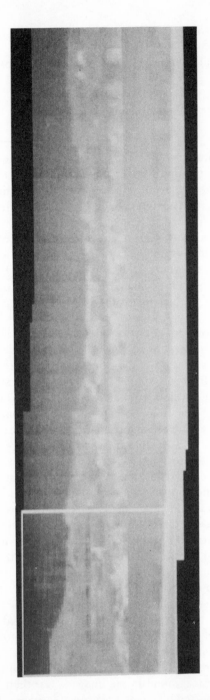

Figure 3.6. Background registration: 24 consecutive images have been registered to a 1-pixel accuracy; the white frame shows the last registered image. The size of the correlation window was only 3 × 45 pixels.

if the motion of the camera is noisy. A possible solution is to detect a subpixel displacement by interpolating the correlation function. Another efficient solution is to perform a registration between two frames separated by an interval larger than one.

4. MOTION SEGMENTATION AND INTERPRETATION BASED ON THE DETECTION OF COOCCURRENCES BETWEEN REGIONS

Because many objects can be encountered in a realistic scene, recovering the 3D motion of each object is a very difficult problem. This problem was addressed by several authors [24, 31, 32, 36] for the particular case of a single rigid object. The usual assumption is that the point correspondences are given as input. However, in real scenes the attribute values are not known exactly, and they do not always provide sufficient discrimination to solve the correspondence problem. A different approach is proposed in this section. This approach tries to interpret the observed changes in the image sequence before establishing the correspondence.

The changes that are observed in the segmented sequence are the result of the relative motion between the IR camera and the objects in the scene. These changes can be also attributed to occlusions, and to the inaccuracy of the segmentation algorithm. Therefore, the motion of the objects in the scene is not always directly related to the transformations that occur in the image plane.

We describe a method that interprets the transformations in the image plane to find a frame to frame correspondence. A simple and reliable analysis of size and shape transformation is performed. This analysis is based on computing the intersections between overlapping regions belonging to two consecutive images. Next, several inferences are described and used to find the motion of each object and establish a correspondence.

4.1 Shape Changes

Change detection can be performed using two different approaches. The first one is very simple and was studied by many researchers [15, 16, 25, 37]. Two consecutive images are subtracted and the areas of change are detected in the difference image. Next, geometrical properties are used to recover the object and its motion. This approach has obvious limitations. It requires registered images and constant illumination. An additional assumption is constant gray levels over each object or high contrast.

The second approach consists in analyzing the unchanged areas in the difference image. To detect such areas, it is necessary to shift one image with respect to the other before subtraction. Anstis [4] suggests a model where one of the images is progressively shifted over the other until minima appear in the difference image. An algorithm that uses a similar idea was recently proposed by Jayaramamurthy and Jain [17]. This algorithm was very successful for detecting textured objects moving against a textured background. However, several difficulties arise in absence of information on the motion characteristics of the camera and the objects; in particular, the displacement of the camera, and the approximate number and sizes of objects must be known a priori. The method proposed in this section does not have the same limitations because it uses previously segmented regions.

The detected regions in an IR-image sequence can be hot or cold parts of the targets, or larger regions that belong to the background. These regions usually do not have a well defined shape because there is always an exchange of heat between a target and its surroundings. Moreover, the image of a target is often split into smaller regions, and the position, size and shape of a given region can change rapidly in the segmented sequence. Based on the observations of specific transformations in the segmented images, we have defined the following classes:

(a) same object,
(b) merging of 2 regions,
(b') splitting of 2 regions,
(c) object entering the field of view,
(c') object leaving the field of view,
(d) foreground occlusion,
(d') end of a foreground occlusion,
(e) approaching object,
(e') receding object,
(f) two objects having the same area but different shapes,
(g) two objects having different areas and different shapes,
(h) occlusion between two objects,
(h') end of an occlusion between two objects,
(i) new object.

Examples of such transformations are depicted in Figure 4.1. Obviously when one of the transformations (a)-(e') is detected, a correspondence can be established between the regions under analysis, whereas the transformations (f)-(i) probably indicate that a match cannot be found.

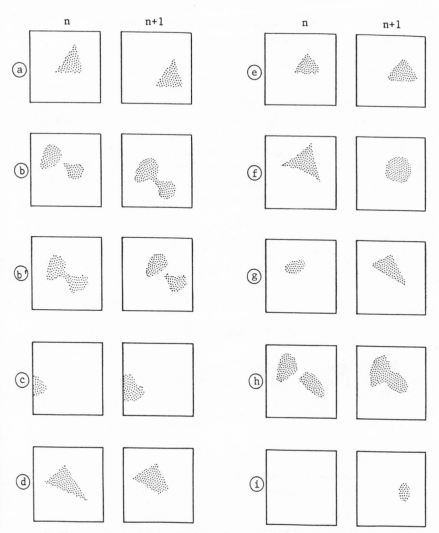

Figure 4.1. Specific transformations of the regions in the image plane.

4.2 The Optimal Intersection between Two Overlapping Regions

Consider the co-occurrence matrix between the labels of the regions:

$$[Cij]_{(u,v)} = \text{number of pairs } (k, l) \text{ such that } Tn(k, l) = i$$
$$\text{and } Tn + 1 \ (k + u, l + v) = j.$$

This matrix gives the intersection between regions ai and bj when there is a displacement (u, v) between image Tn and image $Tn + 1$. If ai and bj

are two corresponding regions, the optimal displacement (u^*, v^*) is given by maximizing the intersection:

$$C^*ij = \max_{u,v} [Cij]. \tag{4.1}$$

A steepest descent like algorithm is used to find this maximum. To have a fast convergence of the algorithm, an initial estimate of the displacement is found by matching the centroids of the two regions. Starting from this initial displacement (u_0, v_0), the algorithm examines 9 possible solutions in the first iteration. In the succeeding iterations, 5 new solutions are examined in the vicinity of the optimal solution found at the previous iteration (see Figure 4.2). The algorithm stops when a maximum is found.

ALGORITHM OPTIMAL DISPLACEMENT
(1) $C(u^*, v^*) = C(u_0, v_0)$
   Compute $C(u + u_0, v + v_0)$ for the eight elementary nonzero vectors $(u, v)/u, v = -1, 0, 1$
   Look for the displacement (u_1, v_1) corresponding to the maximum of $C(u + u_0, v + v_0)$
   If $(C(u_1, v_1) > C(u^*, v^*))$ then $(u^*, v^*) = (u_1, v_1)$ and $C(u^*, v^*) = C(u_1, v_1)$.
   Else, the maximum is detected. Exit.
(2) Compute $C(u_1 + u, v_1 + v)$ for the five vectors (u, v) that are depicted in Figure 4.2.
   Look for the displacement (u_1, v_1) corresponding to the maximum of $C(u + u_1, v + v_1)$
   If $(C(u_1, v_1) > C(u^*, v^*))$ then $(u^*, v^*) = (u_1, v_1)$ and $C(u^*, v^*) = C(u_1, v_1)$.
   Else, the maximum is detected. Exit.
(3) Repeat step 2 until the optimal solution is found.

Figure 4.2.   Two possible configurations of Algorithm Optimal Displacement: + is the optimal solution at step $m - 1$, and ● are the solutions to test at step m.

4.3 Analysis of Overlapping Regions

The analysis of overlapping regions will be used to infer the frame to frame correspondence in the image sequence. We describe several inferences that are derived from elementary properties of the intersection between the regions in the image plane. This analysis is performed by computing several parameters. Let (ai, bj) be a pair of overlapping regions with areas wi and wj, we will first consider the following parameters:

$$S1 = wi; \quad S2 = wj$$

$$\text{MINSUR} = \min(wi, wj)$$

$$\text{INTSUR} = C^*ij$$

$$\left.\begin{array}{l} (H1 = H(ai); L1 = L(ai)) \\ (H2 = H(bj); L2 = L(bj)) \end{array}\right\} \quad \begin{array}{l} \text{The heights and lengths of} \\ \text{the enclosing rectangles.} \end{array}$$

The correspondence can be guided by the use of simple constraints. First, by definition of the intersection between two sets we have the following inequality:

(a) $\text{INTSUR} \leq \text{MINSUR}$,

second, the properties:

(b)   S1 is approximately equal to S2,

(c)   INTSUR is approximately equal to MINSUR,

indicate that the two regions under study have similar sizes and shapes, and thus, can be matched with high confidence. Conversely, if these properties are not satisfied the two regions probably do not belong to the same object.

At this step it is interesting to analyze the splitting and the merging of regions in order to establish a correspondence. Let us assume that the optimal displacement (u^*, v^*) between bj and ai has been detected. If bj overlaps another region ak, the properties (b) and (c) will probably not be satisfied. Therefore, the possibility of merging between the two regions must be considered, and we update the parameters as follows:

$$S1 = wi + wk; \quad S2 = wj$$

$$\text{MINSUR} = \min(S1, S2)$$

$$\text{INTSUR} = [Cij + Ckl]_{(u^*, v^*)}$$

$$H1 = H(ai \cup ak); \quad L1 = L(ai \cup ak)$$

$$H2 = H(bj); \quad L2 = L(bj).$$

An additional constraint is given by:

$$(d) \quad H1/L1 \sim H2/L2$$

if the properties (b), (c) and (d) are satisfied, we infer that the regions bj, ai and ak belong to the same object, and a correspondence is found. If the property (d) is not satisfied we will infer that an occlusion is occurring between two objects.

When a single region ai splits itself into two regions bl and bj, similar inferences can be made to find a correspondence or to detect the end of an occlusion between two objects. Below, the logical parameters DOUBL1 and DOUBL2 are used to indicate the merging and the splitting of regions, respectively.

The logical parameter BORLOG is used to detect if a region is located on the border of the image. If BORLOG = T and the constraint (c) is satisfied, a correspondence is established and $S1$ is compared to $S2$ to find whether the object is leaving or entering the field of view.

A given region can completely overlap another region. To detect this particular situation, Algorithm Optimal Displacement computes another parameter:

INCLU = number of encountered vector (u, v), such that C^*ij = MINSUR.

Different events can be inferred depending on the value of INCLU. If INCLU is equal to one and $S1 = S2$, then the two regions will have the same shape and a correspondence is established. Now, let us assume that the constraint (c) is satisfied but (b) is not. We will have the following inferences:

if INCLU $\leq$ 1   then select (d) or (d')

if INCLU > 1 and $H1/L1 \neq H2/L2$ then select (g)

if INCLU > 1 and $H1/L1 \sim H2/L2$ then select (e) or (e').

To decide whether two overlapping regions have approximately the same size we use the inequality:

$$|S1 - S2| < \text{THS},$$

where THS is a threshold. This threshold can be tuned to account for a particular situation. For example, if the segmentation algorithm gives accurate results and the image is not noisy, then a very low value should be chosen. For processing IR images it seems to be interesting to assume that the noise only affects the pixels on the boundary of the segmented blob. Therefore we define the threshold as:

$$\text{THS} = \gamma \cdot \min(P1, P2),$$

where $P1$ and $P2$ are the perimeters of the two regions, and γ is a constant that should reflect the stability of the segmentation algorithm. The property (c) is verified using the same threshold value, and the property (d) is checked using the parameter γ.

4.4 Motion Detection and the Correspondence

Let us consider a given region bj in the image $n + 1$, and suppose that there is no displacement between the images Tn and $Tn + 1$. If the time interval between consecutive images is sufficiently small, the region bj will overlap one or several regions in the image n. The region in the image n corresponding to bj can be found by analyzing the jth column of the matrix $[Cij]$. Obviously, the entry that has the highest value should give the corresponding region ai. The translation between the two regions ai and bj is then found using Algorithm Optimal Displacement.

However, when the frame rate is low, or when the region sizes are too small, corresponding regions in two consecutive images do not necessarily overlap. Furthermore, when two regions overlap, the maximal intersection cannot always be used as a cue to correspondence. Note also that if an object does not completely displace itself when it moves, the following simple inequalities hold:

$$H(bj) > vj^* \quad \text{and} \quad L(bj) > uj^*. \tag{4.2}$$

At this point, it seems worthwhile formulating some general hypotheses concerning the motion that is observed in the image sequence. A first hypothesis will consider that the image can be decomposed into a small number of components. Each component contains several regions having more or less the same velocity in the image plane. Under this hypothesis, an important task for the motion detection algorithm will be to determine each component in the image sequence. This hypothesis is of great importance in our everyday life vision, because we usually describe the movement of the objects in the visual field using a small number of descriptors for its direction and amplitude. For example, we easily describe the motion of cars in the street; one reason is that the image points of each car have roughly the same velocity. However, the description of the motion of the leaves in a tree seems to be a rather difficult task because adjacent leaves may have different velocity vectors which often change direction. Thus the first hypothesis will not hold in this second example.

To find the velocity field, our first attempt will be to perform a global match between two consecutive images. Our conjecture is that in many situations, this will give the velocity of one component. We call this component the "dominant component." The global displacement (u_G, v_G) between Tn and $Tn + 1$ is the displacement that maximizes the intersection between all the regions

$$\max_{(u,\,v)} \left[\sum_{(i,\,j)} [Cij] \right].$$
(4.3)

This maximization is performed by using an algorithm similar to Algorithm Optimal Displacement. However, to detect the dominant component using this algorithm, a second hypothesis is needed: we will assume that at least one region in the dominant component satisfies the inequalities (4.2).

The algorithm given below looks for potential correspondences between the regions in two consecutive frames. At each iteration, the global displacement is computed, and each region in the current frame is processed if it satisfies the following constraint:

$$H(bj) > f(v_G) \quad \text{and} \quad L(bj) > f(u_G).$$
(4.4)

In the first iteration, $f(u_G) = u_G, f(v_G) = v_G$ and the value of this function is decreased rapidly in the succeeding iterations. This constraint implies that only a few regions are processed when the global displacement is large, and that the small regions that belong to the dominant component are usually not detected in the first iteration. When a potential match is detected, the corresponding regions are deleted from the images; this operation allows one of the remaining components to be detected in the succeeding iterations.

ALGORITHM GLOBAL MOTION

Ⓐ Compute a global displacement (u_G, v_G) between the frames Tn and $Tn + 1$

Ⓑ For each region $bj \in B$ satisfying (4.4), do the following
1. Initialize: DOUBL2 = FALSE, $S2 = wj$, $H2 = H(bj)$, $L2 = L(bj)$
2. Find the region $ai \in A$, which gives the largest intersection with bj
    DOUBL1 = FALSE, $S1 = wi$, $H1 = H(ai)$, $L1 = L(ai)$
3. Starting from the translation (u_G, v_G), search for the optimal translation (ui^*, vj^*) between ai and bj. Then compute INTSUR and MINSUR
4. If there exists a region ak, $k \neq i$, intersecting bj then
    Update $S1$, $H1$, $L1$, INTSUR, MINSUR
    DOUBL1 = TRUE
5. If there exists a region bl, $l \neq j$, intersecting ai then
    Update $S2$, $H2$, $L2$, INTSUR, MINSUR
    DOUBL2 = TRUE
6. If the region bj intersects the border of the image then
    BORLOG = TRUE
7. Store the parameters
    If INTSUR $\sim$ MINSUR or BORLOG = TRUE then
    A potential correspondence is found between ai and bj
    Delete ai from the image Tn and from the set A

> Delete *bj* from the image *Tn* + 1 and from the set *B*
> If DOUBL1 = TRUE then delete *ak* from *Tn*
> If DOUBL2 = TRUE then delete *bl* from *Tn* + 1
> Ⓒ Update $f(u_G)$ and $f(v_G)$
> Repeat steps Ⓐ to Ⓒ until all the regions in the set *B* have been visited at least once.

Algorithm Global Motion computes several parameters that are used by the decision tree (see Figure 4.3) to classify all the regions in the image. Each class corresponds to a particular motion situation or event occurring in the image plane. This classification is used to track the objects throughout the sequence. When one of the classes ⓐ-ⓔ' is detected, a correspondence is established between the regions under analysis. If an occlusion (class ⓗ) is detected, the resulting region keeps the label of the two regions involved in the occlusion. In this case, the sizes and average gray levels of the two regions are stored in order to re-assign the correct labels when the occlusion ends (class ⓗ'). Finally, if one of the classes ⓕ, ⓖ or ⓘ is detected a new label is assigned to the region.

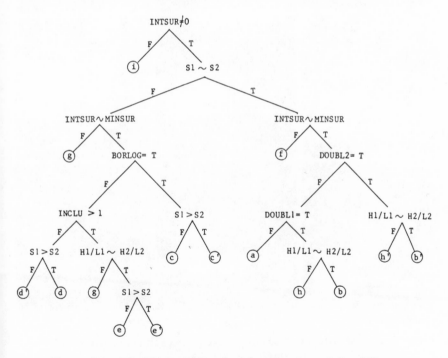

Figure 4.3. Decision tree for the identification of the different transformations shown in Figure 4.1.

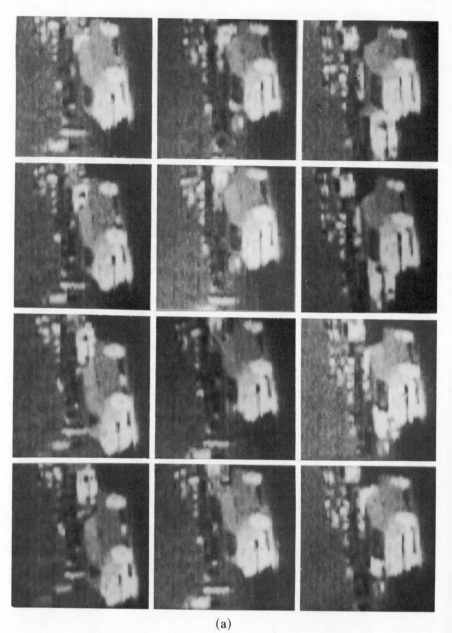

(a)

Figure 4.4. Car sequence: (a) Original sequence, and (b) correspondences.

4.5   Experimental Results

The algorithm was applied to a sequence of 12 image frames (see Figure 4.4a). The frame rate is approximately 12 frames/sec and the resolution 64 × 64. In this short sequence, a car is turning to the left at a crossroad. In each frame, several hot spots have been segmented out using the technique proposed by Keskes [19]. The three wheels and the engine of the car have been extracted, but the body of the car was not found. The correspondence results are shown in Figure 4.4b. In the first image, 9 regions are labeled (the regions smaller than 5 pixels were not processed and are not shown on this Figure). Regions 1, 2, 4 and 6 belong to the car. Good tracking results have been obtained using this sequence. We remark that regions 1 and 2 are merged in image 4. This event is detected by the algorithm which infers that these regions belong to the same object. Therefore, when region 2 is splitted (images 6 and 13), the two resulting regions keep the same label.

The analysis that is performed by Algorithm Global Motion and by the decision tree is described in more detail in Table 1 for the image pairs (1, 2) and (2, 3). Let us consider the image pair (2, 3). In this example, 3 iterations were needed to establish a correspondence and to find the displacement of each object. There are two motion components: the first one contains all

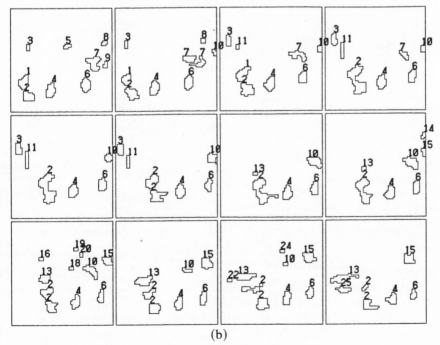

(b)

Figure 4.4.   (cont.)

IMAGES 1 AND 2   IMAGES 2 AND 3

ALGORITHM GLOBAL MOTION :

Ⓐ $(u_G, v_G) = (1,1)$

Ⓑ

ai	bj	ak	bl	(u^*, v^*)
2	2	0	0	(1,2)
4	4	0	0	(0,1)
6	6	0	0	(1,1)
1	1	0	0	(1,2)
7	7	9	7	(5,1)
8	8	0	0	(4,1)

Ⓐ $(u_G, v_G) = (4,2)$

Ⓑ

ai	bj	ak	bl	(u^*, v^*)
3	3	0	0	(4,1)

Ⓐ $(u_G, v_G) = (-6,2)$

Ⓑ

ai	bj	ak	bl	(u^*, v^*)
2	2	0	0	(-6,2)
1	1	0	0	(-6,2)
4	4	0	0	(-6,2)
7	7	0	0	(2,2)

Ⓐ $(u_G, v_G) = (1,2)$

Ⓑ

ai	bj	ak	bl	(u^*, v^*)
3	3	0	0	(1,1)
10	10	0	0	(0,2)

Ⓐ $(u_G, v_G) = (-5,2)$

Ⓑ

ai	bj	ak	bl	(u^*, v^*)
6	6	0	0	(-5,3)

CLASSIFICATION USING THE DECISION TREE :

bj ai	BORLOG	INCLU	DOUBL1	DOUBL2	DECISION
1 —— 1	F	0	F	F	ⓐ
3 —— 3	F	1	F	F	ⓐ
2 —— 2	F	0	F	F	ⓐ
4 —— 4	F	0	F	T	ⓐ
7 ⟍ 7	F	0	T	F	ⓑ
7 ⟋ 9			F	F	
6 —— 6	F	0	F	F	ⓐ
8 —— 8	F	0	F	F	ⓐ
10	T				ⓘ

bj ai	BORLOG	INCLU	DOUBL1	DOUBL2	DECISION
3 —— 3	F	4	F	F	ⓐ
11—11	F	1	F	F	ⓘ
1 —— 1	F	0	F	F	ⓐ
2 —— 2	F	0	F	F	ⓐ
4 —— 4	F	0	F	F	ⓐ
7 —— 7	F	0	F	F	ⓐ
6 —— 6	F	0	F	F	ⓐ
10—10	T	0	F	F	ⓒ

Table 1. Analysis Performed by the Algorithm Global Motion and Classification Obtained Using the Decision Tree for Matching the Image Pairs (1, 2) and (2, 3)

the regions of the car, and its optimal displacement is approximately equal to (−6, 2). The second component contains the other regions that have roughly the same displacement. We remark that region 6, which belongs to the first component, is processed in the last iteration, whereas region 7, which belongs to the second component is processed in the first iteration.

The classification results also indicate that a new region appears in the current frame. In this example, a very high value was selected for the parameter γ; this fact explains why some regions, which change rapidly, are nevertheless correctly labeled. The image sequence was also processed using a smaller value for γ. In this case (see Figure 4.5) only the regions that are similar keep the same label.

5. CONCLUSION

We have presented two different approaches for tracking several targets in low-resolution image sequences. Both approaches are based on a prior segmentation of the images into elementary regions. In the first approach, matching is performed at two different steps of the algorithm. First, a correspondence is established between the detected regions and a model of these regions; second, a correlation technique is used for background registration. Then, a model of the objects is built by analyzing the velocity vectors of neighboring regions and using several inferences. These two models appear to be very efficient to track moving objects through occlusion, and a mutual validation can be performed to detect incorrect matches.

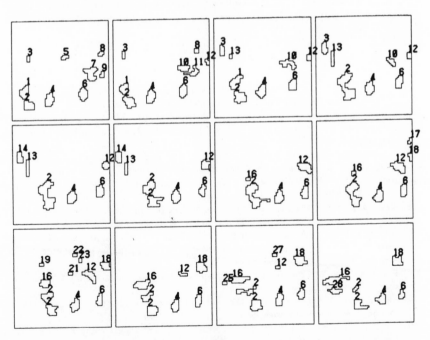

Figure 4.5.   Correspondence analysis using another values for parameter γ.

In the second approach, the computation of motion and the correspondence process are performed simultaneously. An algorithm recursively detects each motion component in the image plane, and forms potential correspondences between regions. Then, several inferences of specific motion situations and shape transformations are made to determine the correct correspondence and interpret the motion. Although this approach only provides an initial interpretation of the dynamic scene, it appears to be a viable one. Actually, some additional experiments [13, 14], using the same image sequences, indicate that rotation in-depth and 3D translations can be recovered, with a good accuracy, by analyzing the changes in the shapes and the relative positions of the segmented regions. Moreover, this approach could be improved by building a model of the objects as in the first approach.

ACKNOWLEDGMENTS

This work carried out at the Etablissement Technique Central de l'Armement (ETCA) was supported by the Direction des Recherches et Etudes Techniques (DRET) under contract 84.1049. The investigation reported in Section 4 was partly performed at MATRA under ESPRIT Project P940.

I thank Dr. G. Ruckebusch for valuable comments on an earlier draft of this paper. The encouragement of Prof. T. S. Huang is also greatly appreciated.

REFERENCES

[1] Aggarwal, J. K., L. S. Davis, and W. N. Martin. "Correspondence Process in Dynamic Scene Analysis," *Proceedings of the IEEE*, 69 (5), pp. 281-291, May 1981.

[2] Aggarwal, J. K., and W. N. Martin. "Analyzing Dynamic Scenes Containing Multiple Moving Objects," *Image Sequence Analysis*, edited by T. S. Huang, Berlin, Springer Verlag, 1981, pp. 355-380.

[3] Aggarwal, J. K., and J. W. Roach. "Computer Tracking of Objects Moving in Space," *IEEE Transaction on Pattern Analysis and Machine Intelligence*, 1 (2), pp. 263-271, 1979.

[4] Anstis, S. M., "Phi Movement as a Substraction Process," *Vision Research*, 10, pp. 1411-1430, 1970.

[5] Ayala, J. L., et al. "Moving Target Tracking using Symbolic Registration," *IEEE Trans. Pattern Analysis and Machine Intelligence*, 4 (5), September 1982.

[6] Bers, K. H., M. Bohner, and P. Fritsche. "Image Sequence Analysis for Target Tracking," *Image Sequence Processing and Dynamic Scene Analysis*, edited by T. S. Huang, Berlin, Springer Verlag, 1982, pp. 493-501.

[7] Brown, D., and W. Frei. "Target Segmentation in Infrared Images," 5th IJCPR Conference, Miami Beach, 1980.

[8] Burt, P., and G. Sperling. "Time, Distance, and Feature Trade-offs in Visual Apparent Motion," *Psychological Review*, 88 (2), pp. 171-195, 1981.

[9] Chen, C. H., and C. Yen. "Object Isolation in FLIR Images using Fisher's Linear Discriminant," *Pattern Recognition*, 15 (3), pp. 153-159, 1982.

[10] Chow, W. K., and J. K. Aggarwal. "Computer Analysis of Planar Curvilinear Moving Images," *IEEE Transaction on Computers*, 26 (2), pp. 179-185, 1977.

[11] Cutting, D. R. "The Minimum Principle and the Perception of Absolute, Common, and Relative Motions," *Cognitive Psychology*, 14, pp. 211-246, 1982.

[12] Gambotto, J. P. "Correspondence Analysis for Target Tracking in Infrared Images," 7th Int. Conf. on Pattern Recognition, Montreal, Canada, 1984.

[13] Gambotto, J. P. "Motion Estimation of Vehicles in an Image Sequence," *Proceedings of the Second Image Symposium CESTA*, pp. 222-231, Nice, France, 1986. [In French]

[14] Gambotto, J. P., and T. S. Huang. "Motion Analysis of Isolated Targets in Infrared Image Sequences," *Pattern Recognition Letters*, 5 (5), pp. 357-363, 1987.

[15] Jain, R. "Dynamic Scene Analysis Using Pixel-Based Processes," *Computer*, pp. 12-18, 1981.

[16] Jain, R., and H. H. Nagel. "On the Analysis of Accumulative Difference Pictures from Images Sequences of Real World Scenes," *IEEE Transaction on Pattern Analysis and Machine Intelligence*, 1 (2), pp. 206-214, April 1979.

[17] Jayaramamurthy, S. N., and R. Jain. "Segmentation of Textured Dynamic Scenes," *Proceedings IEEE Conference PRIP*, pp. 91-93, Dallas, 1981.

[18] Johansson, G., and G. Jansson. "Perceived Rotary Motion From Changes in a Straight Line," *Perception and Psychophysics*, 4 (3), pp. 165-170, 1968.

[19] Keskes, N. "Application of Image Analysis Techniques to Seismic Data," *Proceedings of ICASSP*, pp. 855-858, Paris, 1982.

[20] Kories, R., and G. Zimmerman. "A Class of Stable Feature Extractors for Time-Varying Imagery," *Proc. 7th Int. Conf. on Pattern Recognition*, Montreal, Canada, 1984.

[21] LeGuilloux, Y. "Image Segmentation Using Dynamic Programming," this volume, pp. 39-61.

[22] Martin, W. N., and J. K. Aggarwal. "Survey: Dynamic Scene Analysis," *Computer Graphics and Image Processing*, 7 (3), pp. 356-374, June 1978.

[23] Mitchell, O. R., and S. M. Lutton. "Segmentation and Classification of Targets in FLIR Imagery," *Proc. SPIE*, 155, pp. 83-90, 1978.

[24] Nagel, H. H. "Representation of Moving Rigid Objects Based on Visual Observations," *Computer*, pp. 29-39, August 1981.

[25] Nagel, H. H. "Recent Advances in Motion Interpretation Based on Image Sequences," *Proc. ICASSP*, pp. 1179-1186, Paris, 1982.

[26] Radig, B. M. "Image Region Extraction of Moving Objects," *Image Sequence Analysis*, edited by T. S. Huang, Berlin, pp. 311-351, Springer Verlag, 1981.

[27] Ramachandran, V., and S. M. Anstis. "The Perception of Apparent Motion," *Scientific American*, pp. 80-87, June 1986.

[28] Samy, R. A., and C. A. Bozzo. "Dynamic Scene Analysis and Video Target Tracking," *Proc. 7th Int. Conf. on Pattern Recognition*, pp. 993-995, Montreal, Canada, 1984.

[29] Schunck, B. G. "Image Flow: Fundamentals and Future Research," *Proc. IEEE Conference on Computer Vision and Pattern Recognition*, pp. 560-571, San Francisco, CA, 1985.

[30] Sevigny, L., et al. "Discrimination and Classification of Vehicles in Natural Scene from Thermal Imagery," *Computer Vision Graphics and Image Processing*, 24, pp. 229-243, 1983.

[31] Tsai, R. Y., and T. S. Huang. "Estimating 3D Motion Parameters of a Rigid Planar Patch, I," *IEEE Transactions ASSP*, 29 (6), pp. 1147-1152, December 1981.

[32] Ullman, S. *The Interpretation of Visual Motion*. Cambridge and London, MIT Press, 1979.

[33] Ullman, S. "Analysis of Visual Motion by Biological and Computer Systems," *Computer*, pp. 57-69, August 1981.

[34] Van Santen, J. P. H., and G. Sperling. "Temporal Covariance Model of Human Motion Perception," *Journal of the Optical Society of America*, 1 (5), pp. 451-473, 1984.

[35] Wallach, H., and D. N. O'Connell. "The Kinetic Depth Effect," *Journal of Experimental Psychology*, 45, pp. 205-217, 1953.

[36] Webb, J. A., and J. K. Aggarwal. "Structure and Motion of Rigid and Jointed Objects," *Artificial Intelligence*, 19, pp. 107-130, 1982.

[37] Yalamanchili, S., et al. "Extraction of Moving Object Description Via Differencing," *Computer Graphics and Image Processing*, 18, pp. 188-201, 1982.

Chapter 2

IMAGE SEGMENTATION USING DYNAMIC PROGRAMMING

Le Guilloux, Yann

OUTLINE

Advances in Computer Vision and Image Processing, Vol. 3, pages 39–62.
Copyright © 1988 JAI Press Inc.
All rights of reproduction in any form reserved
ISBN: 0-89232-635-2

ABSTRACT

This chapter presents an algorithm for tracking moving vehicles in an image sequence. The two phases of the algorithm are described. First, consecutive images from the sequence are directly matched using a low-level dynamic programming technique, an idea supported by the observation of natural dynamic vision. Then, using the motion images derived from the first phase, moving vehicles are detected and tracked, allowing eventual partial occlusion and using a one-iteration, split-and-merge technique.

Data involved in experiments consist in 64×64 infrared images, taken at a rate of three images per second. They represent land vehicles moving around in a natural landscape. Experiments prove the robustness of the algorithm, and the capability to simultaneously track multiple vehicles in spite of partial occlusions and changes in shape.

Finally, the extension of the low-level matching technique raises challenging general minimization problems.

1. INTRODUCTION

In the attempt to provide machines with a natural-like vision system, moving from still images to sequences has been an important step. Applications benefiting from such a development include change detection, meteorology, remote sensing, medical imaging, traffic monitoring, surveillance, robot vision . . .

The basic specific issue raised by dynamic vision consists in getting the temporal continuity or discontinuity of the components of the scene, deciding whether such or such element should be matched against a potential counterpart or model from the past. While matching nonidentical elements is an obvious mistake, leaving two representations of the same object unmatched induces failures in the interpretation, involving the disappearance of an object and the sudden apparition of another one.

Solving this problem would allow vehicle tracking, high-level image sequence coding, motion-based segmentation, structure-from-motion determination, next image prediction...

Studies of natural vision suggest that matching is done at a low level of understanding. Here, we take advantage of the horizontal motion constraint and the small volume of data to implement an image-level matching algorithm. It uses a Dynamic Programming technique. Occlusions are modeled and detected, and objects appear as uniform areas in motion images. Once images are mapped, a high-level tracking and segmentation algorithm, using a one-iteration split-and-merge technique, interprets motion images along the sequence in terms of vehicle descriptions, trajectories and occlusions.

In conclusion, the system described performs successfully on very low resolution data. It proves the interest of motion information as a cue for interpretation. The low-level matching is responsible for the robustness of the algorithm.

Finally, extending the matching algorithm to more general motion raises a general minimization problem that may be open.

2. CORRESPONDENCE

2.1   Introduction to the Correspondence Problem

Image sequences might once have only thought as accumulations of images. Then, any image understanding would just have to be applied to each frame.

Actually, it appeared very early that understanding a sequence requires more than understanding all its images. The difference lies in the continuity of the scene, i.e. the same object must be identified throughout the sequence. Although a human observer achieves this task unconsciously, he cannot understand a rapid succession of images having no continuity.

The problem may still look straightforward as presented here, but this is partly because we assumed that single image understanding would provide a perfect object description of the scene. Then, only multiple occurrences of one object would be confusing. Actually, each object to identify often looks different from image to image, because of occlusion, changing light, motion .... Furthermore, no general image understanding algorithm comes out with a perfect object description yet.

However, and this is the major point of image sequence understanding, a different approach can turn the continuity problem to be in favor of sequence analysis. Knowing only partial information derived from the images by single image understanding techniques (like uniform areas, edges, ...) the idea is to match these elements from frame to frame, and to infer from their dynamic behavior (trajectories, occlusions ...) an object segmentation, by gathering similar motions. Now the first and major issue is the correspondence, followed by the analysis from motion (structure, segmentation from motion).

2.2   Correspondence in Natural Vision

Previous studies in natural vision support the correspondence scheme. For instance, Johansson [21] points out that a frog can see only moving preys. Also, a monkey, after ablation of its visual cortex, blind first, becomes quickly able to avoid obstacles and to catch objects as soon as they are moving. However, it remains blind to still objects, and unable to recognize even simple shapes it used to know.

All this suggests that a specific dynamic vision exists, that sees only thanks to motion, i.e. to correspondence information.

Finally, we conducted a simple experiment—random dynamograms— moving a piece of uniformly-distributed random texture in front of a similar uniformly-distributed random texture (background). Thanks to digital image synthesis tools, the piece of texture is perfectly merged with the background as long as no motion is involved. In motion, the visual segmentation is obvious down to the pixel. When it stops, the piece is completely and suddenly merged again. In conclusion, any single image makes the segmentation impossible, although the correspondence set by natural vision when watching the sequence makes it obvious.

Now that the potential power of correspondence information is proved, some experiments reported by Ullman [43] suggest a few basic rules in natural vision, and their limits.

Grayvalue Similarity.   It seems obvious that the correspondence elaborated, in an attempt to represent the physical correspondence, generally tends to match parts of the images with similar grayvalues.

Feature Similarity.   However, an example shows (Figure 1) that the correspondence seen is not always the one achieving the minimal total grayvalue deviation. Here, sharp grayvalue steps are matched though the quadratic deviation suggests no motion.

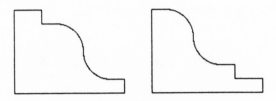

Figure 1. Feature similarity.

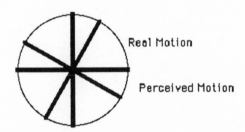

Figure 2. Stroboscopic effect.

Minimal Displacement. The rotation of a cross illustrates the stroboscopic effect (Figure 2). Whenever two correspondences are equally likely to explain the image sequence, the one involving the least total displacement is preferred. In this case, it is not the right one, which leads to the classical aberration.

Existence of Some Structure. Some experiments prove that simple structures—like line segments—can be detected in simple images before association. An example (Figure 3) shows that the correspondence selected is not the one with the minimal displacement but the one matching a line segment to another line segment. This raises the correspondence level issue, that is discussed later.

Minimum of No-Matches. Moreover, the correspondence selected in natural vision usually involves a minimum of no-matches (apparition or

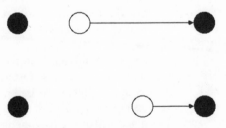

Figure 3. Line-segment matching.

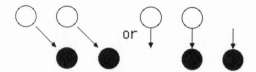

Figure 4.   Ternus configuration.

disappearance). This minimization can cause a conflict with the minimization of displacement pointed above. Such a conflict is exemplified by a Ternus configuration (Figure 4), where two correspondences can be seen. One accounts for a coherent motion of the tokens, the other keeps the middle one still, while the extremes flicker alternatively.

3.   LITERATURE SURVEY

As it was introduced, the correspondence scheme is interesting if it matches parts of objects, not only top-level entities. This leaves open a broad selection for the level of understanding at which matching should be performed. Experiments involving different levels can be found in the literature. We outline a few examples, some of them using image-level matching, others using structural matching.

3.1   Image-Level Techniques

Some people match images at the bottom level by filtering image sequences with a 3D (x, y, t) filter [9, 22, 35, 7]. One of the achievements is, under certain circumstances, the enhancement of areas corresponding to some displacement vector.

Optical flow computation, close in theory to linear filtering of sequence, has been extensively used in coding and dynamic scene analysis [38, 8, 26, 23, 41, 39, 34, 31, 5]. The computations involved require a high-frequency spatial and temporal sampling of the sequence, and little noise. In addition, only partial information about the motion field can in general be found, because of the ambiguity of longitudinal motion. Some ways have been proposed to solve this aperture problem [14, 32, 16, 12, 15, 46, 1] to recover the full velocity field.

The correlation method, often used in tracking, requires a lot of computations [24, 44, 40, 6]. In spite of some improvements (fast algorithms, special purpose architectures), it remains that objects must be known a priori, and that occlusions or changes in size are barely admitted.

A method based on the Fourier transform experimented by Arking [3] did not give good results.

The change detection method, simple and interesting, has been investigated [19, 18, 20, 45, 30]. However, it requires that the background be still, and that a very good quality of images be available.

In short, many method match directly images without any previous understanding. They are generally limited to little and simple evolution between consecutive images. On the other hand, the content of the scene is left open.

3.2 Structural Matching

A number of authors represent images with a set of points, and match lists of points. Unless the images really contains only dots, a first problem is the choice of an interest-point operator. These points must have no equivalent in their neighborhood, and be still surely selected in the next image if they are still visible. Moravec [29], Dreschler and Nagel [10], Maitre and Lopez-Krahe [27] propose examples of such criterions. Generally, because of the little area they represent, points are considered quite noise-sensitive.

Points are matched according to the similarity of some quantitative or qualitative feature. Computing the correspondence often uses also the idea of local consistency of the displacement vector. It is assumed that the displacement vector must be the same over a certain area of the image. Rashid [36] computes a diagram of Voronoï that is matched against predicted positions of points. Aggarwal et al. [2] and O'Rourke [33] use the Hough transform.

Images are also often represented by lines (e.g., contours, edges...). Lines are less noise-sensitive than points. Their ability to represent the scene depends on its content, and is favored by the presence of man-made objects such as buildings or industrial parts. Martin and Aggarwal [28] report an algorithm matching synthetic curves with occlusions. Tsuji et al. [42] match line images minimizing distortion. Several techniques of object detection can be used. For example, Ayache [4] proposes a technique for object recognition that can cope with partial occlusion.

Graphs are another more complete representation of an image. Jacobus et al. [17], Roach and Aggarwal [37], Levine et al. [25] implemented interesting graph matching algorithms for object tracking. Such tools are ideal to render the context of elements. They can handle connectivity, relative positions, inclusions...

3.3 Conclusion

In conclusion, structural matching techniques can generally accept various motions, including rotations, and eventual occlusions. However, their scope is limited to a certain category of scenes, where structures are well defined. On the other hand, image-level techniques, sometimes more robust, less restrictive about the content of the scene, cannot cope with general motion and occlusion.

4. A LOW-LEVEL MATCHING ALGORITHM

As proved by experiments related in the literature, a better robustness can be obtained only from low-level matching schemes, which should be preferred for low-quality low-resolution data. The algorithm we propose [13] makes no assumption about the content of the scene. It assumes horizontal motion. Occlusions are expected, modeled and detected. Using no a priori information, it provides a segmentation of the scene and trajectories of objects.

4.1 Row-to-Row Subproblem

Since we assume horizontal motion, projections of physical points move along image rows. Small deviations from this assumption do not create troubles as long as no strong horizontal texture (like horizontal stripes) is present. Moreover, the coarseness of spatial sampling makes these deviations little visible.

Therefore, we can split the matching problem in N matching subproblems, N being the number of rows. Each subproblem consists in matching two rows from consecutive images. In general, the same principle can be used whenever the direction of motion is known everywhere in the image (roads, rails...). Then lines of fields are globally preserved through motion. These lines can be mapped to rows, which sets the extension.

4.2 Matching

Since we propose an image-level matching scheme, the universe of our search is the set of all possible pixel matches between two rows, which can be represented by a square array (Figure 5).

The correspondence we are looking for is a subset that matches images of the same physical points. Intuitively, as suggested by Figure 5, we can see this subset as path from the upper-left corner to the lower-right corner, except for a few gaps. Along this path, matched pixels, representing the same point, should have about the same grayvalue. This serves as a basis for our path evaluation criterion: the absolute difference between matched pixels integrated along the path should be minimal. So far, we agree with the principle of grayvalue similarity in natural vision, as described in section 2.2. Thus, we translate the problem into picking the path that minimizes an integrated function.

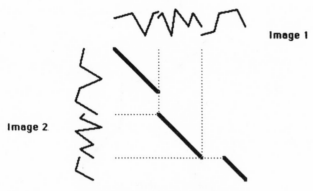

Figure 5. Pixel matches.

4.3 Finding the Optimal Path

To find the optimal path, we use a Dynamic Programming technique, based on the idea that any subpath of the optimal path is itself optimal between its limits. We restrict our search to monotonic paths, i.e. paths that go rightward and/or downward. The algorithm scans the array introduced above row by row, computing the minimal cost from the upper-left corner to the current location. To do so, it just compares the costs to the three possible predecessors of the current location (north, east, northeast), picks the minimum, and adds to it the local cost of the current location. When the lower-right corner is reached, the minimal cost across the array is known, and the optimal path can be easily reconstructed, by backtracking optimal predecessors.

4.4 Interpretation of the Path

As suggested above, the path represents a correspondence between two image rows. The block distance from the diagonal gives the amount of motion of the corresponding image point. Horizontal and vertical segments of the path reflect disappearances and apparitions caused by running occlusions, between two areas having different velocities. Therefore, we can set a displacement value or disappearance/apparition token to each pixel in both rows. Thus, each image is associated with a dense velocity image.

4.5 Stability

To get robust results, a small amount of noise should not change the optimal path drastically. So, we cannot accept for example, in areas of little texture, that a local meaningless grayvalue deviation creating a bump in

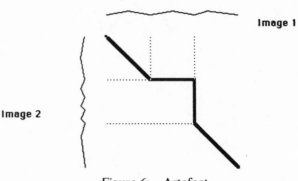

Figure 6.   Artefact.

absolute differences, makes the path go around the bump, therefore giving birth to an artefact (Figure 6). Against this tendency, we add to the original cost of each cell a positive constant, whose effect is to penalize unjustified extra-length, and to favor smooth paths. Since all paths contain the same number of diagonal units, this cost actually penalizes no-matches, i.e. apparitions and disappearances. It agrees with the principle of minimum of no-matches in natural vision (see section 2.2).

The addition of such a cost to make the minimization procedure more stable can be considered as a regularization technique. It is used in a few more occasions in the following.

4.6   Uniform Background Problem

In the simple case of an uniform background, the existence of multiple optimal paths generally confuses the straightforward algorithm (Figure 7).

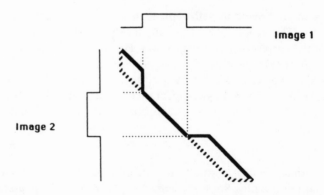

Figure 7.   Uniform background.

It is interesting to note that the *wrong* paths, whose interpretations involve the motion of a piece of background, could actually have generated the image pair. Although we might want to report such ambiguous choices to higher levels of analysis by lack of information, noise makes such situations very unlikely. Practically, one of the theoretically optimal paths is randomly picked as the exact optimal path, due to noise. Thus, we prefer to favor small displacements, minimizing the displacement integrated along the path, or displacement cost. In natural vision, a similar bias is responsible for various effects, including stroboscopic effect. The newly introduced cost is in agreement with the principle of minimal displacement described in section 2.2. Then, since we minimize two criterions—grayvalue difference and displacement cost—a tradeoff must be found: when should we prefer a smaller displacement in spite of larger grayvalue differences, presumably due to noise? We minimize a linear combination of the two, where the coefficients set the tradeoff. They depend naturally on the level of noise in the images.

4.7   Implication of the Displacement Cost

When a large uniform object moves, the expected path is not optimal, due to the integration of the displacement cost (Figure 8). The other path is preferred because it still matches pixels of equivalent grayvalues, and assumes less displacement. Although it does not reflect reality, it leads to a sensible interpretation. The body of the object is still, one end is growing, the other being eroded. The motion of a caterpillar roughly exemplifies such a behavior.

Trying to solve this problem, we realized that the ambiguity can hardly be solved at this level, by lack of a priori segmentation information. To

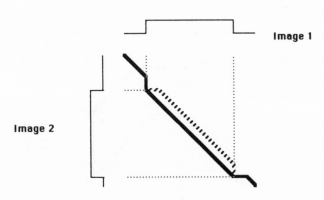

Figure 8.   Large uniform object.

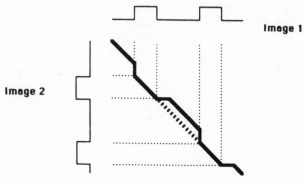

Figure 9.   Parallel motion.

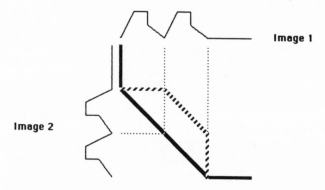

Figure 10.   Ternus-like configuration.

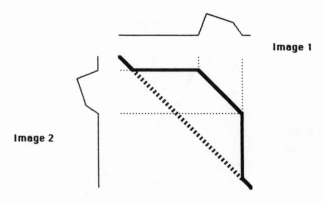

Figure 11.   Large displacement.

illustrate the issue, we consider the parallel motion of two objects before an uniform background (Figure 9). The ambiguity is the same as earlier. The option preferred before leads to fill the gap, as if the background between the objects had moved along with them. Here, we prefer the diagonal path, as opposed to the previous situation.

4.8 Analysis of the Problem

From a theoretical point of view, the ambiguity comes from the absence of local information in nearly uniform areas. At this level, we can just decide to which extent we should fill the gap between two sources of local information (edges, texture . . .). If we do not propagate the displacement, it should be equal to zero.

Finally, looking back at the human visual system, we find that the ambiguity also exists in natural vision: the Ternus configuration, described in section 2.2, analyzed in terms of correspondences, is equivalent to the one displayed in Figure 10, where the paths give the two possible interpretations (coherent/neighborhood motion). Therefore, our matching scheme describes fairly well the lower level of natural dynamic vision up to its ambiguities.

Figure 12.　Image pair.

Figure 13.   Motion image.

4.9   Large Displacements

Due to monotonicity of paths, large displacements involve a lot of no-matches (Figure 11). Because of the displacement and no-match costs, the algorithm actually tends to match slower areas, forgetting about the identity of a fast-moving object.

4.10   Experiments and Postprocessing

The available data are real 64×64 IR images, taken at the rate of three images per second. Vehicles move on a relatively smooth surface, although some hills can hide them at least partially. The camera is itself aboard another vehicle, which explains the fairly shaky camera tracking.

After experimentally tuning the displacement and no-match costs, the output of the algorithm is shown for some consecutive pairs. It proves the ability to differentiate two vehicles based on motion, even though one partially occludes the other, where static information obviously does not allow any discrimination.

Finally, to smooth the results, to get rid of spurious isolated points and to introduce simple interline concurrence, it proves effective to run a 3×3 modal filter on displacement images.

Figure 12 shows an image pair and the corresponding motion images. The poor quality of the sequence can be judged from the original images (top). In the motion images, the color chart is:

1. Green: Rightward motion
2. Red: Leftward motion
3. Blue or White: No match
4. Black or Grey: No motion

In spite of the poor quality of the data, the occlusion of the right vehicle by the left vehicle was found successfully, although no idea of the vehicles is known yet. The blue area between the green and the red areas shows points that will be occluded by motion. Though the camera motion makes the background move in the sequence, it is found still because of its lack of texture, which is consistent with the explanation given in section 4.6.

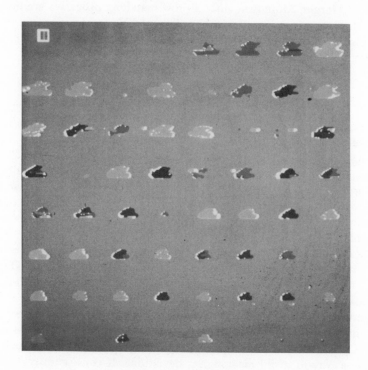

Figure 14. Motion sequence.

Figure 13 shows another difficult case, where two vehicles part behind a low hill that partially occludes both of them. The motion image clearly contains two vehicles having the right direction of motion.

Processing a whole sequence pair by pair gives the result displayed in Figure 14. The first images do not exhibit any motion because the vehicle has not started to move yet. Then, it appears in red, and periodically switches color, eventually becoming invisible. The explanation in terms of motion is that the vehicle sways from side to side in the image, sometimes being still. Physically, this motion represent the residual error of the camera operator tracking. When the motion image is completely gray, the operator tracks it exactly in terms of motion.

4.11   Complexity

Since the algorithm scans an $N \times N$ square for each of N pairs of image rows (assuming square images), the complexity is N^3. However, if we exclude over-large displacements, that we would not recover anyway, only a diagonal band should be scanned. Therefore, the complexity goes down to $N^2 \times$ Margin. Moreover, since all row matching processes are independent, they can run in parallel in N processors. Under these conditions, the processing time comes down to $N \times$ Margin basic iterations (difference/comparisons/sum).

4.12   Further Extensions

We can view the set of correspondence paths as a correspondence surface between two images. Therefore, the problem might as well be stated globally finding the best correspondence surface between two images. The first consequence of this statement is the loss of parallelism. Practically, this new approach takes into account the horizontal patches between two lines, therefore forcing some interline correlation. Finally, finding an optimal surface in a 3D space is not trivial, and might not be feasible within a reasonable complexity.

Another extension might be to match two images globally when any translation is possible. Here, we must find an optimal surface in a 4D space. The issue was a little investigated and raises theoretical difficulties, but would open the way to a general image matcher.

Among more straightforward extensions, an algorithm was implemented that finds the best path with K segments, or K segments at most—where K is a given constant—therefore giving a simple description of the scene. This is a way to avoid meaningless deviations. It consists in scanning K square arrays, each being able to extend a path from its predecessor by eventually creating another segment. Thus, the complexity of this version is K times the original one.

Finally, it is also possible to match three images at a time, row by row, to get more reliable results. The idea is to take the same row in three consecutive images, fill the cube of all three-points matches, and find the best path across the cube. This just involves scanning the cube—or the cube shrunk to the neighborhood of its diagonal, like in the case of the plain algorithm—finding the best out of seven possible predecessors. Then, the complexity is $N \times$ Margin.[2]

5. A MOTION-BASED TRACKING ALGORITHM

5.1 Principle

A motion-based tracking algorithm was implemented [11]. Its originality lies in the fact it uses as an only input motion images computed by the matching algorithm, which clearly carry relevant information. This information is used to detect and update references of the vehicles. The general scheme for a single reference is the following:

- start from a given area of the image (eventually the whole image) as an init value of the reference.
- iterate the following:
  - update the reference by discarding points with different displacements and merge points with the same displacement, under some conditions.
  - match the reference in the current image to the one in the next image, using the correspondence information held in the motion image.

5.2 Initial Reference

The selection of the starting reference is open. It can be done interactively, by thresholding the original image, or segmentation of a motion image . . . . It is not dramatic, since the algorithm splits and merges segments automatically. The point is only to tell the algorithm which area should be processed. One single point of a vehicle is generally enough.

5.3 Updating the Reference

The algorithm maintains a reference for all detected vehicles. It also detects new moving objects. The main idea is to look for a connected component with uniform displacement.

One first estimates the most common D1 and the second most common D2 displacement values in the reference. This allows us to consider the case of two vehicles in the reference, that we want to part thanks to motion. The connected components with displacement D2 sharing too little of their border with D1 areas are detached from the reference as new references.

On the other hand, the reference can also be augmented. To do so, one considers the connected component with displacement D1 extending the reference in the whole displacement image. In general, this component is merged with the reference only if the change of size is reasonable. The reason for this restriction is to avoid to merge the whole image when the vehicle stops, since the whole image has displacement 0. However this test should not be performed when the reference is just a point designating a vehicle to track.

Finally, a modal filter removes isolated points from the background or the reference by imitating the majority of their neighbors.

5.4   Tracking

The updating being done within the current image, one has to match the reference to the next image. This is done using the correspondence represented by the motion image. The amount of horizontal translation of each pixel is obviously its velocity. This eventually shrinks the reference since some points might have the no-match label, meaning that they are occluded in the next image.

5.5   Occlusion Detection

A higher level of understanding might be interested in detecting meaningful occlusions. This can be done by comparing the most common displacement of the reference to the displacement of its center of gravity. Due to the absence of contribution of the hidden part in the next image, the center of gravity relatively moves away from the occluded edge. So the difference between the most common displacement and the displacement of the center of gravity, if meaningful, points toward the occluded edge.

5.6   Results

Tracking through a whole sequence is shown in Figure 15, where the current reference is outline. The partial occlusions by low hills, momentarily altering the visible shape of the vehicle in two occasions, is handled correctly. It should be also pointed that the vehicle does not merge the hot still object it partially masks at the end, which would happen with all single-image algorithms. Figure 16 shows a detail from the sequence.

Figure 15. Tracking sequence.

Figure 16. Detail of the tracking sequence.

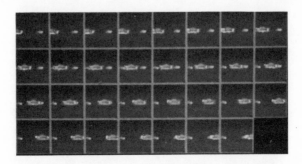

Figure 17.   Crossing.

A test sequence created by inclusion of a synthetic tank in a natural sequence was processed. The result (Figure 17) shows that crossings are easily handled. A detail can be seen in Figure 18.

Finally, Figure 19 shows a short sequence where the vehicle appears and then disappears behind another one. The usual tracking confusion that would lead to switch to the foreground vehicle is avoided.

5.7   Conclusion on the Tracking Algorithm

In conclusion, in spite of a relative simplicity, the tracking algorithm leads to good results, getting the best of its input. Tracking of a reference

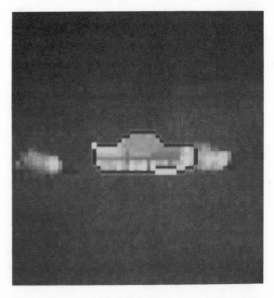

Figure 18.   Detail of the tracking sequence.

Figure 19. Short sequence.

does not interfere with other potential references, and, although the current version handles one reference at a time, the extension to multiple vehicles is just a matter of implementation, since the motion data are available. Depending more specifically on the application, extensions toward higher levels of understanding could be elaborated, including for example recovering a vehicle after a complete occlusion, or building a relative depth map of vehicles based on occlusions.

6. CONCLUSION

Proposing a successful tracking technique in the context of horizontal motion, this work confirms the interest and the feasibility of image-sequence analysis through motion, which proves to be a valuable cue for segmentation and understanding.

The low level of matching, which makes motion even more important, because no a priori information is used to analyze images, is responsible for the robustness of the algorithm. Dynamic Programming provides a low-cost solution to the matching problem, allowing occlusions. The similarity of behavior with natural vision in ambiguous cases seems also positive.

Finally, the motion images provide sufficient information for tracking purpose, as the results of the higher-level algorithm prove it.

Further studies on this algorithm should include a discussion of Dynamic Programming extensions to higher dimensions to accept more general motion.

ACKNOWLEDGMENTS

This research was developed at and supported by Etablissement Technique Central de l'Armement 94114 Arcueil Cedex (France).

REFERENCES

[1] Adiv, G. "Inherent ambiguities in recovering 3-d motion and structure from a noisy flow field," *Proceedings of Computer Vision and Pattern Recognition Conference*, pp. 70–77, 1985.
[2] Aggarwal, J. K., Davis, S., and Martin, W. N. "Correspondence processes in dynamic scene analysis," *Proc. of the IEEE*, pp. 562–572, May 1981.

[3] Arking, A. A. *An Evaluation of Fourier Transform Techniques for Cloud Motion Estimation*, Technical Report TR-351, University of Maryland, Computer Science Department, College Park, MD, January 1975.

[4] Ayache, N., and Darmon, C. "Reconnaissance récursive et localisation de formes planes partiellement visibles dans une image," *Actes du colloque GRETSI*, pp. 611-617, GRETSI, 1983. [In French]

[5] Bergmann, H. C. "Displacement estimation based on the correlation of image segments," *Proceedings of IEE International Conference on Electronic Image Processing*, University of York (U.K.), 1982.

[6] Bers, K. H., Bohner, M., and Fritsche, P. "Image sequence analysis for target tracking," *NATO Advanced Study Institute on Image Sequence Processing and Dynamic Scene Analysis*, pp. 493-501, Berlin, Springer-Verlag, 1982.

[7] Boes, U. "Linear filtering in image sequences," *NATO Advanced Study Institute on Image Sequence Processing and Dynamic Scene Analysis*, pp. 437-447, Berlin, Springer-Verlag, 1982.

[8] Cafforio, C., and Rocca, F. "The differential method for image motion estimation," *NATO Advanced Study Institute on Image Sequence Processing and Dynamic Scene Analysis*, pp. 104-124, Berlin, Springer-Verlag, 1982.

[9] Cano, D., and Bénard, M. "3-d Kalman filtering of image sequences," *NATO Advanced Study Institute on Image Sequence Processing and Dynamic Scene Analysis*, pp. 563-579, Springer-Verlag, 1982.

[10] Dreschler, L. S., and Nagel, H.-H. "On the selection of critical points and local curvature extrema of region boundaries for interframe matching," *NATO Advanced Study Institute on Image Sequence Processing and Dynamic Scene Analysis*, pp. 457-470, Berlin, Springer-Verlag, 1982.

[11] Hildreth, E. *The Computation Of The Velocity Field*, Technical Report AI-Memo 734, Artificial Intelligence Laboratory, Massachusetts Institute of Technology, September 1983.

[12] Horn, B., and Schunck, B. "Determining optical flow," *Artificial Intelligence*, 17, pp. 185-203, 1981.

[13] Ibizon, M. C., and Zapalowski, L. "Structure from motion: an alternative approach," *Proceedings of Computer Vision and Pattern Recognition Conference*, pp. 203-205, 1985.

[14] Jacobus, C. J., Chien, R. T., and Selander, J. M. "Motion detection and analysis by matching graphs of intermediate-level primitives," *IEEE Transactions on Pattern Analysis and Machine Intelligence*, 2 (6), pp. 495-510, November 1980.

[15] Jain, R. "Extraction of motion information from peripheral processes," *IEEE Transactions on Pattern Analysis and Machine Intelligence*, PAMI-3, pp. 489-503, 1981.

[16] Jain, R., Martin, W. N., and Aggarwal, J. K. "Segmentation through the detection of changes due to motion," *Computer Graphics And Image Processing*, (11), pp. 13-34, 1979.

[17] Jain, R., and Nagel, H.-H. "On the analysis of accumulative difference pictures from image sequences of real world scenes, *IEEE Transactions on Pattern Analysis and Machine Intelligence*, PAMI-1, pp. 206-214, 1979.

[18] Johansson, G. "Visual motion perception," *Scientific American*, 232 (6), pp. 76-89, June 1975.

[19] Kretz, F. "Edges in visual scenes and sequences: application to filtering, sampling and adaptative DPCM coding," *NATO Advanced Study Institute on Image Sequence Processing and Dynamic Scene Analysis*, edited by T. S. Huang, pp. 125-155, Berlin, Springer-Verlag, 1982.

[20] Labit, C. *Estimation de mouvement dans une séquence d'images de télévision*, PhD thesis, IRISA, Rennes, FRANCE, 1982. [In French]

[21] Le Guilloux, Y. *Détermination automatique du mouvement dans une séquence d'images. Intérêt pour l'interprêtation.* PhD thesis, Ecole Nationale Supérieure des Télécommunications-Paris, June 1984. [In French]

[22] Le Guilloux, Y. "Structure from motion, acceleration and Taylor series," *Proceedings of Computer Vision and Pattern Recognition Conference,* pp. 400–402, 1986.

[23] Le Guilloux, Y. "Traitement de séquence d'images orienté vers l'analyse de scène," *Actes du colloque GRETSI,* pp. 591–595, GRETSI, 1983. [In French]

[24] Leese, J. A., Novak, C. S., and Clark, B. B. "An automatic technique for obtaining cloud motion from geosynchronous satellite data using cross-correlation," *Journal of Applied Meteorology,* (10), pp. 118–132, 1971.

[25] Levine, M. D., Noble, P. B., and Youssef, Y. M. "A rule-based system for characterizing blood cell motion," *NATO Advanced Study Institute on Image Sequence Processing and Dynamic Scene Analysis,* pp. 663–709, Springer-Verlag, 1982.

[26] Limb, J. O., and Murphy, J. A. "Estimating the velocity of moving images in television signals," *Computer Graphics and Image Processing,* (4), pp. 311–327, 1975.

[27] Maitre, H., and Lopez-Krahe, J. "Transformation de Hough: théorie et application a la détection de symétries circulaires," *Actes du colloque AFCET-INRIA,* pp. 255–264, AFCET, 1984. [In French]

[28] Martin, W. N., and Aggarwal, J. K. "Computer analysis of dynamic scenes containing curvilinear figures," *Pattern Recognition,* (11), pp. 169–178, 1979.

[29] Moravec, H. P. "Toward automatic visual obstacle avoidance," *Proc. of the International Joint Conference on Artificial Intelligence,* p. 584, 1977.

[30] Nagel, H.-H. "Overview on image sequence processing and dynamic scene analysis," *NATO Advanced Study Institute on Image Sequence Processing and Dynamic Scene Analysis,* pp. 2–39, Berlin, Springer-Verlag, 1982.

[31] Nagel, H.-H., and Enckelmann. "Investigations of second order grayvalue variations to estimate corner point displacements," *Proceedings of the International Conference on Pattern Recognition,* pp. 768–773, 1982.

[32] Negahdaripour, S., and Horn, B. "Determining 3-d motion of planar objects from image brightness patterns," *Proceedings of the International Joint Conference on Artificial Intelligence,* 1985.

[33] O'Rourke, J. "Motion detection using Hough techniques," *Proc. of the IEEE Computer Society Conference on Pattern Recognition and Image Processing,* pp. 82–87, 1981.

[34] Prazdny, K. "A simple method for recovering relative depth map in the case of a translating sensor," *Proceedings of the International Joint Conference on Artificial Intelligence,* pp. 698–699, 1981.

[35] Price, C., Snyder, W., and Rajala, S. "Computer tracking of moving objects using a Fourier-domain filter based on a model of the human visual system," *Proceedings of IEEE Conference on Pattern Recognition and Image Processing,* pp. 280–293, Dallas, TX, August 1981.

[36] Rashid, R. F. "Toward a system for the interpretation of moving light displays," *IEEE Transactions on Pattern Analysis and Machine Intelligence,* 2 (6), pp. 574–581, November 1980.

[37] Roach, J. W., and Aggarwal, J. K. "Computer tracking of moving objects in space," *IEEE Transactions on Pattern Analysis and Machine Intelligence,* PAMI-1 (2), pp. 127–135, April 1979.

[38] Robbins, J. D., and Netravali, A. N. "Recursive motion compensation: a review," *NATO Advanced Study Institute on Image Sequence Processing and Dynamic Scene Analysis,* pp. 75–103, Berlin, Springer-Verlag, 1982.

[39] Snyder, W. E., Rajala, S. A., and Hirzinger, G. "Image modeling, the continuity assumption and tracking," *Proceedings of the International Conference on Pattern Recognition*, pp. 1111–1114, 1980.

[40] Spoer, P. "Displacement estimation for objects on moving background," *NATO Advanced Study Institute on Image Sequence Processing and Dynamic Scene Analysis*, pp. 424–436, Berlin, Springer-Verlag, 1982.

[41] Thompson, W. B. "Combining motion and contrast for segmentation," *IEEE Transactions on Pattern Analysis and Machine Intelligence*, 2 (6), pp. 543–549, November 1980.

[42] Tsuji, S., Osada, M., and Yachida, M. "Tracking and segmentation of dynamic line images," *IEEE Transactions on Pattern Analysis and Machine Intelligence*, 2(6), pp. 516–521, November 1980.

[43] Ullman, S. *The Interpretation of Visual Motion*, Massachusetts Institute of Technology Press, Cambridge, MA, 1979.

[44] Wolferts, K. "Special problems on interactive image processing for traffic analysis," *Proc. of the International Joint Conference on Pattern Recognition*, pp. 1–2, 1974.

[45] Yalamanchili, S., Martin, W. N., and Aggarwal, J. K. "Differencing operations for the segmentation of moving objects in dynamic scenes," *Computer Graphics and Image Processing*, (18), pp. 188–201, 1982.

[46] Yuille, A. *The Smoothest Velocity Field and Token Matching Schemes*, Technical Report AI-Memo 724, Artificial Intelligence Laboratory, Massachusetts Institute of Technology, August 1983.

Chapter 3

A REGIONAL APPROACH TO TRACKING 3D MOTION IN AN IMAGE SEQUENCE

T. Y. Young and S. Gunasekaran

OUTLINE

Advances in Computer Vision and Image Processing, Vol. 3, pages 63–99.
Copyright © 1988 JAI Press Inc.
ISBN: 0-89232-635-2

ABSTRACT

Three-Dimensional (3D) motion of an object in an image sequence taken from a camera at a fixed location is considered. An object image is segmented into regions, each corresponding to an object face. 3D rotation and translation parameters are estimated via linear and/or nonlinear parameters that describe the shape changes of object faces. Iterative algorithms for estimation of the shape-change parameters are derived, using an operator formulation.

A multi-stage segmentation scheme is developed that combines edge detection and relaxation with region-based methods. The segmented faces are converted into binary images to emphasize shape information and to simplify subsequent computation. With orthographic projections, a set of linear shape-change parameters for a planar face is sufficient to determine motion parameters during tracking. The problem of initial orientation is discussed in some detail. For perspective projections, under the conditions of small rotation angles and small translation toward the camera, shape changes of planar faces can be taken into account by including quadratic parameters. Experimental results on segmentation and parameter estimation are presented.

1. INTRODUCTION

Motion analysis has emerged as an important research area in computer vision studies. Consider the three-dimensional (3D) motion of an object and a sequence of images taken from a camera at a fixed location. As the object translates and rotates, the projections of its visible faces change gradually in size and shape. A human is capable of perceiving the 3D orientation of an object from the shapes of its visible faces. Here, we are concerned with extracting 3D motion information by regional analysis of 2D shape changes of object faces.

Recent studies on 3D motion by other authors are mostly based on finding and comparing corresponding points in consecutive images. Roach and Aggarwal [1] discussed a method using two views of six corresponding points or three views of four points to produce 22 equations in 21 unknowns. The set of nonlinear equations are solved iteratively with a modified least-square procedure. A recent paper by Mitiche and Aggarwal [2] used the principle of conservation of distances between the points on a rigid object for motion analysis.

Tsai and Huang [3, 4] discussed the uniqueness problem and the estimation of 3D motion parameters. A set of eight pure parameters are defined for a planar patch, and two different ways to estimate these parameters are discussed. The direct method is for small motion parameters only. It does not require estimating the point correspondences first, while the indirect, two-step method does. For curved surfaces, eight or more point correspondences are needed. Experimental results obtained [5, 6] indicated that image resolution must be quite high to estimate motion parameters with reasonable accuracy. A similar technique was discussed by Longuet-Higgins [7].

Another popular approach to motion analysis is optical flow computation and interpretation [8–12]. A computed optical flow field is an estimation of local velocities subject to certain constraints. The object surfaces considered are usually not smooth and the contrast in the object image is high so that local variations of gray-level values can be utilized to estimate local velocities. It becomes more difficult to compute if object surfaces are smooth and optical flow must be computed from moving edges [10].

In an effort to estimate 3D motion of a planar patch without knowing correspondence of points, Kanatani [13, 14] presented two methods for tracing its orientation. The first method estimates the motion by measuring "diameters" of the contour, and it involves various approximations. The other scheme uses line and surface integrals, and it is exact in principle. As noted by the author, the estimation is accurate when the motion is small but cannot be applied to cases with large motion. Jerian and Jain [15] discussed a hypothesize-and-verify approach to recover-motion parameters. The authors suggested that none of the existing methods was robust enough to function independently in real images, and showed the difficulties introduced by noise, the lack of resolution, and the need for better low-level processing techniques.

In this chapter, we consider moving objects with smooth, planar faces. An object image is segmented into regions, with each region corresponding to an object face. Regional shape changes in consecutive images are analyzed, and linear and nonlinear parameters are estimated from the shape changes using an iterative procedure. 3D motion parameters are then estimated from the shape-change parameters. The iterative procedure searches systematically among feasible solutions for a solution that provides the best match. The mean-square matching error is evaluated during the search to ensure that the estimated parameters are accurate. The segmented object faces are converted into binary images, which preserve the 2D shape information while subsequent computations can be reduced significantly.

There are several reasons to suggest that estimation of 3D motion parameters by region analysis of shape changes could be more robust and more accurate than the point-correspondence approaches. Identification of corresponding regions accurately is much easier than finding a number of corresponding points. A region usually consists of a large number of pixels, and therefore region analysis utilizes effectively regional motion information and it is less sensitive to noise and other causes of inaccuracy. The physical meaning of shape changes of a region is intuitively much clearer than that of position changes of isolated points; a person is capable of recognizing the orientation of an object from the shapes of its visible faces. Finally, it is noted that several authors [16-20] presented algorithms for estimation of 2D translation and rotation parameters, using region-analysis approaches, and some of the techniques may be extended and generalized for 3D motion analysis. On the negative side, the method is limited to moving objects with at least one planar face, and an approximation is required for objects in perspective view.

In the following section, the basic relationship between linear shape-change parameters and 3D rotation of a planar face is established for orthographic projections. Iterative parameter estimation algorithms is derived in section 3, using an operator formulation. The operator description of shape changes is essentially a compact representation of a Taylor series expansion. Motion analysis of an object in perspective view is discussed in section 4, where quadratic terms are added for the description of shape changes. Segmentation and experimental results are presented in sections 5 and 6, respectively. 2D motion analysis is treated as a special case and an occlusion problem in 2D motion is briefly discussed in section 7.

2. MOTION AND LINEAR SHAPE-CHANGE PARAMETERS

In this section, we show that with orthographic projection, 3D rotation angle of an object can be computed from a set of linear shape-change parameters of one of its faces. The analysis demonstrates a fundamental relationship between 3D rotation of a rigid object and its projections.

2.1. Linear Shape Changes

Let (x_t, y_t) denote an image point of a moving object in the tth frame of an image sequence. We adopt the vector notation $\mathbf{x}_t^T = [x_t, y_t]$, where the superscript T denotes transpose. The point x_t is moved to x_{t+1}, and it is assumed that their relationship can be expressed by an affine transformation,

$$x_{t+1} = Ax_t + c. \tag{1}$$

Affine transformations have interesting implications to shape changes. For example, under 2D affine transformations, rectangles (or parallelograms) are transformed into parallelograms, triangles into triangles, circles (or ellipses) into ellipses, and conic sections into conic sections of the same type. For this reason, elements of the matrix A are regarded as linear shape-change parameters.

Clearly the vector c in (1) represents translation and has no effect on shape changes. Special cases of matrix A include linear size change (dilation), angular deformation, and 2D rotation, which are denoted by A_s, A_A, and A_R, respectively. Linear size change and 2D counterclockwise rotation of an object by an angle θ may be represented by

$$A_S = \begin{bmatrix} \sigma_1 & 0 \\ 0 & \sigma_2 \end{bmatrix}, \qquad A_R = \begin{bmatrix} \cos\theta & -\sin\theta \\ \sin\theta & \cos\theta \end{bmatrix}. \tag{2}$$

In a similar manner, we may define an angular deformation by

$$A_A = \begin{bmatrix} \cos\alpha & \sin\alpha \\ \sin\alpha & \cos\alpha \end{bmatrix}. \tag{3}$$

It is easy to show that an arbitrary A can be decomposed into the form,

$$A = A_s A_A A_R. \tag{4}$$

Affine transformations for 3D motion analysis have gained attention recently [12, 21-23]. Young and Wang [21] developed the relationship between 3D rotation and the linear parameters in affine transformations. Bamieh and DeFigueiredo [23] were interested in moments that are invariant to a class of affine transformations and to 3D object motion. Adiv [12] used affine transformations and nonlinear transformations for segmenting the optical flow field into connected sets of flow vectors, where each set was consistent with a rigid motion of a roughly planar patch.

2.2   3D Rotation

For 3D motion analysis, let us assume orthographic projections and use an object coordinate system that translates with the translation of the moving object. The center of a certain visible face of the object is chosen as the origin, which can be located easily. The 2D translation of the coordinate system can be evaluated accurately from two consecutive images by region analysis; however, the z-direction translation is not identifiable with the orthographic projection assumption. With this formulation, we may assume without loss of generality that the origin is the center of rotation that can be represented by a 3×3 orthogonal matrix $\mathbf{R}$, i.e.,

$$\begin{bmatrix} x_{t+1} \\ y_{t+1} \\ z_{t+1} \end{bmatrix} = \mathbf{R} \begin{bmatrix} x_t \\ y_t \\ z_t \end{bmatrix}. \tag{5}$$

If we use the Euler angle representation [24], the matrix $\mathbf{R}$ may be expressed as

$$\mathbf{R} = \mathbf{R}_z(\phi)\mathbf{R}_y(\theta)\mathbf{R}_z(\psi), \tag{6}$$

where the subscripts indicate the axes of rotations.

A plane in the 3D space can be expressed as

$$z = -px - qy - s, \tag{7}$$

where (p, q) is a point in the well-known gradient space [25]. A substitution of (7) into (5) yields

$$\begin{bmatrix} x_{t+1} \\ y_{t+1} \end{bmatrix} = \begin{bmatrix} r_{11} - pr_{13} & r_{12} - qr_{13} \\ r_{21} - pr_{23} & r_{22} - qr_{23} \end{bmatrix} \begin{bmatrix} x_t \\ y_t \end{bmatrix} + \begin{bmatrix} -sr_{13} \\ -sr_{23} \end{bmatrix}, \tag{8}$$

which is in the form of (1), the 2D affine transformation.

For a planar face, all points on the face must satisfy the planar equation. Suppose the values of p, q and s of a certain face are known at the instant t. The values of $\mathbf{A}$ and $\mathbf{c}$ in (1) can be evaluated by analyzing shape change of the face in the tth and $(t + 1)$th frames of the images. A comparison of (1) and (8) yields

$$r_{11} = a_{11} - pc_1/s, \qquad r_{21} = a_{21} - pc_2/s,$$
$$r_{12} = a_{12} - qc_1/s, \qquad r_{22} = a_{22} - qc_2/s, \tag{9}$$
$$r_{13} = -c_1/s, \qquad r_{23} = -c_2/s.$$

We note that s is nonzero as long as the plane does not pass through the origin.

With the six elements of $\mathbf{R}$ obtained, it is now possible to calculate the rotation angles and the values of p, q and s for the plane at $t + 1$. In terms of Euler angles, the nine elements of $\mathbf{R}$ are [24],

$$r_{11} = \cos \phi \cos \theta \cos \psi - \sin \phi \sin \psi,$$
$$r_{12} = -\cos \phi \cos \theta \sin \psi - \sin \phi \cos \psi,$$
$$r_{13} = \cos \phi \sin \theta,$$
$$r_{21} = \sin \phi \cos \theta \cos \psi + \cos \phi \sin \psi,$$
$$r_{22} = -\sin \phi \cos \theta \sin \psi + \cos \phi \cos \psi, \tag{10}$$
$$r_{23} = \sin \phi \sin \theta,$$
$$r_{31} = -\sin \theta \cos \psi,$$
$$r_{32} = \sin \theta \sin \psi,$$
$$r_{33} = \cos \theta.$$

Clearly, the values of the six elements in (7) are more than sufficient to solve for ϕ, θ and ψ. A relatively simple solution is

$$\phi = \arctan(r_{23}/r_{13}), \qquad -90° < \phi < 90°,$$
$$\theta = \arcsin(r_{13}/\cos\phi), \qquad -90° < \theta < 90°, \tag{11}$$

and after simple manipulations,

$$\psi = \arcsin(r_{21}\cos\phi - r_{11}\sin\phi), \qquad -90° < \psi < 90°. \tag{12}$$

Note that the solutions for ϕ, θ and ψ are unique under the assumption that all three angles are between $-90°$ and $90°$. The assumption is reasonable for tracking object motion. We also note that there will be difficulty to solve for ϕ using (11) if θ equals zero; however, an examination of (6) and (11) shows that in this case the problem in fact reduces to the simple problem of 2D rotation.

For the computation of p, q and s at $t + 1$, it is more convenient to use a homogeneous transformation,

$$\mathbf{R}_H = \begin{bmatrix} \mathbf{R} & \mathbf{0} \\ \mathbf{0}^T & 1 \end{bmatrix}, \tag{13}$$

where $\mathbf{0}$ is a 3D zero vector. Since $\mathbf{R}_H$ is an orthogonal matrix, $\mathbf{R}_H^{-1} = \mathbf{R}_H^T$. Let

$$\mathbf{p}_t^T = [p_t, q_t, 1, s_t],$$
$$\mathbf{p}_{t+1}^T = [p_{t+1}, q_{t+1}, 1, s_{t+1}]. \tag{14}$$

Then

$$\mathbf{p}_{t+1} = \frac{1}{K}\mathbf{R}_H\mathbf{p}_t, \tag{15}$$

where K is a normalization constant so that the third elements of the resulting $\mathbf{p}_{t+1}$ equals one. Thus, with ϕ, θ and ψ known, the values of $\mathbf{p}_{t+1}$ can be computed easily from $\mathbf{p}_t$.

2.3   Tracking and Initial Orientation

We take the point of view of tracking object motion in an image sequence, and assume that the values of $\mathbf{p}_t$ of a certain object face are known. The center of another visible face is chosen as the origin of the 3D coordinate system. The tracking algorithm is summarized as follows:

- Step 1.   Set $t \leftarrow 1$ and segment the first frame of the image sequence into object faces. Obtain the initial value of $\mathbf{p}_1$ of a certain visible face.

- Step 2. Segment the $(t + 1)$th frame of the image sequence into object faces (see section 5) and identify the corresponding faces.
- Step 3. Estimate the values of $\mathbf{A}$ and $\mathbf{c}$ using an iterative algorithm (see section 3).
- Step 4. Compute the six elements of $\mathbf{R}$ from $\mathbf{A}$, $\mathbf{c}$ and $\mathbf{p}_t$, using (9), and calculate the Euler angles ϕ, θ and ψ from (11) and (12). Also, calculate the remaining three elements of $\mathbf{R}$.
- Step 5. Calculate $\mathbf{p}_{t+1}$ from $\mathbf{R}$ using (13) and (15).
- Step 6. Set $t \leftarrow t + 1$ and $\mathbf{p}_t \leftarrow \mathbf{p}_{t+1}$, and return to Step 2.

Now, suppose $\mathbf{p}_t$ is not known, and let us drop the subscript t for simplicity of notation. It is noted that the orthogonal matrix property of $\mathbf{R}$ provides additional equations, which can be used as auxiliary equations to help finding the orientation $\mathbf{p}$. With a substitution of the elements of $\mathbf{R}$ by (9), the normalization and orthogonality conditions become,

$$
\left(\frac{p}{s} - \frac{a_{11}}{c_1}\right)^2 + \left(\frac{q}{s} - \frac{a_{12}}{c_1}\right)^2 = \frac{1}{c_1^2} - \frac{1}{s^2},
$$

$$
\left(\frac{p}{s} - \frac{a_{21}}{c_2}\right)^2 + \left(\frac{q}{s} - \frac{a_{22}}{c_2}\right)^2 = \frac{1}{c_2^2} - \frac{1}{s^2}, \tag{16}
$$

$$
\left(\frac{p}{s} - \frac{a_{11}}{c_1}\right)\left(\frac{p}{s} - \frac{a_{21}}{c_2}\right) + \left(\frac{q}{s} - \frac{a_{21}}{c_1}\right)\left(\frac{q}{s} - \frac{a_{22}}{c_2}\right) = -\frac{1}{s^2}.
$$

There are three unknowns, p, q, s, in (16); however the three equations are dependent. A proper linear combination of the three equations in (16) results in a constraint equation on $\mathbf{A}$ and $\mathbf{c}$,

$$
\left(\frac{a_{11}}{c_1} - \frac{a_{21}}{c_2}\right)^2 + \left(\frac{a_{12}}{c_1} - \frac{a_{22}}{c_2}\right)^2 = \frac{1}{c_1^2} + \frac{1}{c_2^2}. \tag{17}
$$

Taking the difference of the first two equations yields

$$
\frac{p}{s}\left(\frac{a_{11}}{c_1} - \frac{a_{21}}{c_2}\right) + \frac{q}{s}\left(\frac{a_{12}}{c_1} - \frac{a_{22}}{c_2}\right)
$$

$$
= \frac{1}{c_1^2}(1 - a_{11}^2 - a_{12}^2) + \frac{1}{c_1 c_2}(a_{11}a_{21} + a_{12}a_{22}), \tag{18}
$$

which is linear in p/s and q/s. This same equation can be obtained by taking the difference of any two of the three equations in (16) and using (17). Note that the first two equations are equations of circles in the $(p/s, q/s)$ plane, and it can be shown that

$$
\frac{1}{s^2} \leq \frac{1}{c_1^2 + c_2^2}. \tag{19}
$$

For a given value of $1/s$ within the range specified by (19), the values of p/s and q/s can be easily calculated using (18) and one of the circular equations in (16).

Clearly an additional equation is needed to determine the initial orientation. Some ideas used in the recovery of 3D object shape and orientation from a single view [26, 27] can be adopted for this purpose. These ideas include regularity assumptions or a priori knowledge on parallel lines, perpendicular lines and symmetry. For example, one of the regularity heuristics proposed by Kanade [26] is the following: A skewed symmetry in the 2D image plane depicts a real symmetry viewed from some view direction. Figure 1 shows an example of skewed symmetry and the angles, β_1 and β_2, between the skewed-symmetry axes and the x-coordinate. Thus, if the object face under consideration is symmetric by assumption or by a priori knowledge, the two axes of symmetry must be perpendicular in the

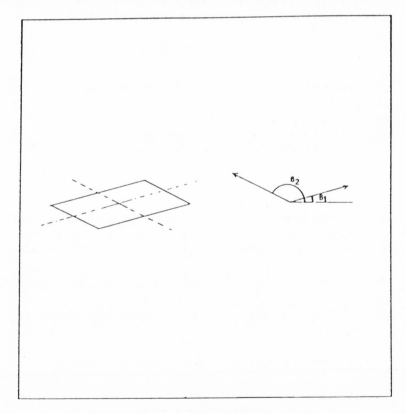

Figure 1. An example of skewed symmetry in the image of a regular symmetric face of an object. β_1 and β_2 are the angles subtended by the axes of symmetry with x-axis of the image.

3D space, and as a result [26],

$$\cos(\beta_1 - \beta_2) + (p \cos \beta_1 + q \sin \beta_1)(p \cos \beta_2 + q \sin \beta_2) = 0. \quad (20)$$

With β_1 and β_2 measured from this image, the set of values p can be obtained by solving (16) and (20). An example of such a case is in section 6.

3. ALGORITHMS FOR PARAMETER ESTIMATION

Linear shape-change parameters can be estimated from segmented images iteratively. An operator formulation is adopted. The operators are, in a sense, compact representations of the infinite number of terms in Taylor series expansions. The operator concept allows us to describe, in a simple and compact way, the dynamic equation of motion, and it facilitates the derivation of the iterative parameter estimation algorithms.

3.1   Operator Formulation

It is convenient to use a $(x, y; t)$ coordinate system to describe object motion in an image sequence. Consider the tth frame and let $F(\mathbf{x}; t)$ denote a segmented face of the object on a zero background. We assume for convenience that $\mathbf{c} = \mathbf{0}$ in (1). The time evolution of the face in the image sequence is described by an operator $L(t)$ so that

$$F(\mathbf{x}; t + 1) = L(t)F(\mathbf{x}; t). \quad (21)$$

Note that in the simple case of 2D translation, a 2D object moving in a certain direction is equivalent to the coordinate system moving in the opposite direction. Similarly, linear shape change of the face can be interpreted as the coordinate system undergoing an inverse transformation. Let

$$\mathbf{A}^{-1} = \mathbf{I} + \mathbf{B}, \quad (22)$$

where $\mathbf{I}$ is the identity matrix. To describe the shape of the face at $t + 1$ in terms of its functional form at t, we have, with inverse transformation of the coordinate system,

$$F(\mathbf{x}; t + 1) = F((\mathbf{I} + \mathbf{B})\mathbf{x}; t). \quad (23)$$

Thus, the operator equation (21) becomes

$$L(\mathbf{B})F(\mathbf{x}) = F(\mathbf{x} + \mathbf{Bx}). \quad (24)$$

In (24), $\mathbf{B} = \mathbf{B}(t)$ is time varying, and $F(\mathbf{x}) = F(\mathbf{x}; t)$, with t suppressed for simplicity of notation.

To find the form of the operator L, consider an infinitesimal $\Delta\mathbf{B}$. Ignoring the higher-order terms,

$$
\begin{aligned}
L(\Delta\mathbf{B})F(\mathbf{x}) &= F(\mathbf{x} + \Delta\mathbf{B}\mathbf{x}) \\
&= F(\mathbf{x}) + (\Delta\mathbf{B}\mathbf{x})^T \nabla F(\mathbf{x}),
\end{aligned}
\tag{25}
$$

where

$$
\nabla = \begin{bmatrix} \partial/\partial x \\ \partial/\partial y \end{bmatrix}.
\tag{26}
$$

Therefore, according to (25)

$$
\begin{aligned}
L(\mathbf{B} + \Delta\mathbf{B})F(\mathbf{x}) &= L(\Delta\mathbf{B})L(\mathbf{B})F(\mathbf{x}) \\
&= [1 + (\Delta\mathbf{B}\mathbf{x})^T \nabla]L(\mathbf{B})F(\mathbf{x}).
\end{aligned}
\tag{27}
$$

In the limit, as $\Delta\mathbf{B}$ approaches zero, we have the operator equation,

$$
\begin{aligned}
dL(\mathbf{B}) &= \lim_{\Delta\mathbf{B}\to 0}[L(\mathbf{B} + \Delta\mathbf{B}) - L(\mathbf{B})] \\
&= [(d\mathbf{B}\mathbf{x})^T \nabla]L(\mathbf{B}).
\end{aligned}
\tag{28}
$$

Dividing by $L(\mathbf{B})$ and integrating yield the solution

$$
L(\mathbf{B}) = \exp[(\mathbf{B}\mathbf{x})^T \nabla],
\tag{29}
$$

which satisfies the boundary condition of $L(\mathbf{0}) = 1$. An expansion of $\exp[\cdot]$ in (29) generates a generalized 2D Taylor series.

To include the translation term $\mathbf{c}$, it can be shown by going through the same procedure that

$$
L_c(\mathbf{B}, \mathbf{d}) = \exp[(\mathbf{B}\mathbf{x} - \mathbf{d})^T \nabla],
\tag{30}
$$

with $\mathbf{d}$ defined by

$$
\mathbf{d} = \mathbf{A}^{-1}\mathbf{c} = \mathbf{c} + \mathbf{B}\mathbf{c}.
\tag{31}
$$

Special cases of L_c include L in (29) and 2D translation and rotation operators [20].

3.2 Iterative Parameter Estimation

Given $F(\mathbf{x}; t)$ and $F(\mathbf{x}; t + 1)$ segmented from two consecutive images. Since the centers of gravity of the two faces can be located easily, we assume without loss of generality that $\mathbf{c} = \mathbf{0}$ and use the operator $L(\mathbf{B})$. We seek iteratively the value $\hat{\mathbf{B}}$ that minimizes the mean-square error defined as

$$
\varepsilon(\hat{\mathbf{B}}) = \sum_{\mathbf{x}} [\hat{F}(\mathbf{x}; t + 1) - F(\mathbf{x}; t + 1)]^2,
\tag{32}
$$

where $\hat{F}(\mathbf{x}; t + 1)$ is estimated from $F(\mathbf{x}; t)$ by

$$\hat{F}(\mathbf{x}; t + 1) = L(\hat{\mathbf{B}})F(\mathbf{x}; t). \tag{33}$$

Using the notation of differentiation with respect to a matrix, we obtain

$$\frac{\partial \varepsilon(\hat{\mathbf{B}})}{\partial \hat{\mathbf{B}}} = 2 \sum_{\mathbf{x}} [\hat{F}(\mathbf{x}; t + 1) - F(\mathbf{x}; t + 1)] \frac{\partial \hat{F}(\mathbf{x}; t + 1)}{\partial \hat{\mathbf{B}}}, \tag{34}$$

where $\partial \varepsilon / \partial \hat{\mathbf{B}} = [\partial \varepsilon / \partial \hat{b}_{ij}]$ is a 2×2 matrix. It follows from (33) and (29) that

$$\frac{\partial \hat{F}(\mathbf{x}; t + 1)}{\partial \hat{\mathbf{B}}} = \frac{\partial L(\hat{\mathbf{B}})}{\partial \hat{\mathbf{B}}} F(\mathbf{x}; t)$$

$$= [\nabla \hat{F}(\mathbf{x}; t + 1)]\mathbf{x}^{\mathsf{T}}. \tag{35}$$

The iterative estimation algorithm is

$$\hat{\mathbf{B}}_{k+1} = \hat{\mathbf{B}}_k - \rho_k \frac{\partial \varepsilon(\hat{\mathbf{B}}_k)}{\partial \hat{\mathbf{B}}_k}, \tag{36}$$

with the positive ρ_k chosen somewhat arbitrarily. It seeks iteratively the minimum of ε by adjusting $\hat{\mathbf{B}}$.

The iterative scheme is a gradient method, and it may converge to a local minimum or it may diverge. The convergence condition of an algorithm for estimating 2D translation parameters has been studied by Netravali and Robbins [18]; the condition is essntially for a local minimum since the higher-order terms of a Taylor series expansion were neglected. Generally speaking, convergence to à global minimum will depend upon the goodness of the initial estimate. This initial estimation problem is largely solved for our tracking scheme, since at t we may simply use $\hat{\mathbf{B}}(t - 1)$ as an initial estimate of $\hat{\mathbf{B}}(t)$. This initial estimate will be good, as long as the linear and angular velocities change gradually. In addition, the mean-square error ε will be evaluated during the estimation process, and a small ε will indicate a fairly accurate estimation.

After the iterative estimation of $\mathbf{B}$, the matrix $\mathbf{A}$ is computed from the inverse of $(\mathbf{I} + \mathbf{B})$. The vector $\mathbf{c}$ has already been obtained from the centers of gravity of the segmented faces at t and $t + 1$, and the matrix $\mathbf{R}$ can be calculated from $\mathbf{A}$ and $\mathbf{c}$ using (9) and the known values of p, q and s.

3.3   Binary Images

Since we are interested in moving objects with smooth faces, the segmented faces $F(\mathbf{x}; t)$ and $F(\mathbf{x}; t + 1)$ are converted into binary images by a simple masking process that preserves 2D shape information. Estimation of $\mathbf{B}$ using binary images emphasizes the shape change aspect of 3D rotation, and it improves the speed of computation of the iterative algorithm.

The iterative algorithm presented in (34)–(36) is for continuous functions. We first notice that since the elements of $\mathbf{x}$ are integer-valued in a digital image, the gradient ∇ should be replaced by a difference δ defined by

$$\delta \hat{F}(\mathbf{x}; t+1) = \begin{bmatrix} \hat{F}(\mathbf{x} + \mathbf{u}_1; t+1) - \hat{F}(\mathbf{x}; t+1) \\ \hat{F}(\mathbf{x} + \mathbf{u}_2; t+1) - \hat{F}(\mathbf{x}; t+1) \end{bmatrix}, \tag{37}$$

where $\mathbf{u}_1^T = [1, 0]$ and $\mathbf{u}_2^T = [0, 1]$. With F and $\hat{F}$ assumed binary, $\delta \hat{F}(\mathbf{x}; t+1)$ is zero everywhere except at the edge points of $\hat{F}(\mathbf{x}; t+1)$. An examination of (34), (35) and (37) shows that (34) is reduced to

$$\frac{\partial \varepsilon(\hat{\mathbf{B}})}{\partial \hat{\mathbf{B}}} \sum_{\mathbf{x}_e} [\hat{F}(\mathbf{x}; t+1) - F(\mathbf{x}; t+1)][\delta \hat{F}(\mathbf{x}; t+1)]\mathbf{x}^T, \tag{38}$$

where $\mathbf{x}_e$ denotes edge points of $\hat{F}(\mathbf{x}; t+1)$. Thus, the iterative estimation algorithm (36) is implemented using (38) instead of (34). Since the summation is over the edge points only and since much of the computation deals with the numbers -1, 0 and 1, the computation time required is reduced significantly.

4. MOTION ANALYSIS FROM PERSPECTIVE VIEWS

Let (X, Y, Z) represent a Cartesian coordinate system with the camera at the origin, and let (x, y) represent the corresponding coordinate system of the image. The focal length of the camera is normalized to 1 without loss of generality. Then, the perspective projection (x, y) of a points (X, Y, Z) is [4].

$$x = X/Z, \qquad y = Y/Z. \tag{39}$$

A 3D rigid body motion can be represented by a rotation $\mathbf{R}$ followed by a translation $\boldsymbol{\mu}$. Thus we have, in the object space,

$$\begin{bmatrix} X_{t+1} \\ Y_{t+1} \\ Z_{t+1} \end{bmatrix} = \mathbf{R} \begin{bmatrix} X_t \\ Y_t \\ Z_t \end{bmatrix} + \boldsymbol{\mu}. \tag{40}$$

Combining (39) and (40) yields [4],

$$x_{t+1} = \frac{X_{t+1}}{Z_{t+1}} = \frac{r_{11}x_t + r_{12}y_t + r_{13} + \mu_1/Z_t}{r_{31}x_t + r_{32}y_t + r_{33} + \mu_3/Z_t},$$

$$y_{t+1} = \frac{Y_{t+1}}{Z_{t+1}} = \frac{r_{21}x_t + r_{22}y_t + r_{23} + \mu_2/Z_t}{r_{31}x_t + r_{32}y_t + r_{33} + \mu_3/Z_t}. \tag{41}$$

The 2D velocity of the point in the image plane is $(x_{t+1} - x_t, y_{t+1} - y_t)$, and from (41) we obtain,

$$x_{t+1} - x_t = \frac{r_{13} + (r_{11} - r_{33})x_t + r_{12}y_t - r_{31}x_t^2 - r_{32}x_ty_t + (\mu_1 - \mu_3 x_t)/Z_t}{r_{33} + r_{31}x_t + r_{32}y_t + \mu_3/Z_t},$$

$$y_{t+1} - y_t = \frac{r_{23} + r_{21}x_t + (r_{22} - r_{33})y_t - r_{31}x_ty_t - r_{32}y_t^2 + (\mu_2 - \mu_3 y_t)/Z_t}{r_{33} + r_{31}x_t + r_{32}y_t + \mu_3/Z_t}. \tag{42}$$

Under certain conditions, 3D motion of a planar patch in perspective images can be represented by a quadratic transformation with linear and quadratic parameters.

4.1   Quadratic Transformation

The planar equation of an object face at t is

$$Z_t = -pX_t - qY_t - s. \tag{43}$$

If we divide (43) by sZ_t, we obtain

$$1/Z_t = -(px_t + qy_t + 1)/s. \tag{44}$$

A substitution of $1/Z_t$ by (44) would eliminate Z_t in (42). Let

$$\xi^T = [1, x, y, x^2, xy, y^2] \tag{45}$$

be an augmented vector, which can be easily calculated from $x^T = [x, y]$. It is assumed that the motion of the planar face satisfies the equation,

$$x_{t+1} = x_t + G\xi_t, \tag{46}$$

where $G = G(t)$ is a 2×6 matrix, and its elements include linear and quadratic parameters.

The assumption (46) is valid for a planar patch [12, 28], if the following conditions are satisfied: (1) the rotation angles are small, (2) the Z-direction translation μ_3 is small relative to the distance of the object from the camera, and (3) the field of view of the camera is not very large. The first two conditions are reasonable if the time interval between the two image frames is short or if the motion is slow.

For small rotation angles, $r_{11} = r_{22} = r_{33} = 1$, and $r_{12} = -r_{21}$, $r_{23} = -r_{32}$, and $r_{31} = -r_{13}$ are small. With $|\mu_3/Z_t|$ small and $1/Z_t$ substituted by (44), (42) reduces to (46) with $g_{15} = g_{23} = 0$, and

$$
\begin{aligned}
g_{10} &= r_{13} - \mu_1/s, & g_{20} &= r_{23} - \mu_2/s, \\
g_{11} &= (\mu_3 - p\mu_1)/s, & g_{21} &= -r_{12} - p\mu_2/s, \\
g_{12} &= r_{12} - q\mu_1/s, & g_{22} &= (\mu_3 - q\mu_2)/s, \\
g_{13} &= r_{13} + p\mu_3/s, & g_{24} &= r_{13} + p\mu_3/s, \\
g_{14} &= r_{23} + q\mu_3/s, & g_{25} &= r_{23} + q\mu_3/s.
\end{aligned}
\tag{47}
$$

In our tracking scheme, it is assumed that p, q and s are known at t, and the matrix $\mathbf{G}$ is evaluated iteratively from the shape change of the face in consecutive images. Thus, (47) is linear in r and μ, and the six unknowns, r_{12}, r_{13}, r_{23}, μ_1, μ_2, and μ_3 can be solved easily. If the initial orientation of the face is unknown, we note that s in (47) is essentially a scale factor and define $\nu_i = \mu_i/s$, $i = 1, 2, 3$. With $g_{13} = g_{24}$ and $g_{14} = g_{25}$, there are eight unknowns that can be solved from the eight nonlinear equations in (47). It is noted that similar to the orthographic projection case, regularity assumptions or a priori knowledge on parallel lines and perpendicular lines can provide additional equations for determining initial orientation. In particular, for 3D objects that are rich in parallel lines, the direction of the parallel lines can be calculated from the common vanishing point of these lines, and in many cases, the shape and orientation of the visible faces can be determined from a single perspective view [27].

4.2   Parameter Estimation by Time Reversal

With the affine transformation, we interpreted the linear shape change as the coordinate system undergoing an inverse transformation and estimated first the matrix $\mathbf{B}$. A difficulty in estimating quadratic parameters is that unlike the linear affine transformation, inverses of nonlinear transformations are not unique. To circumvent this difficulty, we adopt a time reversal technique and estimate the set of linear and nonlinear parameters by examining shape change of a visible face backwardly from the $(t + 1)$th image frame to tth frame.

With the quadratic transformation $\mathbf{G}$ shown in (46), we define a time-reversed quadratic operator Q^{-1} by

$$F(\mathbf{x}; t) = Q^{-1}(t)F(\mathbf{x}; t + 1), \tag{48}$$

where, as in section 3, we use the $(\mathbf{x}; t)$ coordinate system to describe motion in the image sequence. To express the shape of the face at t backwardly by the functional form at $t + 1$, we use the forward transformation $\mathbf{G}$ for the coordinates, i.e.,

$$F(\mathbf{x}; t) = F(\mathbf{x} + \mathbf{G}\boldsymbol{\xi}; t + 1). \tag{49}$$

Thus, the operator equation (48) becomes

$$Q^{-1}(\mathbf{G})F(\mathbf{x}; t + 1) = F(\mathbf{x} + \mathbf{G}\boldsymbol{\xi}; t + 1), \tag{50}$$

where Q^{-1} is time-varying via $\mathbf{G}(t)$. Using a procedure similar to the derivation of the linear operator, we obtain

$$Q^{-1}(\mathbf{G}) = \exp[(\mathbf{G}\boldsymbol{\xi})^T\boldsymbol{\nabla}], \tag{51}$$

which is similar in functional form to $L(\mathbf{B})$.

For the time-reversal method, we wish to minimize the mean-square error,

$$\varepsilon(\mathbf{G}) = \sum_{\mathbf{x}} [\hat{F}(\mathbf{x}; t) - F(\mathbf{x}; t)]^2, \tag{52}$$

where $\hat{F}(\mathbf{x}, t)$ is estimated from $F(\mathbf{x}; t+1)$ by

$$\hat{F}(\mathbf{x}; t) = Q^{-1}(\hat{\mathbf{G}})F(\mathbf{x}; t+1). \tag{53}$$

The iterative algorithm,

$$\hat{\mathbf{G}}_{k+1} = \hat{\mathbf{G}}_k - \rho_k \frac{\partial \varepsilon(\hat{\mathbf{G}}_k)}{\partial \hat{\mathbf{G}}_k} \tag{54}$$

seeks the minimum of ε with

$$\frac{\partial \varepsilon(\hat{\mathbf{G}})}{\partial \hat{\mathbf{G}}} = 2 \sum_{\mathbf{x}} [\hat{F}(\mathbf{x}; t) - F(\mathbf{x}; t)][\nabla \hat{F}(\mathbf{x}; t)]\boldsymbol{\xi}^{\mathrm{T}}. \tag{55}$$

The estimation procedure is almost identical to that of estimating **B**, except for time reversal. In the implementation of the algorithm for experimental study, the segmented faces were converted into binary images to improve the speed of computation, and (55) was replaced by

$$\frac{\partial \varepsilon(\hat{\mathbf{G}})}{\partial \hat{\mathbf{G}}} = 2 \sum_{\mathbf{x}_e} [\hat{F}(\mathbf{x}; t) - F(\mathbf{x}; t)][\delta \hat{F}(\mathbf{x}; t)]\boldsymbol{\xi}^{\mathrm{T}}, \tag{56}$$

where $\mathbf{x}_e$ were edge points of $\hat{F}(\mathbf{x}; t)$.

5. SEGMENTATION

Segmentation plays an important role in low-level processing of any vision system, and it is essential to the success of the proposed motion analysis scheme, which is based on the shapes of the segmentated regions. Most of the recent work on segmentation can be broadly classified into two basic approaches. First, edge-detection and contour-tracing–based methods, in which a local evaluation of the edge strength at a pixel is carried out resulting in an edge-feature vector at each point, which are then grouped into meaningful contours at higher global levels to form a set of boundaries that divide the image into final segments. The second approach is mainly the dual of the above. In the region-based approach, often a seed point (any pixel for that matter) is chosen to be a region, and at each stage its adjacent, unassigned points is added in such a way that certain uniformity criteria are satisfied; alternatively one may start with the entire picture as one region and recursively splitting/partitioning each region such that a connected subset of points in a region, over which uniformity is satisfied locally but fails globally is removed to form a new region, at each recursion. A careful inspection of both methods reveals that the region-based methods are somewhat equivalent to edge-detection–based schemes, when the latter employs nonmaximum-edge suppression for consolidating the locally consistent edge segments as a global boundary.

We adopt a multistage segmentation method that takes advantage of the strength of both approaches. The method is divided into three phases: (1) preprocessing, which reduces noise and fine textures in image data by edge-preserving smoothing, (2) edge detection and evaluation including nonmaxima suppression and relaxation, and (3) boundary formation, which connects edge elements to form lines, splits inhomogeneous regions; eliminates insignificant holds, and merges small regions into larger ones. Figure 2 shows an example of an image at various stages of segmentation.

5.1 Preprocessing

The method employed in this stage is essentially the same as that described in Prager [29]. Let N_0 be the point at which we are smoothing the image; define a set of neighboring pixels as a 3×3 square block centered at the current pixel, label the center as N_0, and the rest N_1, N_2, ... N_8. Then select only those N_is whose absolute difference with N_0 is less than certain predefined threshold T, and replace N_0 by the average of these N_is.

This operator results in the following improvements. Random noise that is present in the homogeneous regions are smoothed out if the noise variance is less than T. Pixels at the inside of a boundary are not affected by the outward neighbors (that is the pixels that belong to the neighboring region), if the contrast is more than T. Also, within a textured region, if the texture elements differ by an amount less than T, they are smoothed out resulting in a homogeneous region.

Clearly the choice of threshold value T plays an important role in the final segmentation. An optimum value of T was chosen experimentally by passing the whole segmentation process with different values of T and choosing the one that led to better results; however, there are some techniques discussed elsewhere to select T from the spatial statistics of the image. The original picture was uniformly distributed over the 8-bit gray-scale range, and the chosen T was 25, while the camera noise was estimated to be 2.5; all in gray units. If the nature of the noise is known a priori, a suitable method of smoothing may be applied.

5.2 Edge Detection and Evaluation

An edge, by definition, is a representation of spatial discontinuities in the gray values of the image function. A detailed discussion on various

a

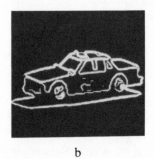

b

c

Figure 2. (a) An example image being segmented. (b) Raw edge output after applying the edge masks, followed by normalization. The edge strength have been thresholded for display purpose. (c) Edges, after compatibility checking, partial thinning and nonmaxima suppression. (d) Each completely closed contours in 2c is represented by a distinct gray level. (e) Several boundaries are broken and the small regions in 2d are melted. (f) After merging some similar, adjacent regions; also breaking weak boundaries in 2e. (g) Final, segmented image. Boundary representation of 2f.

canonical representations of edges, and the problem associated with each one may be found in [30]; also the connectivity paradox over rectangular grids is emphasized in [31]. The satisfying representation for our purpose turns out to be the one used by Brice and Fennema [32]. In this model the edges are constrained to fall between pixels. However, the definition of edge under gradient standpoint suffers with this representation when diagonal gradients are encountered. The problem is readily circumvented by viewing the edges as the boundary between two regions, that is, between two adjacent pixels that belong to two different regions (see Figure 3).

With this representation, the following observation can be made: Let (x, y) be the coordinate of a given pixel, where x, y are both integers in the

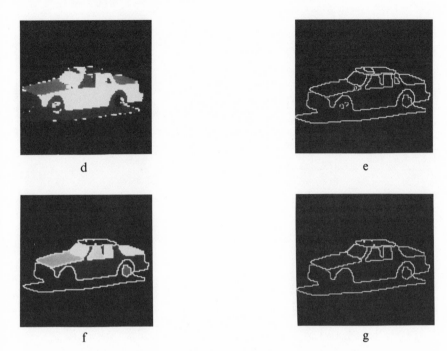

d

e

f

g

Figure 2. (cont.)

valid range. Then there are four edges associated with each pixel that may exist independently, identified as follows:

$$
\begin{aligned}
E_1 &- \text{Dist}((x, y)(x + 1, y)) \\
E_2 &- \text{Dist}((x, y)(x, y + 1)) \\
E_3 &- \text{Dist}((x, y)(x - 1, y)) \\
E_4 &- \text{Dist}((x, y)(x, y - 1)),
\end{aligned}
\tag{57}
$$

where $\text{Dist}((x, y), (x', y'))$ is defined as the distance between two pixels in certain metric, indicating that they belong to different regions. In the edge detector that is used in the following, Dist is a signed quantity indicating the direction and the magnitude of the edge along the chosen direction, i.e.,

$$
\text{Dist}((x, y), (x', y')) = -\text{Dist}((x', y'), (x, y)).
\tag{58}
$$

This leads to a canonical representation of edges in which only E_1 and E_2 need to be stored at each pixel.

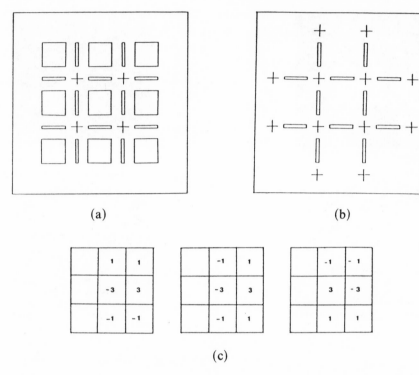

Figure 3. An illustration of interpixel representation of edges. The □ represents pixels, the ▭ represents edge strokes and + represents the vertices joining adjacent edges. (b) A system of boundary paths over a 3 × 3 window. (c) Three masks used to compute E_1 the edge strength along x-direction.

A. Edge Detection

The edge strength at each pixel is computed by a general masking procedure. The family of masks is designed to interact efficiently with the relaxation refinement to be explained later. Given the interpixel representation of edges, one needs to compute edge strength only at two directions (vertical and horizontal). Henceforth these elements will be called as edge-elements or strokes. The masks for computing edge strength in x direction would be presented below, while the ones for y direction are the result 90° rotation of the same.

The masks being used are designed with the following assumptions: First, for a stroke to be a part of a boundary, there has to be at least one stroke in each end assuring continuity. Secondly, larger mask size would have to be avoided as they tend to pick up variations at faraway pixels and result in multiple edges. Finally, the resulting contours have to be smooth enough, that is, the curve does not change directions at 3 successive stroke–stroke junctions. The masks are shown in Figure 3; and at the given pixel the maximum magnitude of the responses for these three masks is chosen to be the result.

It is suggested in [30], that a 2×1 mask is desired since the possibility of multiple edges is ruled out. However, the problem manifests in a different form at the gradient collection process. Also there is a potential possibility that a globally consistent line may get broken or dislocated; and it was felt reasonable to modify the mask reflecting the constraint. Also, this turns out to have the advantage of responding to diagonal variations.

B. Edge Tracing

Edge tracing for boundary detection can be reformulated as the problem of finding an optimal path in a weighted graph. Montanari [33] devised a method in which an objective function is developed based on the properties of the boundary curves. A dynamic programming approach is then developed, that maximizes the objective function, satisfying certain constraints on the resulting boundaries. An exhaustive search may be used if desired, to find the truly optimal solution. However, the complexity considerations at the problem sizes incurred in practice claim the merits of this approach.

Consider a 3×3 window superimposed on the stroke cells as shown in Figure 3b. One can consider the stroke-junctions as nodes of a graph, and cost of travelling to an adjacent node as the strength of the linking stroke, and formulate the longest path problem to find the maximum discriminatory boundary. Any boundary line passing through the window does not enter and leave both in one side of the window, as it would violate the smooth-boundary assumptions. Any meaningful boundary passing through the block must involve at least one of the four inner strokes, where at most only two can take part in the activity. Furthermore, a single pixel region is not permitted (that is, all the four edges do not coexist). All these facts, in the form of constraints, result in only few possible system of paths, are used to prune the search tree considerably. These were implemented in a 16-level, mutually exclusive conditional execution blocks.

The algorithm does to a certain degree, connectivity-preserving-thinning; weakest boundary breaking (alternatively, smallest region melting), non-maxima suppression all partially. In the process a set of compatible and consistent paths are given a confidence incentive, and those paths that are competing with some strong alternatives are decremented by an amount. In either case the increment and decrement quantities are judiciously chosen.

C. Relaxation

Relaxation is a classical iterative method applied to solve boundary value problems in numerical solutions of partial differential equations. A similar approach [34] can be used to iteratively refine the edge-strength values that are obtained in the foregoing section. The underlying assumption in this process is that if the resulting edge-elements satisfy local compatibility (or consistency) everywhere, then global consistency is implicitly exhibited. The relaxation model used in Hanson and Riseman [30] was implemented with no major modifications. In normalizing the output from the foregoing section to match the present relaxation, the following process was used: the histogram of the edge occurrence was constructed as a 1-dimensional edge-strength distribution density; instead of the highest strength incurred (global maximum) for normalizing, a reasonable value was chosen as the global maximum. If the global maximum is considered for normalizing, a large response due to noise or a strong edge results in lower probability values for those edges that are in right places. Secondly, the higher the global average, and inherent compatibility due to our edge masks, lead to less iterations for relaxation, avoiding the possibility of enhancing spurs. The effect of static increment/decrement values were observed experimentally by using different values and repeating the whole process. The values of delta $= 0.15$ $q$min $= 0.05$, $q$max $= 0.95$ (see [30]) were found to be effective; however, a different set of values is expected to result if other edge masks are used.

5.3   Boundary Formation

The result of the previous phase is an array of edge-stroke values that exhibit a certain degree of global consistency; however, the information about the underlying structures and details are yet scattered all over the image. The purpose of this phase of segmentation is to consolidate the above data into a meaningful semantic network that cogently describes the scene.

The process first involves a bind process, which identifies lines. A line is a sequence of edges connecting two points that are junctions of 1, 3 or 4 lines. Then a boundary-interaction graph (BIG) to be described later would be developed, which is an indirect representation of the regions of our final segmentation. A dual of BIG, is readily observed to be the region adjacency graph (RAG), with one exception of few loops at some region-nodes. Information available in the dual-graphs system can be used recursively to split and merge regions, or alternatively to bridge two vertices or break a link in BIG, respectively. Popular algorithms exist in graph-theory to solve these problems individually at varied levels of complexities.

A. Bind Process

We define a line as a sequence of strokes such that each stroke meets exactly one stroke at each end except the extreme elements, The lines are then characterized by the number of lines incident on these vertices; also associated with each line is a feature vector that may include the length, boundary strength or confidence, total curvature, and so on. Clearly, under this representation each vertex is located at center of its 4 nearest pixels; the degree of these vertices at the end of a line can, at most, be 4; and any vertex of order 0 or 2 do not exist in the final representation of lines. However, vertices of degree 1 may exist, which in fact corresponds to broken boundaries. We call these lines as cracks, spurs and borders if their vertices are of $1 - 1$, $x - 1$, $x - x$ (x nor 0 or 2), respectively. The lines formed by binding these edges are uniquely labeled, and the features are computed. The first two steps are represented in an algorithm. Complete information about these lines is available, in the form of a graph, when the algorithm completes traversing the entire array of strokes. We call this graph a boundary interaction graph. Also note that BIG does indeed contain some unconnected subgraphs, those with only two vertices for each spur detected, and one corresponding to each maximal connected set of lines (borders); also to be observed is that vertices of degree 1 exist, corresponding to open ends of each crack encountered.

Parallel to the above step, one may apply a raster-scanned depth first filling algorithm, to identify closed regions; that is, cycles in the boundary interaction graph are identified, that correspond to regions of our final segmentation. We shall call them as pseudo regions, since a spur or crack may exist within the face encircled by the cycles in the BIG, hence a potentially false region. This step is twofold: First, it is evident that the BIG is planar, since it indirectly represents a system of spatially adjacent regions. Note that any straightforward cycle-finding algorithms would not be able to associate a spur with the cycle that encircles it. Secondly, if one were to construct the pseudo regions from the BIG, then connectivity problem is expected in deciding which of those pseudo regions are adjacent and/or connected to each other.

We conclude the description on the bind process with the following observation: BIG and RAG contain some spatial interaction information in the form of graphs; both are partially dual to each other and they carry information of complementary nature, that is, none of them contains complete description of the scene.

B. Region Splitting

The set of pseudo regions and the RAG developed above contain partial result of our segmentation. Pathological situations may exist where there are one or more breaks in the boundary between two spatially adjacent homogeneous regions, resulting in nonuniform regions that may be the union of two or more true regions. The purpose of this step is to develop a reliable and acceptable segmentation from the BIG and pRAG described above. The process involves bridging a broken boundary path in BIG or alternatively splitting a pseudo region in pRAG.

The singular vertices in the BIG are identified, which correspond to the vertices of degree 1; the parent pseudo regions, that is the pseudo regions within which the vertex is spatially present or contained is identified. A set of all such vertices is formed, which we call as singular vertices set (SVS); the SVS is then partitioned, such that each partition corresponds to one pseudo region.

For each partition in SVS the following steps are carried out: First, apply a uniformity test over the corresponding pseudo region. If an acceptable degree of uniformity is observed, then delete all those vertices in BIG that are in the current partition of SVS; mark confidence for that pseudo region and repeat the above procedure if there are more partitions in SVS. If nonuniformity resulted in the test, then the current pseudo region is a potential candidate for split; alternatively the vertices in SVS are the candidates for bridging.

There are basically two approaches that are possible at this stage. The first approach is to resegment the current pseudo region by any of the classical but simple methods such as histogram-based techniques. It is reasonable to expect acceptable performance as explained in [35]. Other methods may be used if desired. In the second approach, an optimal curve fitting may be devised such that, a minimal-length curve passes through most of the vertices in current SVS partition.

The histogram-based region split method was implemented in our system. The old pseudo region is removed from pRAG and two new pseudo regions are created and added to pRAG, and the BIG is updated by bridging the broken boundaries. If no meaningful partitioning of the pseudo region resulted in the above process, flag the pseudo region as less confident, and repeat the process until there is no SVS or pseudo region to be examined.

C. Merging

This is the final step of our segmentation system. The purpose of this step is to construct the regions from the set of pseudo regions that are marked confident by the previous stage, and examine and accept/reject those that were not examined in the last stage. In the resulting set of regions, there may still be some adjacent regions whose union exhibits an acceptable degree of homogeneity. These regions may be merged optionally. The operation, in the region-based terminology represents melting a small region;

and in the boundary-based approach corresponds to breaking of a boundary. This stage was implemented using region-based approach, i.e., from pRAG instead of BIG. Note that the order in which pRAG is traversed results in different outcomes that are not significantly different.

6. EXPERIMENTAL RESULTS

We present here experimental verification of the proposed schemes for 3D motion analysis. Two separate cases are considered. The first case assumes orthographic projections. A pair of images of an automobile under motion is chosen as a candidate for the linear-parameter estimation algorithm. The initial orientation as well as the motion parameters are estimated from the images. In the second case, the camera is placed closer to the moving automobile to obtain perspective views. Motion parameters are then estimated from linear and quadratic shape-change parameters. In addition, a pair of images is generated synthetically to verify the estimation algorithm and estimation accuracy.

6.1 Orthographic Projections

Two fairly complex images of a moving automobile recorded at different times are presented in Figures 4a and 4b. The images are 128×128 pixels in size, and were acquired from a standard video camera through an 8-bit digitizer. It is worth mentioning that some camera-digitizer combinations introduce certain problems related to aspect-ratio considerations. In such cases, a pixel in the sampled image does not represent a square area in the image plane of the camera. A suitable combination of bilinear interpolation or a simple supersampling followed by averaging can be devised to counter the problem.

The images in Figures 4a and 4b were segmented using the multistage segmentation procedure presented in section 5. The segmented images are given in Figures 4c and 4d, respectively. The labeled regions or segments corresponding to the left-side view and the hood of the automobile were chosen for subsequent analysis.

The centroids of the left-side view in both images were found, and the difference was treated as the translation component. Henceforth, the images were represented in object coordinate systems whose origins were located at the centroids of this face in both instants. The shape-change information of the hood segment from time t to $t + 1$ was chosen for iterative parameter estimation. We note that the hood is a large, nonoccluded surface, and it exhibits a skewed symmetry that is amenable for developing auxiliary constraint as in (20).

Two binary-image functions, $F(\mathbf{x}; t)$ and $F(\mathbf{x}; t+1)$ were created representing the hood. For a given $\mathbf{x}$ at time t, $F(\mathbf{x}; t)$ was set go 1 if $\mathbf{x}$ was contained in the hood segment, and was set to zero otherwise. The iterative parameter estimation algorithm developed in section 3 was then applied over $F(\mathbf{x}; t)$ and $F(\mathbf{x}; t+1)$ to compute the values of $\mathbf{A}$ and $\mathbf{c}$. The values thus obtained are:

$$\mathbf{A} = \begin{bmatrix} 1.006 & .000 \\ .015 & 1.000 \end{bmatrix}, \qquad \mathbf{c} = \begin{bmatrix} -6.736 \\ -2.829 \end{bmatrix}.$$

These values are in agreement with (17), the constraint equation on $\mathbf{A}$ and $\mathbf{c}$, within a reasonable accuracy. As explained in section 2.3, the values $\mathbf{A}$, $\mathbf{c}$ alone are not sufficient to determine the 3D structure that includes initial orientation. The partial information contained in $\mathbf{A}$ and $\mathbf{c}$ is well revealed in a parameter plane $(p/s, q/s)$ as illustrated in Figure 5.

The following comments apply to possible solutions for a given value of $\mathbf{A}$ and $\mathbf{c}$, as exhibited in Figure 5. With each value of s, we have a pair of circles centered at $(a_{11}/c_1, a_{12}/c_1)$ and $(a_{21}/c_2, a_{22}/c_2)$, intersecting always on a straight line satisfying (18). The circles represent the first two of the three relationships in (16). It is also apparent that for a given value of $1/s$

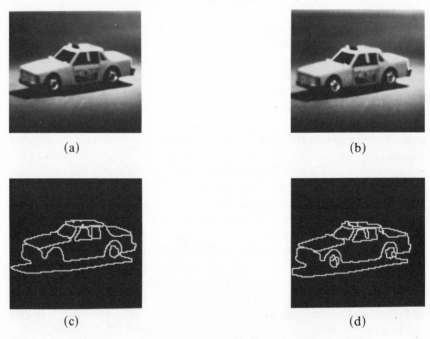

(a)   (b)

(c)   (d)

Figure 4. (a) Automobile at time t. (b) Automobile at time $t+1$. (c) Segmented version of (a). (d) Segmented version of (b).

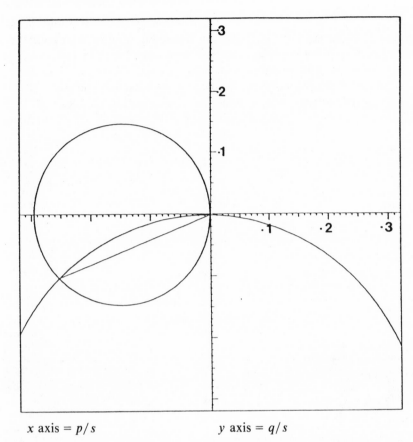

x axis = p/s y axis = q/s

Figure 5. Mutual constraints on **A** and **c** illustrated through a pair of intersecting circles. The common chord contains all the possible solution instances. Both the circles represent the largest possible circles about the corresponding centers.

within the range specified by (19), there is a pair of points in the parameter plane satisfying the above. The distance between the centers of the two circles is given by (17); as a result, a geometrical interpretation of the equations, for a limiting value of $1/s^2 = 0$, leads to a right-angled triangle formed by the centers of the circles and the solution point on the line. This places a limit on the solutions (18) to a line segment that is the common chord of the two circles with radius $|c_1|^{-1}$ and $|c_2|^{-1}$, respectively, as shown in Figure 5. Each point on the line segment satisfies completely the equations in (16).

Since **A** and **c** are known, for a given point $(p/s, q/s)$ on the line segment, $1/s^2$ can be calculated from any one of the equations in (16). Dividing

$(p/s, q/s)$ by $1/s$ will give us a solution point (p, q). A large number of (p, q)-points corresponding to the points on the line segment were computed in this way, and the resulting solution curve was plotted in Figure 6. The solution curve is hyperbolalike with high curvature at the two vertices.

To seek an unique solution, the two axes of skewed-symmetry of the hood segment at time t were obtained. The resulting angles of skewed-symmetry were: $\beta_1 = 14.0°$ and $\beta_2 = 152.5°$. The hyperbola of (20), for these

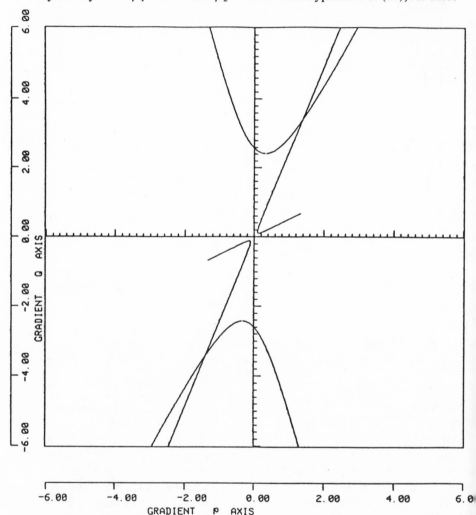

Figure 6. The solution curve and the hyperbola, intersecting at the final solution pairs. The highly asymptotic curve is the solution curve. The hyperbola represents $\beta_1 = 14°$ and $\beta_2 = 152.5°$.

values of β_1 and β_2, is also shown in Figure 6, and the hyperbola cut the solution curve developed earlier. The above two curves intersect at a pair of points, each corresponding to $+/-$ values of s. The initial orientation thus obtained was

$$(p, q, s) = (-1.4, -3.4, \pm 278) \quad \text{or} \quad (1.4, 3.4, \pm 278).$$

These values were then substituted into (9) for computing the coefficients of the matrix $\mathbf{R}$. The resulting rotation angles computed from (11) and (12) are

$$(\phi, \theta, \psi) = (22.8°, 1.5°, -22.1°).$$

The relatively large values of ϕ and θ may raise some doubt for some readers, but it is noted that they are both about the z-axis, and in opposite directions. In fact, the results agree reasonably to the scene instances that were recorded.

Much of the computations discussed above are for the initial orientation that needs to be computed only once during tracking. It is also noted that other a priori knowledge may be used instead of symmetry. Another possibility is to use shape changes of two or more faces, providing additional equations for determining initial orientations.

6.2   Perspective Projections

A computer-generated image pair of an automobile undergoing a composite motion is shown in Figure 7. The images demonstrated a certain degree of perspectiveness. The purpose of the simulation is to examine the applicability of the quadratic parameter-estimation algorithm and the motion-parameter extraction from the linear and quadratic shape-change parameters.

The hood patch of the automobile at t was considered, and the values of (p, q, s) for the planar equation (43) were taken from the simulation model. Taking the binary images corresponding to time t and $t + 1$, and applying the iterative parameter estimation algorithm (54) and (56), the G matrix was computed to a reasonable accuracy. Substituting the values of (p, q, s) and g_{ij}'s in (47) yielded eight equations in six unknowns. The eight linear equations were solved through linear least-square techniques using a standard subroutine.

It is more convenient to use rotation angles $\boldsymbol{\omega}^T = (\omega_x, \omega_y, \omega_z)$ for perspective views since for small rotation angles [12, 28], we have

$$\omega_x = -r_{23} = r_{32},$$

$$\omega_y = -r_{31} = r_{13}, \tag{59}$$

$$\omega_z = -r_{12} = r_{21}.$$

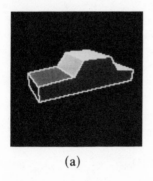   

(a)   (b)

Figure 7.   (a) Computer generated image of an automobile under perspective projection. (b) The automobile of Figure 7a after a composite motion.

The results obtained were $\omega^{T} = (6.1°, 16.0°, -10.9°)$ and $\mu^{T} =$ $(-4.5, -5.5, -10.3)$, which agreed reasonably with the actual values of rotation $(5.0°, 15.0°, -10.0°)$ and translation $(-4.0, -5.0, -7.5)$.

We next considered a pair of perspective images shown in Figures 8a and 8b. This experiment differs from the previous one in that real images were considered and that the initial orientation (p, q, s) was unknown. With s treated as a scaling parameter, the orientation parameters (p, q) can be computed from the matrix $\mathbf{G}$ in such instances.

Consider (47) and let $v_i = \mu_i/s$, $i = 1, 2, 3$. With (p, q) unknown, (47) is a set of eight nonlinear equations in eight unknowns. By a series of substitutions, the eight equations can be reduced to

$$p = \frac{(q^2 + 1)(qh_1 - h_2)}{(q^2 h_3 + 2qg_{22} - h_3)},$$

$$q = \frac{(p^2 + 1)(ph_3 - h_2)}{(p^2 h_1 + 2pg_{11} - h_1)},$$
(60)

where

$$h_1 = g_{13} - g_{10},$$

$$h_2 = -(g_{12} + g_{21}),$$
(61)

$$h_3 = g_{25} - g_{20}.$$

Further reduction of (60) is possible by substituting for q in the first expression by the second equation and then simplifying the result. The reduction process leads to a polynomial of 8th degree in p that needs to be solved. It is easy to see from (60) that two of the solutions are $(p = 0, q =$

h_2/h_1) and ($p = h_2/h_3, q = 0$). The remaining six roots can be solved using any of the standard techniques of finding the zeros of a polynomial. It is noted that at each step of reducing the original set of equations, only linear substitutions were required. Thus for each root of the polynomial, only one set of values of q, $\boldsymbol{v}$, and $\mathbf{R}$ exists. However, among the solution sets corresponding to distinct real roots of the polynomial, the choice of a specific solution set is somewhat arbitrary.

In our experiment, we encountered only four real roots. As expected, ($p = 0, q = h_2/h_1$) and ($p = h_2/h_3, q = 0$) represent two of the four real-valued solutions; however, they are not meaningful in our case. The root that was chosen as the solution yielded small values of r_{12}, r_{13}, and r_{23}. Thus, for this example,

$$(p, q) = (-1.67, 5.39)$$

$$(r_{12}, r_{13}, r_{23}) = (-.19, .08, .07)$$

$$(v_1, v_2, v_3) = (-.078, .072, .199).$$

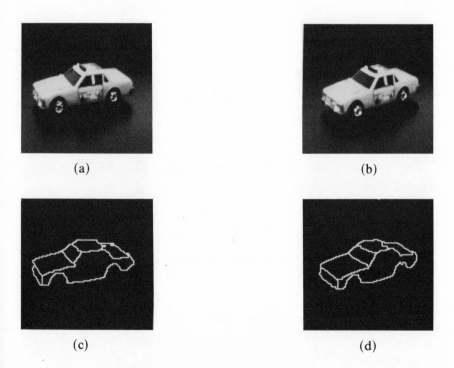

(a) (b)

(c) (d)

Figure 8. (a) Automobile at time t. (b) Automobile at time $t + 1$. (c) Segmented version of (a). (d) Segmented version of (b).

The resulting rotation angles, $\boldsymbol{\omega}^T = (-10.95°, 5.1°, 4.04°)$ are small, even though the object in Figures 8a and 8b appears to undergo a larger angular displacement. This is expected, since with the $\boldsymbol{\omega}$ representation, the rotation angles are measured with respect to the camera location at a certain distance from the moving automobile. Additional experimental studies are needed for this initial orientation problem.

7. 2D MOTION ANALYSIS

The regional approach discussed here lends itself easily to 2D object motion analysis, a problem that has been studied by many authors [16-20]. 2D translation and rotation operators have been developed by Legters and Young [20], which can be treated as special cases of the linear operator L_c in (30). Also discussed briefly in this section is the occlusion problem and the use of predictive Kalman filter to keep the tracking on course during severe occlusion.

7.1   2D Rotation and Translation

We consider a 2D moving object in an image sequence. An object point $\mathbf{x}_t$ is moved to $\mathbf{x}_{t+1}$, and under the assumption of a rigid 2D object, their relationship can be expressed as

$$\mathbf{x}_{t+1} = \mathbf{A}_R \mathbf{x}_t + \mathbf{c}, \tag{62}$$

where $\mathbf{A}_R$ has been given in (2) for a counterclockwise rotation angle θ. Clearly, (62) is a special case of the affine transformation discussed in section 2. The 2D object does not change in size or in shape.

The matrix $\mathbf{A}_R$ is an orthogonal matrix, and hence $(\mathbf{A}_R)^{-1} = \mathbf{A}_R^T$. A matrix $\mathbf{B}_R$ may be defined, similar to (22),

$$\mathbf{A}_R^T = \mathbf{I} + \mathbf{B}_R \tag{63}$$

and the linear operator for 2D motion becomes, similar to (30),

$$L_2(\mathbf{B}_R, \mathbf{d}) = \exp[(\mathbf{B}_R \mathbf{x} - \mathbf{d})^T \nabla], \tag{64}$$

with $\mathbf{d} = \mathbf{c} + \mathbf{B}_R \mathbf{c}$.

Two special cases are of interest. For the pure translation case, $\mathbf{A}_R = \mathbf{I}$, $\mathbf{B}_R = \mathbf{0}$, $\mathbf{d} = \mathbf{c}$, and (64) reduces to

$$L_T(\mathbf{c}) = \exp(-\mathbf{c}^T \nabla), \tag{65}$$

which corresponds to the standard Taylor series expansion [17, 19]. The second special case deals with pure rotation about a center of rotation $\mathbf{c}_o$.

We have, in this case

$$\mathbf{x}_{t+1} = \mathbf{A}_R(\mathbf{x}_t - \mathbf{c}_o) + \mathbf{c}_o. \tag{66}$$

With $\mathbf{c} = \mathbf{c}_o - \mathbf{A}_R\mathbf{c}_o$, we obtain after simple manipulations a rotation operator,

$$L_R(\mathbf{B}_R, \mathbf{c}_o) = \exp[(\mathbf{B}_R(\mathbf{x} - \mathbf{c}_o))^T\nabla]. \tag{67}$$

If the rotation angle θ is small, we may approximate $\mathbf{B}_R$ by

$$\mathbf{B}_R = \begin{bmatrix} 0 & \theta \\ -\theta & 0 \end{bmatrix}. \tag{68}$$

These results are consistent with the translation and rotation operators in [20].

Iterative algorithms to track the dynamic parameters for 2D motion were derived [20]. It should be noted that the matrix $\mathbf{A}_R$ depends on a single variable θ only. Therefore, the iterative algorithms were for direct estimation of θ and the two translation parameters.

7.2 Kalman Filters to Aid Tracking

When the 2D moving object is occluded by another object or by the background, the iterative algorithms will yield inaccurate estimates of the motion parameters. In fact, erratic and unrealistic estimates may result, in case of severe or total occlusion, causing instability of the algorithm. A predictive Kalman filter may be used to alleviate this difficulty and to predict the point of reappearance of an object occluded in several consecutive scenes [20].

A Kalman filter algorithm is a statistical approach to estimate a time-varying state vetor $\boldsymbol{\eta}(t)$ from noisy measurements, based on a model of linear-vector differential or difference equation [36]. It is an estimation scheme that minimizes the mean-square estimation error. We are interested in using predictive Kalman filters to help tracking, and the state vector $\boldsymbol{\eta}(t)$ is simply the time-varying motion parameters (i.e., linear and/or angular positions, velocities, accelerations, etc.) of interest. The iterative algorithm provides measurements of motion parameters by comparing consecutive images, and the resulting mean-square error gives an indication of the measurement uncertainty. The Kalman filter is designed to match the dynamic system model of the moving object, the statistics of the error between the model and reality, and the uncertainty associated with the measurements.

The overall 2D tracking algorithm that incorporates a Kalman filter to aid tracking is summarized as follows:

- Step 1. Obtain an initial estimate of the state vector $\eta(t -)$ from $\eta(t - 1)$ (see Step 4).
- Step 2. Estimate 2D motion parameters iteratively from consecutive binary images until the iterative algorithm converges or terminates after a predetermined number of iterations.
- Step 3. Evaluate the mean-square error $\varepsilon(t)$.
- Step 4. Estimate $\eta(t)$ from the Kalman filter with the Kalman gain $\mathbf{K}(t)$ controlled by $\varepsilon(t)$. Predict $\eta(t + 1 -)$ from $\eta(t)$ using a system-dynamics model.

As noted before, the state vector $\eta(t)$ contains 2D motion parameters. The minus sign in Steps 1 and 4 indicates estimation of the system state before the measurement process. When there is no occlusion, object tracking is done primarily by the iterative algorithm that is similar to (36) except that it is designed for 2D motion parameters, and the resulting mean-square error $\varepsilon(t)$ will be small. The Kalman gain $\mathbf{K}(t)$ is designed in such a way that for small $\varepsilon(t)$, estimation of $\eta(t)$ is dominated by the measurement process (i.e., the iterative algorithm). On the other hand, a large $\varepsilon(t)$ indicates instability and/or occlusion, and $\mathbf{K}(t)$ allows the system dynamics model to take over the estimation and prediction. It is noted that the selection of a system dynamics model is not critical, since the Kalman filter approach allows errors in system dynamics, and since the iterative algorithm that is responsible for the tracking most of the time, is independent of the system dynamics model.

Details of applying Kalman filters to aid tracking 2D objects in an image sequence can be found in [20]. Experimental results using synthesized binary images indicate that under fairly severe occlusion conditions, the Kalman filter is capable of keeping the tracking on course and predicting the point of reappearance of the object occluded in several consecutive frames of the image sequence. The idea can be extended to tracking 3D motion.

8. CONCLUSIONS

We have presented a regional approach for tracking 3D translation and rotation of a rigid object in an image sequence. An object image is segmented into regions corresponding to the visible faces. Assumably the moving object has at least one planar face.

The regional approach has the following salient features: (1) It requires the identification of corresponding regions in the image sequence instead of corresponding points. A major advantage is that the identified regions will lead naturally to the construction of a 3D object model that can be used to facilitate recognition and 3D tracking under conditions such as occlusion, hidden faces, and so on. (2) 3D motion parameters are computed via linear and/or quadratic parameters that provide a description of shape changes of object faces caused by motion. (3) Mean square errors are minimized and evaluated during the tracking process, giving some assurance on the accuracy of the estimation. (4) A multistage segmentation method has been developed and implemented that combines edge detection and relaxation with region-based methods. The segmented faces are converted into binary images to emphasize the shapes of the faces and to simplify computation.

With orthographic projections, a set of linear shape-change parameters is sufficient to determine motion parameters during tracking. To find the initial orientation, however, an additional equation is needed that can be obtained from a priori knowledge such as symmetry. For perspective projections, under the condition of small rotation angles and small z-direction translation, shape changes of planar faces can be taken into account by including quadratic parameters. 2D motion is treated as a special case. Remaining problems to be investigated include estimation accuracy, utilization of two or more faces, and construction of a 3D object model from the sequence of images.

ACKNOWLEDGMENT

This research was supported by a National Science Foundation Grant DCR-8509737, and by a Florida High Technology and Industry Council Grant no. 585.

REFERENCES

[1] Roach, J. W., and J. K. Aggarwal. "Determining the movement of objects from a sequence of images," *IEEE Trans. Pattern Anal. Machine Intell.*, vol. PAMI-2, pp. 554-562, 1980.

[2] Mitiche, A., and J. K. Aggarwal. "A computational analysis of time-varying images," *Handbook of Pattern Recognition and Image Processing*, edited by T. Y. Young and K. S. Fu, pp. 311-332, Academic Press, 1986.

[3] Tsai, R. Y., and T. S. Huang. "Estimating three-dimensional motion parameters of a rigid planar patch," *IEEE Trans. Acoustics, Speech, and Signal Processing*, vol. ASSP-29, pp. 1147-1152, 1981.

[4] Tsai, R. Y., and T. S. Huang. "Uniqueness and estimation of three-dimensional motion parameters of rigid object with curved surfaces," *IEEE Trans. Pattern Anal. Machine Intell.*, vol. PAMI-6, pp. 13-27, 1984.

[5] Fang, J. Q., and T. S. Huang. "Some experiments on estimating the 3D motion parameters of a rigid body from two consecutive image frames," *IEEE Trans. Pattern Anal. Machine Intell.*, vol. PAMI-6, pp. 545-554, 1984.

[6]   Huang, T. S. "Determining three-dimensional motion and structure from two perspective views," *Handbook of Pattern Recognition and Image Processing*, edited by T. Y. Young and K. S. Fu, pp. 333–354, Academic Press, 1986.

[7]   Longuet-Higgins, H. C. "A computer algorithm for reconstructing a scene from two projections," *Nature (Lond.)*, vol. 293, pp. 133–135, 1981.

[8]   Horn, B. K. P., and B. G. Schunck. "Determining optical flow," *Artificial Intelligence*, vol. 17, pp. 185–203, 1981.

[9]   Prazdny, K. "Egomotion and relative depth map from optical flow," *Biol. Cybernetics*, vol. 36, pp. 87–102, 1980.

[10] Hildreth, E. C. "Computations underlying the measurement of visual motion," *Artificial Intelligence*, vol. 23, pp. 309–354, 1984.

[11] Thompson, W. B., K. M. Mutch, and V. A. Berzins. "Dynamic occlusion analysis in optical flow fields," *IEEE Trans. Pattern Anal. Machine Intell.*, vol. PAMI-7, pp. 374–383, 1985.

[12] Adiv, G. "Determining three-dimensional motion and structure from optical flow generated by several moving objects," *IEEE Trans. Pattern Anal. Machine Intell.*, vol. PAMI-7, pp. 384–401, 1985.

[13] Kanatani, K. I. "Tracing planar surface motion from a projection without knowing the correspondence," *Computer Vision, Graphics, and Image Processing*, vol. 29, pp. 1–12, 1985.

[14] Kanatani, K. I. "Detecting the motion of a planar surface by line and surface integrals," *Computer Vision, Graphics, and Image Processing*, vol. 29, pp. 13–22, 1985.

[15] Jerian, C., and R. Jain. "Determining motion parameters for schemes with translation and rotation," *IEEE Trans. Pattern Anal. Machine Intell.*, vol. PAMI-6, pp. 523–530, 1984.

[16] Nagel, H. H. "Analysis techniques for image sequences," *Proc. 4th Int. Conf. Pattern Recognition*, pp. 186–211, 1978.

[17] Cafforio, C., and F. Rocca. "Methods of measuring small displacements of television images," *IEEE Trans. Inform. Theory*, vol. IT-22, pp. 573–579, 1976.

[18] Netravali, A. N., and J. D. Robbins. "Motion-compensated television coding: Part 1," *Bell Systems Tech. J.*, vol. 58, pp. 631–670, 1979.

[19] Schalkoff, R. J., and E. S. McVey. "A model and tracking algorithm for a class of video targets," *IEEE Trans. Pattern Anal. Machine Intell.*, vol. PAMI-4, pp. 2–10, 1982.

[20] Legters, G. R., Jr, and T. Y. Young. "A mathematical model for image tracking," *IEEE Trans. Pattern Anal. Machine Intell.*, vol. PAMI-4, pp. 583–594, 1982.

[21] Young, T. Y., and Y. L. Wang. "Analysis of three-dimensional rotation and linear shape changes," *Pattern Recognition Letters*, vol. 2, pp. 239–242, 1984.

[22] Young, T. Y., and S. Gunasekaran. "Three-dimensional motion analysis using shape change information," *Proc. SPIE Conf. on Applications of Artificial Intelligence III*, pp. 318–326, 1986.

[23] Bamieh, B., and R. J. P. DeFigueiredo. "Efficient new techniques for identification and 3D attitude determination of space objects from a single image," *Proc. IEEE Conf. on Robotics and Automation*, pp. 67–72, 1985.

[24] Paul, R. P. *Robot Manipulators*, Cambridge, MA, MIT Press, 1981.

[25] Nevatia, R. *Machine Perception*, Englewood Cliffs, NJ, Prentice-Hall, 1982.

[26] Kanade, T. "Recovery of the three-dimensional shape of an object from a single view," *Artificial Intelligence*, vol. 17, pp. 409–460, 1981.

[27] Nelson, R. N., and T. Y. Young. "Determining three-dimensional object shape and orientation from single perspective view," *Optical Engineering*, vol. 25, pp. 394–401, 1986.

[28] Longuet-Higgins, H. C., and K. Prazdny. "The interpretation of a moving retina image," *Proc. R. Soc. London, B.*, vol. 208, pp. 385–397, 1980.

[29] Prager, J. M. "Extracting and labeling boundary segments in natural scenes," *IEEE Trans. Pattern Anal. Machine Intell.*, vol. PAMI-2, pp. 16–27, 1980.

[30] Hanson, A. R., and E. M. Riseman. "Segmentation of natural scenes," *Computer Vision Systems*, edited by A. R. Hanson and E. M. Riseman, pp. 129-163, Academic Press, 1978.

[31] Pavlidis, T. *Structural Pattern Recognition*, Berlin, Springer-Verlag, 1977.

[32] Brice, C., and C. Fennema. "Scene analysis using regions," *Artificial Intelligence*, vol. 1, pp. 205-226, 1970.

[33] Montanari, U. "On the optimal detection of curves in noisy pictures," *Commun. ACM*, vol. 14, pp. 335-345, 1971.

[34] Zucker, S. W., R. A. Hummel, and A. Rosenfeld. "An application of relaxation labeling to line and curve enhancement," *IEEE Trans. Computers*, vol. C-26, pp. 394-403, 1977.

[35] Rosenfeld, A., and A. C. Kak. *Digital Picture Processing*, Second Edition, vol. 2, Academic Press, 1982.

[36] A. Gelb, editor, *Applied Optimal Estimation*, Cambridge, MA, MIT Press, 1974.

Chapter 4

OBJECT RECOGNITION AND ORIENTATION DETERMINATION BY TENSOR METHODS

D. Cyganski and J. A. Orr

OUTLINE

Advances in Computer Vision and Image Processing, Vol. 3, pages 101–144.
ISBN: 0-89232-635-2

ABSTRACT

Tensor mathematics is a compact and well-suited means for the expression and manipulation of relations connected with the identification of objects and their orientations from image data. By means of tensor operations, the problem of finding an object's orientation can be solved from image data not including any form of feature correspondence information. Furthermore, the solution process does not involve search or iterative error-minimization techniques. Image normalizations also can be developed which decouple the object identity problem from the object orientation problem, considerably reducing the complexity and effort associated with both problems.

In this chapter, the basic notions of tensor theory are developed within the context of image data and arbitrary orientations of objects in three-space. Solutions of the identity and orientation problems are constructed for a number of object and data types. Solutions are developed for planar object projections using image moments. This method is extended for use with image features, first with and then without the condition of coplanarity. A distinctly different application of tensors is used to generalize the Fourier decomposition method for contour data. Here differential tensors are used to derive a contour matching and transform-estimation procedure that is applicable where the curves have been skewed as well as scaled and rotated.

1. INTRODUCTION

Considerable attention has been given to finding means by which objects may be recognized from their images regardless of their position or orientation in space. In the following, an approach is developed that solves this problem as well as the related orientation-determination problem for several classes of objects and image types. The method will be developed with the use of a tensor representation for image data. This representation provides' not only a compact notation for the expression of image measures and their transformation, but also assists in the development of solution methods for these image transformations.

The methods to be derived will depend only on the direct manipulation and reduction of image data. That is, these techniques will not attempt to find the transformations that relate images by any sort of search or iterative optimization scheme. Likewise, no use will be made of correspondence information relating features in one image to those in another.

As an introductory example, consider one of the most elementary forms of a direct method, one which solves for the translations an object has undergone parallel to the imaging plane. Assume a background image-function value of zero and either uniform illumination or consistent binary object/background discrimination by thresholding. Then the translations of the object may be found directly from the change in image-function center of gravity.

This method effectively decouples the identification problem from the translation estimation problem. An image function can be normalized with respect to translation, for example, by shifting the center of gravity to the origin. Now all images of the object for any translation will agree after this normalization. Hence, one image distance calculation for each member of a library of normalized images will suffice to identify a normalized image as corresponding to one of the library object images. Below, we will introduce image normalizations that realize the same decoupling between object identification and more general object motions in three-space. These results will be achieved for the group of all rigid body motions consisting of the rotations and translations associated with each of three orthogonal spatial axes. Several of the methods to be discussed will achieve this by normalizing the images themselves with respect to image translation, rotation and skew. From the normalizing transform, it will be possible to calculate the transformations relating the images of an object in different positions and orientations, and from these the change in object orientation.

One of the first direct methods to be proposed that was more general than the center-of-gravity method was that of Hu [15]. Here the principle axis method was proposed as a means for image normalization against rotation of the image (corresponding to object rotation on the image-projection axis). Coupling this method with normalization of the center of gravity and scaling according to total optical mass, the effects of object translation, scaling and rotation on the imaging axis could be removed.

Hu also proposed the use of moment invariants. The moment invariant is a combination of moments determined by the forms of the theory of algebraic invariants. These values are unaffected by the transformations of moments that take place on rotation of the object on the imaging axis. While such invariants do not contribute to our knowledge about the rotation, they can be used as points in a feature space for object identification that is independent of rotation of the object on the imaging axis.

The method of moments due to Hu has been tested [6] and rederived in various forms [1, 20, 22] and the invariants generalized to include the case of wholly specified three dimensional (3D) objects [21].

The first of the tensor-based methods to be derived below can be thought of as the generalization of this method of moments. The algebraic invariants are in fact a subset of tensors known as the Cartesian tensor densities or rank zero Cartesian tensors. In the following we see that using a more general tensor setting will result in the formulation of a normalization which separates the identification problem from the estimation of the object's rotations on all three-spatial axes and its translations.

Furthermore, the tensor representation will be found applicable to other generalizations. In one section we will see that the method of Fourier descriptors that has been used to align or identify contours that differ by imaging axis rotation and shifts can be generalized. Using a curve parameterization based on a tensorial differential, the method can be made to apply to general linear transformation (rotation, scale, shift and skew) of the contours.

After introducing some fundamental notions in the next section regarding object and image space transformations, some basic tensor theory will be reviewed. Next, the basic tensor-reduction method for orientation determination and image normalization will be developed. Finally, applications of the method to the case of general 3D objects in three-space and the generalization of the Fourier descriptor method will be examined.

2. OBJECT AND IMAGE SPACE TRANSFORMATIONS

The coordinate system to be used throughout the following and the relationship between three-space object rotations and the image transformations that result will be described here.

Assume that an orthogonal set of axes corresponding to coordinates x^1, x^2 and x^3 are erected in the 3D object space. An index system will be used to denote the axes rather than the typical x, y, z designations to comply with the index-oriented notation of tensors to be introduced later. With each axis we associate a natural direction of positive rotation, Figure 1, by application of the right-hand rule taking γ, β, α, respectively, as the rotation angles about the x^1, x^2 and x^3 axes. These angles are often called the Euler angles. Furthermore, restrict α, β and γ to the intervals

$$-\frac{\pi}{2} < \alpha \leq \frac{\pi}{2}$$

$$-\pi < \beta \leq \pi$$

$$-\pi < \gamma \leq \pi.$$

This restriction results in there being a unique set of angles associated with any general three-space rotation.

Any rigid body motion can be described as a combination of shifts along the three axes and rotations about the axes. However, the group of shifts and each of the rotations do not commute. Therefore, it is important to specify the order in which rotations are taken and whether these are before or after the translation.

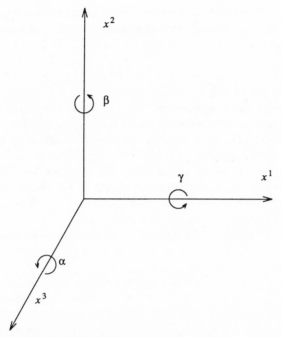

Figure 1. The object space coordinate system and the associated directed rotation angles.

We will assume that rotations are applied about the x^1, x^2 and x^3 axes, in that order. Let the column vector **p** denote the coordinates of an object point in three-space. If $\bar{p}$ denotes its location after rotation about the origin of our coordinate system, then let

$$\begin{bmatrix} \bar{p}^1 \\ \bar{p}^2 \\ \bar{p}^3 \end{bmatrix} = \begin{bmatrix} B^1_1 & B^1_2 & B^1_3 \\ B^2_1 & B^2_2 & B^2_3 \\ B^3_1 & B^3_2 & B^3_3 \end{bmatrix} \begin{bmatrix} p^1 \\ p^2 \\ p^3 \end{bmatrix},$$

be the matrix transformation describing the rotation. Here we again use an array element indexing scheme designed to agree with tensor notation practice. Composing B from the assumed coordinate system and rotation convention, we have that

$$B = \begin{bmatrix} \cos\alpha\cos\beta & -\sin\alpha\cos\gamma + \cos\alpha\sin\beta\sin\gamma \\ \sin\alpha\cos\beta & \cos\alpha\cos\gamma + \sin\alpha\sin\beta\sin\gamma \\ -\sin\beta & \cos\beta\sin\gamma \end{bmatrix}$$

$$\begin{bmatrix} \sin\alpha\sin\gamma + \cos\alpha\sin\beta\cos\gamma \\ -\cos\alpha\sin\gamma + \sin\alpha\sin\beta\cos\gamma \\ \cos\beta\cos\gamma \end{bmatrix}.$$

Below, the order in which rotation and translation are applied will be obvious from the expression for the complete point transformation formula. Typically we will say

$$\bar{p} = B(p - q) + \bar{q},$$

indicating that the object is first translated so that the point q now falls at the origin (often taken as the center of gravity of the object). Then it is rotated about the origin in agreement with three given Euler angles. Finally, it is again translated so that the object feature located before the first step at point q, is now located at point $\bar{q}$.

Later, when developing the method of 3D moments, we will be solving for point transformations of the above form. It will be shown that given several views of an object in three-space, the translations and rotation matrix, B can be found.

We will also explore several methods in which information regarding the Euler angles of rotation and the object translation can be found from a single view of an object if it is flat or possesses features (vertices, holes, markings) that are coplanar. To support this development we will discuss the relationship among the three-space rotations of a planar object and its projections.

An object image function will be taken as the result of the parallel projection of some object features (e.g., spatial extent, surface color) onto an image plane that is parallel to the x^1, x^2 plane of the three-space coordinate system,

$$\begin{bmatrix} p^1 \\ p^2 \\ p^3 \end{bmatrix} \rightarrow \begin{bmatrix} p^1 \\ p^2 \end{bmatrix}.$$

We will denote both of these vectors by p, and let context indicate the dimensionality of the vector to which we are referring.

Now, if the three-space feature set is planar then for every point p in this set we have that

$$p^3 = r_1 p^1 + r_2 p^2,$$

where r_1 and r_2 define the plane of the object and the plane is taken as passing through the origin without loss of generality. Hence the third coordinate of each object point is redundant given the first two coordinates, r_1 and r_2, and hence given its projection. By using this condition, we see that a transformation matrix, A, which takes each 2D image-space point p onto $\bar{p}$ can be found from the 3D transformation, B.

$$A = \begin{bmatrix} A_1^1 & A_2^1 \\ A_1^2 & A_2^2 \end{bmatrix}$$

$$= \begin{bmatrix} \cos \alpha \cos \beta & -\sin \alpha \cos \gamma + \cos \alpha \sin \beta \sin \gamma \\ \sin \alpha \cos \beta & \cos \alpha \cos \gamma + \sin \alpha \sin \beta \sin \gamma \end{bmatrix}$$

$$+ \begin{bmatrix} (\sin \alpha \sin \gamma + \cos \alpha \sin \beta \cos \gamma) \\ (-\cos \alpha \sin \gamma + \sin \alpha \sin \beta \cos \gamma) \end{bmatrix} [r_1, r_2]$$

$$= C + D.$$

Here we see that C is the transformation that would take place if the feature set were parallel to the image plane, while the introduction of D provides the general result for an image lying on the plane defined by r_1 and r_2. Thus, for a planar object, the effect of a general reorientation in three-space about some origin is a linear transformation of the image function feature locations about the projection of that origin. Obviously the x^1 and x^2 translations of the object become like translations of the object image and translation in x^3 has no effect on the image.

While the whole development that follows assumes parallel projection, we can introduce an approximation for the effects of perspective distortion given a large object to point-of-focus distance. Suppose the size of the object is small with respect to its distance from the camera point of focus. In this case, the perspective distortion of the image can be approximately represented by a simple scaling with the scale factor, k, being inversely proportional to the distance of the object from the point of focus. Therefore, the image transformation can still be represented by a linear transformation matrix, A.

In the later development, we will show how the linear transformation, A, relating two images of an object can be found. Typically it is the change of orientation in three-space of the object which is of direct concern, however. To what extent are the Euler angles recoverable from A?

Because the derivation is somewhat tedious, we will repeat here only the final result of the solution for α, β, γ and the scale factor k from the A matrix. Furthermore, to greatly simplify the form of the expression, we will assume that $A = kC$. That is, we will assume that the original orientation of the planar object is such that it is parallel to the x^1, x^2 plane. This result can be used without modification even for the case where two object images are given with neither object orientation qualifying under the above restriction. In this case we can find the transformation mapping each of these images to a library image fulfilling the parallelism constraint. Then, the Euler angles relating the original two images are given by the differences between the angles relating them to the library image.

Under the above constraints we have that

$$\alpha = \tan^{-1}(A_1^2/A_1^1)$$

$$k = \left(\frac{(a^2 + b^2 + c^2) + \sqrt{(a^2 + b^2 + c^2)^2 - 4a^2b^2}}{2} \right)^{-1/2}$$

$$\beta = \pm\cos^{-1}(A_1^1/(k \cos \alpha))$$

$$\gamma = \arg(a/k, c/(k \sin \beta)),$$

where

$$a = -A_2^1 \sin \alpha + A_2^2 \cos \alpha$$

$$b = A_1^1 / \cos \alpha$$

$$c = A_2^2 \sin \alpha + A_2^1 \cos \alpha$$

and the argument function is defined by

$$arg(x, y) = \begin{cases} \tan^{-1}(y/x) & x \geq 0 \\ \tan^{-1}(y/x) + \pi & x < 0. \end{cases}$$

Examining these results we see that the angle, β is two-valued. That a unique value for β cannot be determined from A is fairly obvious. The image distortions that result from a rotation of a planar object that is parallel to the image plane in either direction on the x^2 axis are identical. (The similar uncertainty regarding rotation on the x^1 axis is also accounted for by the unknown sign in β.) Therefore α, β and γ can be found from a single image pair only to within this one sign uncertainty. But a second image pair from a second viewing angle can resolve this. That is, binocular vision is needed to complete our knowledge about the object's change in orientation. Given binocular vision, one can also find the x^3 translation directly from the correspondence in the origins of the two image rotations. Thus, all rotation and translation uncertainty can be resolved if two viewing projections are used.

3. INTRODUCTION TO TENSOR THEORY

The representation of image information (such as moments and certain curve differentials) in tensor form will greatly simplify the algebraic manipulation of these quantities and their transformations under change in the orientation of the object being described. More important, new solution approaches to significant problems will become obvious in this representation. In this section the general notion of a tensor will be introduced.

A tensor is a collection of values associated with a particular coordinate system such that under a change of coordinate systems the new values can be calculated from the old values by a linear transformation. That is, each new value can be obtained as a linear combination of all the old values. The transformation that is applied to the sets of measurements is typically related in a nonlinear fashion with the matrix elements that define the transformation of the coordinate systems.

The algebra and calculus of tensors was put to extensive use by non-Euclidean geometers, for example in the formulation of the theory of relativity, because of the compactness and the structure of the notation. The structure that tensor mathematics contributes is connected with the guarantee that after any allowed manipulations of tensors, the result will be a tensor. That is, the result will behave in a fixed and well-known way upon change of coordinate systems. In effect, tensor equations can be thought of as providing a means for coordinate-independent mathematical expression for quantities that they can describe.

Most texts that derive the tensor theory are strongly influenced by the work of these mathematicians and typically develop the theory in a very general form related to differential transformations of differential quantities. The tensor-vision methods to be developed later will deal with arbitrary linear transformations and not nonlinear transformations that require a description in terms of differentials. For this reason we will review here the tensor properties associated with this subset of tensor theory that are both conceptually and notationally simpler. The differential transformation formulation not considered here may have important applications in vision; it seems an appropriate tool for example in developing means for image tracking given a distorting visual medium or a nonrigid target.

The tensor is a special case of the mathematical entity known as the form. Consider a form to be an array of values with one or more indices each ranging from 1 to the dimensionality of the space in which the form is defined. We will refer to the number of such indices as the rank of the form. Thus a form with k indices in an n dimensional space has n^k components. The form corresponds to the programming construct typically called the multidimensional array (where, unfortunately, it is common use to refer to the number of indices and not the range of an index as the dimension of the array). The tensor is a form with the property that the components are not just numbers, but rather measurements associated with a particular coordinate system. Thus the tensor must be given with reference to a coordinate system just like a vector (which is a unit rank tensor).

Let e_i for $i = 1, \ldots, n$ be a basis for an n dimensional linear space. That is, any element in our space may be constructed from a linear combination of the e_i. In signal theory the basis elements might be a certain set of time functions. In our case we take them to be directed displacements from some origin. Let x be an element or a point in this space. While x has a well-defined meaning without any reference to other points in the space, for the sake of manipulation and communication we can describe it numerically with respect to the basis. Any point, x, may be represented as:

$$x = \sum_{i=1}^{n} x^i e_i.$$

That is, a given point in space may be located by a linear combination of the basis elements (displacements). The numerical values, x^i are called the coordinates of the point x with respect to the basis set e_i.

We shall now introduce a short hand notation for representing sums over all values of a given index. Let

$$x = \sum_{i=1}^{n} x^i e_i = x^i e_i.$$

The rightmost expression uses the Einstein summation convention to represent the same summation over the index i as is given to the left. Throughout the following this convention will be used wherein summation is understood to take place over any repeated index in an expression over the full range of that index. Indices may appear either in upper (contravariant) or lower (covariant) positions. A purpose for the distinction between these will soon be obvious.

We need to be able to refer to the same point in space given a different choice of basis set. Suppose we are given a new basis set $\bar{e}_i$ related to the old set by the linear transformation

$$e_i = A_i^j \bar{e}_j \quad \text{or} \quad \bar{e}_i = a_i^j e_j,$$

where

$$a_k^j A_j^i = \delta_k^i,$$

which for the case of two dimensions is the tensor notation for the matrix equality

$$\begin{bmatrix} a_1^1 & a_2^1 \\ a_1^2 & a_2^2 \end{bmatrix} \begin{bmatrix} A_1^1 & A_2^1 \\ A_1^2 & A_2^2 \end{bmatrix} = \begin{bmatrix} 1 & 0 \\ 0 & 1 \end{bmatrix}.$$

The Kronecker delta function δ_k^i in this expression obeys the classic definition as a selector function (that is, it is nonzero only when both indices are equal) and can be thought of as the matrix identity function as seen above. The Kronecker delta as written here in tensor form is in fact a tensor participating in all the tensor transformation and combination rules to be developed below. From the matrix equation above it is also easy to see that

$$a_i^j A_k^i = \delta_k^j.$$

Now let the same point x, as defined above, represented by the coordinate pair x^i in the basis set e_i be expressed by new coordinate values $\bar{x}^i$ in the new basis set $\bar{e}_i$:

$$x = \bar{x}^i \bar{e}_i.$$

We will find that the new coordinates are related to old ones by the linear transformation

$$\bar{x}^i = A_j^i x^j.$$

This can be found by substituting for the new basis set its representation in terms of the old basis set and likewise for the coordinate pairs using the proposed relationship

$$\bar{x}^i \bar{e}_i = x^i A_i^j a_j^k e_k$$
$$= x^i \delta_i^k e_k = x^i e_i$$

by the definitions of a and A and the properties of the Kronecker delta that results from their contraction by summation.

Note that the new basis vectors $\bar{e}_i$ are obtained from the old, e_i, by the a_j^i transformation. Any quantities that transform according to a like rule will be said to be covariant with the basis. Notice that the point coordinates x^i are related by the inverse transformation, A_i^j. Such quantities are said to be contravariant with the basis. Under these transformation rules and the choice of notation, the covariant quantities will always end up being indexed by indices in the covariant (lower) position and similarly contravariant components will always be indexed by contravariant (upper) indices.

By a tensor product (often called the outer product) of two tensor quantities is meant the creation of a new form with elements produced by multiplying the components of every pairwise combination of elements taken from the two original forms (with one taken from each). In the notation for forms which we have been using, the tensor product of two coordinate vectors, for instance, can be written as

$$\zeta^{ij} = x^i x^j.$$

That is, the tensor product produces a new form with as many indices as the sum of the indices of the component forms. We reserve the title tensor product for the case in which attention is given to keeping covariant and contravariant indices in agreement with their origins in the component forms. If the component forms of the tensor product are tensors (possess the tensor transformation property) then the components of the elements of the new form will transform linearly among themselves. Thus, a new tensor has been formed with a transformation property that is immediately evident; the four quantities $x^i x^j$ transform as

$$(\bar{x}^i \bar{x}^j) = A_k^i A_l^j (x^k x^l)$$

under the change in basis. Note that because the elements to be summed, and the elements on either side of an equation to be equated, are all identified by correspondences of index names, the tensor notation provides greater freedom than matrix notation in the ordering of the components of such an expression. Notice that the components of $x^i x^j$ transform as a set according to a linear transformation defined by the elements of a new form which is the tensor product of the transformations of the original tensors

x^i that were combined. A short hand notation for this new composite transform, which occurs often, is given by

$$A^{j_1 j_2 \cdots j_n}_{i_1 i_2 \cdots i_n} \equiv A^{j_1}_{i_1} A^{j_2}_{i_2} \cdots A^{j_n}_{i_n}.$$

Thus, we say that any set of quantities indexed as a form ξ is a (an) (absolute) tensor of covariant rank m and contravariant rank n if it transforms upon change of basis as

$$\bar{\xi}^{i_1 i_2 \cdots i_n}_{j_1 j_2 \cdots j_m} = A^{i_1 i_2 \cdots i_n}_{k_1 k_2 \cdots k_m} a^{l_1 l_2 \cdots l_n}_{j_1 j_2 \cdots j_m} \xi^{k_1 k_2 \cdots k_n}_{l_1 l_2 \cdots l_m}. \tag{1}$$

There are several generalizations of the absolute tensor which will be used later. Some physical quantities transform in a more complicated fashion than the point coordinates we have examined so far. For example, directed areas, such as can be associated with the usual notion of a cross product, require a compensation of scale under general transformation. This is familiar from the scaling accompanying a change of variables on a double integral, which requires the introduction of a Jacobian factor.

Suppose we define a Jacobian for the case of the transformation of a tensor as $J = \det(a)$. Then if

$$\bar{\xi}^{i_1 i_2 \cdots i_n}_{j_1 j_2 \cdots j_n} = J^W A^{i_1 i_2 \cdots i_n}_{k_1 k_2 \cdots k_n} a^{l_1 l_2 \cdots l_n}_{j_1 j_2 \cdots j_n} \xi^{k_1 k_2 \cdots k_n}_{l_1 l_2 \cdots l_n}, \tag{2}$$

we say that ξ is a relative tensor of weight W. Finally if

$$\bar{\xi}^{i_1 i_2 \cdots i_n}_{j_1 j_2 \cdots j_n} = J^W sgn(J) A^{i_1 i_2 \cdots i_n}_{k_1 k_2 \cdots k_n} a^{l_1 l_2 \cdots l_n}_{j_1 j_2 \cdots j_n} \xi^{k_1 k_2 \cdots k_n}_{l_1 l_2 \cdots l_n}, \tag{3}$$

where sgn is the function of unit magnitude and possesses the sign of its argument then we say that ξ is an oriented, relative tensor of weight W.

Suppose that ξ and η are tensors of the same type (contravariant and covariant ranks agree and they are both absolute or relative of the same weight and orientation attribute) then $\xi + \eta$ is a tensor of the same type and weight. This is true because both tensors obey the same linear transformation; hence, their sum will obey this transformation also.

The tensor product of any two tensors ξ and η of any types is a new tensor of the composite type. For example, if ξ^{ij}_k is an oriented relative tensor of weight 2 and η_l is an oriented relative tensor of weight -1 then with

$$\mu^{ij}_{kl} = \xi^{ij}_k \eta_l.$$

μ is a relative (not oriented) tensor of unit weight. Here the $sgn(J)$ functions cancel and the weights obviously add when the new tensor transformation is composed by the tensor multiplication of the old transformations.

The inner product of two tensors is formed by summing over one or more pairs of indices of opposite type; that is, a covariant index must be paired with a contravariant index (hence the importance of the notational distinction between them). As with the tensor product operation the result is a new tensor of composite type and rank two less than the sum of the component ranks for every pairing of indices (contractions). Using ξ and μ above, if

$$\nu_k = \xi_k^{ij} \eta_i \eta_j$$

then ν is an oriented absolute tensor. We can contract indices of different types and have a tensor as a result because the transformation matrices associated with the contracted indices contract with each other to form the Kronecker delta, which can be removed from the expression entirely. For example, in the case above,

$$\bar{\nu}_k = sgn(J) A_l^i A_m^j a_k^a \xi_q^{lm} a_i^r \eta_r a_j^s \eta_s$$

$$= sgn(J) \delta_l^r \delta_m^s a_k^a \xi_q^{lm} \eta_r \eta_s = sgn(J) a_k^q \xi_q^{rs} \eta_r \eta_s$$

$$= sgn(J) a_k^q \nu_q = \bar{\nu}_k.$$

Contraction of like indices (where both are covariant or contravariant) would not result in the removal of the transformations in this fashion and the result is generally not a tensor.

Finally we will introduce an important "numerical" tensor, ε_{ij}. It can be shown that under any transformation of basis sets the permutation tensor defined by

$$\varepsilon_{ij} = \begin{cases} 1 & \text{if } i = 1, j = 2 \\ -1 & \text{if } i = 2, j = 1 \\ 0 & \text{if } i = j \end{cases} \tag{4}$$

if treated as a relative tensor of weight -1 reproduces itself as a result. To show this, let us evaluate

$$\bar{\varepsilon}_{ij} = a_i^k a_j^l \varepsilon_{kl} J^{-1}.$$

Taking the elements of ε_{ij} one at a time we have

$$\bar{\varepsilon}_{11} = (a_1^1 a_2^1 - a_2^1 a_1^1) J^{-1} = 0,$$

$$\bar{\varepsilon}_{12} = (a_1^1 a_2^2 - a_2^1 a_1^2) J^{-1} = J J^{-1} = 1,$$

$$\bar{\varepsilon}_{21} = (a_1^2 a_2^1 - a_2^2 a_1^1) J^{-1} = -J J^{-1} = -1,$$

$$\bar{\varepsilon}_{22} = (a_1^2 a_2^2 - a_2^2 a_1^2) J^{-1} = 0,$$

so that in fact $\bar{\varepsilon} = \varepsilon$. That this should be true is a remarkable and useful result. The existence of a numerical tensor is important because it allows us to use it to form a new, true, tensor expression from other tensors without having to know anything about our current basis or coordinate system.

4. IMAGE-MOMENT TENSOR

We will now show that the 2D moments of an image are the components of tensors with respect to affine transformation of that image. Since, for planar objects and orthographic projection, shifts and rotations of the object in three-space result in affine transformations of the object image, moment tensors are a well suited representation for this image data.

Let $f(x^1, x^2)$ be an image function. This function might be an intensity function or a binary valued selector function related to the presence/absence of optical mass at this point in the projection as might be derived by image thresholding.

By an image moment we mean a quantity derived from $f(x^1, x^2)$ of the form

$$m_{pq} = \int (x^1)^p (x^2)^q f(x^1, x^2) \, dx^1 \, dx^2.$$

Note the use of parentheses to distinguish exponentiation from superscript indices. Rather than use the classic designation, m_{pq}, for the (p, q) moment of the image function, we will introduce instead a set of forms that collect all moments of a given order $(p + q)$ into a single indexed array. Let the mth order moment form (which will be shown to be a tensor) be given by

$$M^{i_1 i_2 \cdots i_m} = \int x^{i_1} x^{i_2} \cdots x^{i_m} f(x^1, x^2) \, dx^1 \, dx^2.$$

Obviously the components of M are the m_{pq} with $p + q = m$, of which only $^2C_m^{(r)}$ (using the standard notation from combinatorics) are unique, the remainder being repetitions introduced by the various permutations of the indices that involve the same numbers of each index value. (The form of the redundancy leads to these being called symmetric tensors. If the order of the indices is permuted the value of a symmetric tensor does not change.) This notation seems overly cumbersome at first because of the inherent redundancy, but as will now be seen, it leads to great economy in expressing the change in the moments under linear transformation of the image.

Suppose the object being viewed undergoes a change in position which results in a linear transformation of the locations of each point in the object image function. So, we now have an image function $\bar{f}$ related to f by

$$\bar{f}(\bar{x}^1, \bar{x}^2) = f(x^1, x^2), \tag{5}$$

where

$$\bar{x}^i = A_j^i x^j. \tag{6}$$

That is, $\bar{f}$ is a new image related to f by the fact that an image feature formerly found at a point x^j in the image f can now be found at point $\bar{x}^j$ in the image $\bar{f}$.

Treating the variables $\bar{x}^i$ as the new dummy variables of integration, we see that the image moment tensor of the new image is given by

$$\bar{M}^{i_1 i_2 \cdots i_m} = \int \bar{x}^{i_1} \bar{x}^{i_2} \cdots \bar{x}^{i_m} \bar{f}(\bar{x}^1, \bar{x}^2)\, d\bar{x}^1\, d\bar{x}^2.$$

Now by applying a change of variables suggested by (5) and (6) we see that

$$\bar{M}^{i_1 i_2 \cdots i_m} = \int A^{i_1}_{j_1} x^{j_1} A^{i_2}_{j_2} x^{j_2} \cdots A^{i_m}_{j_m} x^{j_m} f(x^1, x^2) |J^{-1}|\, dx^1\, dx^2,$$

where J is the Jacobian factor introduced in (2). By grouping the linear transformations of the coordinates outside the integral we see that

$$\bar{M}^{i_1 i_2 \cdots i_m} = A^{i_1 i_2 \cdots i_m}_{j_1 j_2 \cdots j_m} |J^{-1}| M^{j_1 j_2 \cdots j_m}. \tag{7}$$

Comparison with (3) reveals that the form M of image moments of order m transforms as an oriented relative tensor of weight -1 with respect to the linear transformation of the image. We have departed a little here from the usual definition of the tensor as this transformation was induced not by a change in coordinate systems but by an actual transformation of the image. However, since the image transformation could have been induced by a change in viewer coordinate systems, the usual tensor manipulation rules and interpretation will be appropriate.

Equation (7) indicates that under linear transformation of an image, all moments of a given order may be found by a simple linear transformation of all such moments of the original image. Unfortunately, a shift of the image does not give rise to such elegant behavior. In general, a given moment of a shifted image can only be derived as a combination of all equal and lower order moments of the original image.

Fortunately, the central moments of an image μ_{pq} are fixed under image translation. Let

$$\mu_{pq} = \int (x^1 - g^1)^p (x^2 - g^2)^q f(x^1, x^2)\, dx^1\, dx^2,$$

where

$$g^1 = m_{10}/m_{00} \qquad g^2 = m_{01}/m_{00}$$

are the center of gravity components of the image. A translation of f gives rise to an identical translation of the g components. Thus, by a simple change of variables it can be seen that the μ_{pq} remain constant. Furthermore, by resorting to tensor notation we see that

$$g^i = \frac{M^i}{M},$$

which transforms according to the rule

$$\bar{g}^i = \frac{A_j^i M^j |J^{-1}|}{M|J^{-1}|} = A_j^i g^j$$

is an absolute contravariant tensor like the coordinates x^i. Hence the central moment form

$$\bar{T}^{i_1 i_2 \cdots i_m} = \int (\bar{x}^{i_1} - \bar{g}^{i_1})(\bar{x}^{i_2} - \bar{g}^{i_2}) \cdots (\bar{x}^{i_m} - \bar{g}^{i_m}) \bar{f}(\bar{x}^1, \bar{x}^2) \, d\bar{x}^1 \, d\bar{x}^2$$

$$= \int A_{j_1}^{i_1} (x^{j_1} - g^{j_1}) A_{j_2}^{i_2} (x^{j_2} - g^{j_2}) \cdots$$

$$A_{j_m}^{i_m} (x^{j_m} - g^{j_m}) f(x^1, x^2) |J^{-1}| \, dx^1 \, dx^2$$

$$= A_{j_1 j_2 \cdots j_m}^{i_1 i_2 \cdots i_m} |J^{-1}| T^{j_1 j_2 \cdots j_m}$$

transforms as an oriented relative tensor of weight -1 under general affine transformation in accordance with the linear part of that transformation, A_j^i.

Thus, when later solving for the general affine transformation that relates two images, we can use central moment tensors to ascertain the linear component of transformation. Next this information may be used with the image center of gravity information to find the translation component of the transformation

$$\bar{B}^i = \bar{g}^i - A_j^i g^j, \tag{8}$$

where the transformation that relates the locations of point features in the two images is given by

$$\bar{x}^i = A_j^i x^j + \bar{B}^i. \tag{9}$$

5. TENSOR REDUCTION OF THE ORIENTATION PROBLEM

In this section we will develop a method by which the affine transformation that relates two images may be determined from only image-moment information. Later sections will demonstrate that this basic technique will lead to a separation of the object identification and orientation estimation problems. Furthermore, several generalizations will be described that allow this method to be applied to several kinds of image feature sets.

Recall the relationship between the image moment tensors:

$$\bar{T}^{i_1 i_2 \cdots i_m} = A_{j_1 j_2 \cdots j_m}^{i_1 i_2 \cdots i_m} |J^{-1}| T^{j_1 j_2 \cdots j_m}.$$

We wish to find the transformation A_j^i. For the first order moment tensor we have a system of linear equations in the components of the A_j^i. However, as the components of a first order central moment tensor are identically zero, this system of equations provides no useful information. Considering the higher rank moment tensors we see that in general, the moments T and $\bar{T}$ are related by a linear transformation which itself is a tensor product composition of the desired transformation matrix A^i_j.

Because of the redundancy noted earlier, T and $\bar{T}$ each involve at most $m + 1$ independent values, giving rise to at most $m + 1$ independent linear equations in the mth order products of the A^i_j components appearing in the tensor transformation array. There are ${}^4C^{(r)}_m = (m^3 + 6m^2 + 11m + 6)/6$ unique such combinations of these unknowns appearing in the full transformation form for the moment tensor. Thus, direct solution for the moment transformation leading to resolution of the desired A^i_j transform is not possible. For example, if $m = 3$, the moment tensor would have four independent components. This would at first glance seem to provide a sufficient number of equations for the solution of the four A^i_j components. However, the unique composite variable unknowns making up the tensor transformation, $A^{i_1 i_2 i_3}_{j_1 j_2 j_3}$, will number twenty.

To obtain more equations in the composite transformation components one could consider using more moment tensors of other orders. But the fact that these transform according to a different composite transformation (as A^i_j must occur to a different tensor product power equal to the new moment order) these equations cannot be simply used to augment the current collection.

Another approach to the solution of this problem would be to treat it as a nonlinear system of equations in the four unknowns A^i_j. This approach bears the usual set of problems associated with any attempt to solve simultaneous nonlinear equations connected with the behavior of iterative methods near local minima, and so on.

Fortunately, there is a means by which several tensor systems of equations may be combined to form a new system involving a smaller tensor product power of the desired transform A^i_j. By proceeding properly, one can obtain systems in A^i_j alone, reducing the overall problem of solving for the components of A^i_j into a linear one.

The authors originally developed the method to be shown below by writing out the solution of a simple linear system of equations in tensor form and then extending the form of the expression of an inverse matrix to tensor forms. The permutation tensor ε_{ij} that enters linear system theory as the basis for the tensorial expression of the adjoint and the determinant will again play a special role in this new solution method. Rather than duplicate the extension argument, we will follow a more straightforward derivation here based solely on the properties of tensors.

Earlier, in (4), the numerical permutation tensor ε_{ij} was introduced as a covariant relative tensor of weight -1. It is immediately tempting to contract two indices of a given moment tensor, say T^{ijk} with ε_{ij} to form a tensor of reduced rank, $S^k = T^{ijk}\varepsilon_{ij}$, which would participate in a simpler transformation $\bar{S}^i = A^i_j \, sgn(J)J^{-2}S^j$. However, the symmetry of the moment tensors causes any such reduction in rank via the so-called antisymmetric permutation tensor, to produce tensors with each component identically zero. Any attempt to contract two indices of one symmetric tensor or any tensor that is symmetric in that index pair (invariant to exchange of that pair of index values) will result in the formation of a tensor with all elements equal to zero. Except for singular instances, however, moment tensors of different orders can be reduced by means of inner products with the permutation tensor.

Let s^{ij} and t^{ijk} be used to denote second- and third-order moment tensors. By summing the weights of the participants in the following equations, we see that

$$\mu^m = s^{ij}\varepsilon_{ik}\varepsilon_{jl}t^{klm} \tag{10}$$

and

$$\eta^i = t^{ijk}\varepsilon_{jl}\varepsilon_{lm}\mu^l\mu^m \tag{11}$$

are relative tensors of weight -4 and -11, respectively. But the zero-order moment tensor z (which has no indices) possesses a weight -1; that is, $\bar{z} = z|J|^{-1}$. Hence, we can construct a pair of unit rank absolute moment tensors

$$\begin{aligned} u^i &= \mu^i/(z)^4 \\ v^i &= \eta^i/(z)^{11}, \end{aligned} \tag{12}$$

which participate in the simple transformation

$$\begin{aligned} \bar{u}^i &= A^i_j u^j \\ \bar{v}^i &= A^i_j v^j. \end{aligned} \tag{13}$$

Thus, we see that from the moment tensors of order zero, two and three we can obtain four linear equations in the four desired unknowns. In fact, the form of the equations in (13) are such that the systems may be decoupled into two pairs of two equations in two unknowns

$$\begin{aligned} \bar{u}^1 &= A^1_1 u^1 + A^1_2 u^2 \\ \bar{v}^1 &= A^1_1 v^1 + A^1_2 v^2 \end{aligned} \tag{14}$$

and

$$\begin{aligned} \bar{u}^2 &= A^2_1 u^1 + A^2_2 u^2 \\ \bar{v}^2 &= A^2_1 v^1 + A^2_2 v^2. \end{aligned} \tag{15}$$

Given the solution of these equations and the old and new center of gravity tensors g and $\bar{g}$, which are obtained from the zero- and first-order (noncentral) moment tensors, we can obtain the complete image affine transformation

$$\bar{x}^j = A^i_j(x^j - g^j) + \bar{g}^i. \tag{16}$$

Earlier work on the tensor-reduction method [11, 12] made use of a construction similar to that in (12), but used contractions of moment tensors to form the weight-normalization constant rather than the zero-order moment tensor. This form of normalization arose from direct analogy with the matrix inverse. However, normalization by z has proven to be more robust when using camera-acquired data and requires considerably fewer computations.

Note that the moment vectors μ and η were formed from just the second- and third-order moments. In fact, any combination of higher-order moment tensors could be used in a similar scheme, as well, in theory. Our experience is that the robustness of the solution to image distortion is greatest when the lesser-order moment tensors are used. If, however, the systems formed are accidently singular with a given choice of moments then these other combinations can be used to otherwise solve the problem. Several such systems could be formed and solved by a least-squares method also as a means of achieving robustness.

An alternate construction for the unit rank absolute tensor v^i in (13) above that we have found useful is

$$v^i = \frac{s^{ij}\varepsilon_{jk}\mu^k}{sgn(J)(z)^6}.$$

The vector that results from this construction, apparently because of the smaller number of factors involved in the construction of its elements, is more robust to image noise than that given above. Unfortunately, the sign of the Jacobian is required for its construction to cancel the $sgn(J)$ factor introduced by the use of a single permutation tensor in the contraction. One can obtain this information, for example, by first forming u and v as before and using the fact that

$$\bar{u}^i\varepsilon_{ij}\bar{v}^j = u^i\varepsilon_{ij}v^jJ^{-1}$$

as a result of the permutation tensor being a relative tensor of weight -1. Thus this value can be used in the construction of the alternate v^i vector.

The linear equations developed by tensor reduction will always be singular when the image function can be mapped into a function which possesses any k-fold rotational symmetry. That this must be so can be easily seen. Take the case of one of the vectors, say u^i, resulting from the tensor contraction and normalization of the moments associated with a k-fold

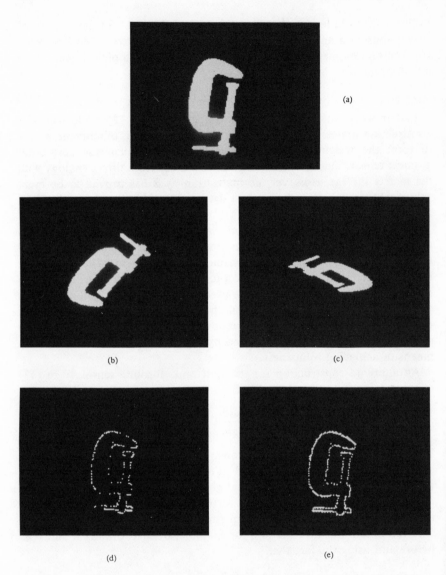

Figure 2. Illustration of the application of the affine transform estimation procedure to determine the orientation of an unknown view of an object with respect to a standard view. Image (a) represents the standard view. Images (b) and (c) represent unknown orientations. Images (d) and (e) result from the EXCLUSIVE OR operation with (a) of the result of application of the inverses of the estimated affine transforms to (b) and (c), respectively. The accuracies of the calculated affine transforms are evident.

symmetric object. By the symmetry of the object, there are k-linear mappings of the image into itself. But since the vector u^i transforms according to the same rule, there are k independent linear transforms that take u^i into itself. But this can only be true if u^i is the zero vector. Hence, the vectors associated with such objects do not result in useful systems of equations.

Operation of the affine transform estimation technique with images of actual objects is illustrated in Figure 2. Figure 2a is the result of video camera acquisition of an image of a C-clamp, followed by sampling on a 128×128 grid, and thresholding. This first image will be assumed to be in a standard orientation, to which new images will be compared. Figure 2b represents the result of image inversion about the x axis, followed by a 45-degree rotation of the object in a plane parallel to the image plane. Figure 2c represents the result of an object rotation of 135 degrees with parallel image and object planes, followed by an oblique camera view (60 degrees with respect to the object plane). Both of these transformations were accomplished synthetically on the Figure 2a image so that the actual transforms would be exactly known.

The actual affine transforms representing the above reorientations, together with the transforms calculated from the images by the method described here, are given in Table 1. The small errors in the results arise from spatial quantization due to image sampling and from finite numerical precision in the algorithm. Figures 2d and 2e illustrate the effect of application of the inverses of the estimated transforms to Figures 2b and 2c, respectively, followed by an exclusive or operation with the Figure 2a image to illustrate the accuracy of each match.

6. CURVE AND POINT FEATURES

The above development assumes that an image of the object is available in which the object's image is completely isolated from the background and that the object-intensity map undergoes exactly the affine transformation dictated by the object motion and parallel projection. In typical situations this isolation does not naturally occur, and is sometimes difficult to achieve by simple preprocessing. In these cases it is more convenient to work with well-behaved (or consistently extractable) features of the object image. Examples of such features are contours of planar areas on the object, centers of gravity of cutouts in the object, the corners of a convex hull around the object, or colored alignment markers on the object surface.

Methods analogous to those developed above for "whole" images can be used to produce similarly unit-rank absolute tensors from which orientation estimates may be derived [12, 13].

Table 1.   Affine Transforms for Images in Figure 2

Figure	Actual Transform	Estimated Transform
2(b)	$\begin{bmatrix} 0.707 & -0.707 \\ -0.707 & -0.707 \end{bmatrix}$	$\begin{bmatrix} 0.749 & -0.710 \\ -0.686 & -0.725 \end{bmatrix}$
2(c)	$\begin{bmatrix} -0.707 & 0.707 \\ -0.354 & -0.354 \end{bmatrix}$	$\begin{bmatrix} -0.705 & 0.687 \\ -0.338 & -0.348 \end{bmatrix}$

The extension to the contour case is simple. Suppose that from each image we obtain either a single planar nonsymmetric contour or a set of any coplanar planar contours that are unsymmetrically arranged. Now any open contour may be closed with a straight line. Since lines remain lines under any affine transformation, this closure behaves as if truly a part of the object.

Now a function $c(x^1, x^2)$ may be constructed by assigning c the value 1 for any point that falls inside one of the closed contours and 0 otherwise. This selector function obviously behaves under change in object orientation just like the object projection itself as described by (5) and (6). Thus, image tensors derived from c may now be treated as before and the linear and translation components of the curve projection transform can be found. An alternate approach using the differential geometry of the contours and not relying upon a moment development is presented in a later section.

The use of contours extracted from an image rather than whole images provides several benefits. As mentioned before, preprocessing used to extract the contours may be effective in isolating the object from a non-null background. In addition, our previous requirement that the object be planar is relaxed; only the contours need be planar. Thus, outlines of windows or markings on buildings or vehicles can be used with the method even though the whole object image might be ineligible. Furthermore, considerable reduction in the computational effort required to form the moment tensors can be obtained for the case of contours by not evaluating the moments of c as if it were an image, but rather by employing the contours directly and applying Green's theorem to find the moments.

Point-type image features may also be available as a result of image preprocessing. We can form moment tensors from such point-feature sets by treating them as optical masses of infinitesimal size but finite mass. There will be some important inherent differences between these moment tensors and those previously examined. The features in the set that result from projections of coplanar features of the object must not display any symmetry and must number at least four (since there are three affine transforms that take any three points into themselves). More than the minimal number of points would normally be used to reduce sensitivity of the results to perturbations such as those due to spatial quantization of the image.

Techniques that find the transformation-relating object images, given sets of feature points, are well known for the case where the correspondences between the features are known. In this simple case, a number of linear equations can be solved for the transformation relating the old and new point positions. Such methods can also be used as the basis for a solution in the case of features with unknown correspondences by testing each transformation calculated on the basis of possible correspondences of a subset of the points against the remainder of the points. Feature labels (information regarding the type of feature such as corner, curve radius, and so on) can be used to reduce the number of trials in such an approach. This method of moment tensors sidesteps the feature labeling and assignment of correspondence problems by solving for the transformation without any special information about the feature set.

Suppose that an image $f(x^1, x^2)$ has N features at locations $_ky^i$ for $k = 1$ to N, where we use the pre-script k to index the features to avoid confusion with tensor indices. We can represent the collection of these features by an image functional consisting of unit optical masses at the feature locations,

$$p(x^i) = \sum_{k=1}^{N} \delta(x^i - {}_ky^i).$$

With the object in its new position, we expect the features to be found in positions $_k\bar{y}^i$ related to the original locations by an affine transformation. Considering first only a linear transformation we have that

$$_k\bar{y}^i = A^i_j \, {}_ky^j$$

resulting in the new image functional

$$\bar{p}(\bar{x}^i) = \sum_{k=1}^{N} \delta(\bar{x}^i - {}_k\bar{y}^i).$$

Applying the well-known properties of the impulse functional δ we see that

$$\delta(\bar{x}^i - A^i_j \, {}_k\bar{y}^j) = |J|\delta(a^i_j\bar{x}^j - {}_ky^j),$$

where

$$A^i_j a^k_i \equiv \delta^k_j$$

as was defined earlier and J is likewise the Jacobian, det(a). Hence, unlike the case of the image function we have that the image functional g transforms as

$$\bar{g}(\bar{x}^i) = g(x^i)|J|.$$

Thus, the moment tensors associated with the image functionals transform as

$$\bar{P}^{i_1 i_2 \cdots i_m} = A^{i_1 i_2 \cdots i_m}_{j_1 j_2 \cdots j_m} P^{j_1 j_2 \cdots j_m},$$

that is, as absolute moment tensors.

As in the case of whole image moment tensors, we may extend our results to affine transformations by using central moments. With central moments defined exactly as before, equations like those in (13) will again be found for the linear part of the transformation. The translation component of the transformation can again be found from the shift in the center of gravity of the point set once the linear transformation has been found as in (16).

Because the image functional moment tensors are absolute tensors the formation of the unit rank tensors by reduction will take a slightly different form. Again denoting second- and third-order moment tensors by s^{ij} and t^{ijk} we have that

$$\mu^m = s^{ij} \varepsilon_{ik} \varepsilon_{jl} t^{klm}$$

and

$$\eta^i = t^{ijk} \varepsilon_{jl} \mu^l \varepsilon_{km} \mu^m$$

are unit-rank relative tensors of weight -2 and -6, respectively. We seek to normalize these to produce absolute unit-tank tensors. However, the zero-rank, zero-order moment tensor is no longer useful since being an absolute tensor it preserves no information about the Jacobian of the transformation. Fortunately we can construct such a normalization constant from the other moment tensors; for example

$$\bar{z} = \bar{s}^{ij} \varepsilon_{ik} \varepsilon_{jl} \bar{s}^{kl} = z|J|^{-2}.$$

With z as above, we obtain the desired unit rank absolute tensors

$$u^i = \mu^i / (z)^2$$

$$\nu^i = \eta^i / (z)^6$$

from which the linear transform A^i_j can be found as before in (14) and (15). As before, other tensor reductions can be used if these result in a singular system of equations, or if more robustness is sought.

As with contour features there are several attractive aspects associated with the use of point sets. Again object isolation from background information can sometimes be achieved for some features despite difficulties with isolating the whole object image. Furthermore, the object need not be planar but rather only the features need be coplanar on the object surface. Finally, there is a tremendous economy involved with calculating the moments of feature sets rather than of the whole image.

Operation with point features is illustrated in Figure 3. In this example the features are selected by the algorithm as the centers of the white circular regions. The pair, u^i and v^i, which results from the tensor operations on each image are represented as a pair of vectors attached to the center of the object's optical mass. This vector pair forms a convenient and compact representation of all of the orientation information in each image. It may be used as the basis for image normalization, as in the object-identification operation. Also the affine transform relating two images of an object may be found from the associated vector pairs.

The figure shows two views of an actual planar object with the vectors calculated by the algorithm superimposed. It is evident that the vector orientation matches the object orientation in each case, indicating correct operation in these oblique views. Quantization in the vector display system used in this example limits the apparent accuracy of the vectors.

The images shown in Figure 3 were generated by a program executing on a GE PN2304 Optomation II industrial vision system. The program was written in the system's built-in Vision Programming Language that is a variant of the BASIC language supporting the special vision features of the machine. The under-one-hundred-line program that generated the pictures in the figure executes the following set of tasks at a rate of once per second:

1. Acquires a gray scale image from the camera.
2. Thresholds the image array and finds the coordinates the center of gravity of each hole in the object.

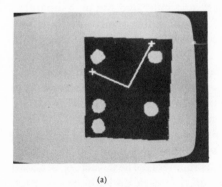 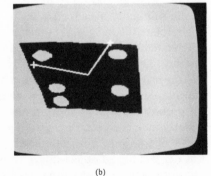

(a) (b)

Figure 3. Thresholded views of a planar object with features selected as the centers of the white circular regions. Vector pairs representing the size and orientation of the feature set are superimposed. Between views (a) and (b) the object was translated and rotated in three-space.

3. Forms the point feature moments and solves for the associated unit rank tensors by the means described above.
4. Displays the threshold image with the unit rank tensors plotted as vectors from the object's center of gravity.

This demonstration indicates the applicability of the moment-tensor reduction system for real-time industrial vision systems.

7. SEPARATING IDENTITY FROM ORIENTATION

In the previous sections, techniques were developed that can be used to determine the affine transform relating projections of a planar object or of coplanar object features. Typically the orientation-determination problem is a complication added to the object recognition problem. In this section we will show that the tensor methods developed so far can be used to disassociate effectively the object recognition problem from the orientation problem.

Consider a naive approach to object identification. Given a projection of a planar object we could use some image metric to determine the distance between this image and each image in a library of standard objects. Unfortunately, the given image may differ from that of the same object in the library by an affine transform if the object under observation has undergone translation and rotations in three-space (including scaling due to perspective distortion). Hence, to determine properly the degree of similarity between the given image and those in the library one must find the pair separated by the minimum distance found by testing all affine transformations that might relate the images. By matching centers of gravity of each image pair, one can remove two degrees of freedom. Despite this economy, the minimum distance-determination still requires a search for a minimum over four transformation parameters. Such a search is tedious at best and owing to the complicated behavior of typical image distances versus transformation, the problems posed by local minima may be extreme.

In the object orientation-determination algorithms previously discussed, a pair of unit-rank absolute tensors, which may be considered as vectors, was derived for an object image from its moments. These vectors, we saw, transform exactly as does the object projection itself under object rotation in three-space and scaling. As indicated by the fact that four degrees of freedom are available in the affine transform and that there are four components associated with the vector pair, one can find an image transformation that will match the associated moment vectors with any given pair of vectors.

Suppose an independent but otherwise arbitrary pair of forms (ordered pairs), η and ζ, are chosen. Furthermore, suppose that we are given an image $f(x^1, x^2)$ with which can be associated the vector pair u^i and v^i found by means of tensor reduction. Then a linear transformation can be found relating u^i and v^i with the "standard" ordered pairs:

$$u^i = A^i_j \eta^j$$
$$v^i = A^i_j \zeta^j. \tag{17}$$

The inverse transformation, A^{-1}, could be applied to the image f to obtain a "normalized" object image f^* for which the associated vectors are now equal to η^i and ζ^i. Now, suppose a second image $\bar{f}(x^1, x^2)$ of the same object is processed. A transformation may also be found taking its vector pair $\bar{u}^i$, $\bar{v}^i$ into η^i and ζ^i.

$$\bar{u}^i = B^i_j \eta^j$$
$$\bar{v}^i = B^i_j \zeta^j.$$

It should be obvious that the new image is related to the old one by the image transformation $B^{-1}A$. Hence, object orientation can be determined from the two normalizing transformations. But consider that if we apply the transformation B^{-1} to the image $\bar{f}$ to form $\bar{f}^*$ then owing to the uniqueness of the solutions A and B we have that $f^* = \bar{f}^*$. Therefore, the normalized images will match regardless of the object orientations associated with each original image. Thus it is possible to standardize the presentation of object image information without knowledge of the identity or orientation of the object before normalization.

Now, given a set of 2D image functions $s_n(x^1, x^2)$ representing the complete library of objects ($n = 1, \ldots, N$), we can form a set of normalized images $s_n^*(x^1, x^2)$ from the transformations $_nB$, which relate a standard pair of forms, η^i and ζ^i, with the vectors $_nu^i$ and $_nv^i$, derived from each image:

$$_nu^i = {}_nB^i_j \eta^j$$
$$_nv^i = {}_nB^i_j \zeta^j.$$

Now, given an image of an object $f(x^1, x^2)$ unknown in both orientation and identity, a transform, A, relating its vector pair, u^i and v^i, and the standard forms may be found as in (17) and a normalized image can be formed, $f^*(x^1, x^2)$. Now, an image similarity metric can be applied to f^* and to each member of the set s_n^*. Given image data of sufficient quality, this metric will take on its optimum value for the correct selection from the library. Now, given this match occurs for image s_m^* then we have immediately that

$$u^i = A^i_j b^i_{k\,m} u^k$$
$$v^i = A^i_j b^j_{k\,m} v^k,$$

where

$$B_j^i b_k^j = \delta_k^i.$$

That is, $A_j^i b_k^j$ is the affine transform that relates the new image to the library image of the same object. This transform may in turn be used to find the three-space rotations relating the orientations of the object in the case of the two images. Thus, upon identification, the transformation relating the object image and its library image may be resolved from their normalizing transformations.

The flow chart for an object identification and orientation estimation algorithm based upon the normalization method is shown in Figure 4. The fact that the largest part of the computational effort, the assembly of a normalized set of library images and their normalizing transforms, can be executed offline is stressed in the flow chart.

Performance of the identification algorithm using actual camera acquired images for the standard library and unknown objects is illustrated in Figures 5-9. A sample library of planar patch objects is shown in Figure 5, and Figure 6 illustrates the result of standardization of these images to a moment form derived from the object in Figure 5a. Figure 7 contains images of four randomly chosen views of objects whose identity is to be determined by the algorithm. The normalized versions of the images in Figure 7 are shown in Figure 8.

The normalized unknown images are to be compared to the known images in Figure 6 to perform the identification. A variety of different comparison metrics could be used. The following form derived from the normalized correlation coefficient for discrete binary images was used for these tests:

$$K_n = \frac{b_{\text{com}} \cdot n_{\text{tot}} - n_{\text{lib}} \cdot n_{\text{unk}}}{\sqrt{(n_{\text{lib}} \cdot n_{\text{tot}} - n_{\text{lib}}^2) \cdot (n_{\text{unk}} \cdot n_{\text{tot}} - n_{\text{unk}}^2)}},$$

where n_{lib} and n_{unk} represent the total number of logical one picture elements in the library and unknown images, respectively. Also, n_{com} is the number of logical one picture element locations in common between the two images, and n_{tot} is the total number of picture elements in the area of each image.

The results of this comparison are given in Table 2. Here it is clear that the correct object has been identified via a maximum correlation value in each row. Examples of matching and nonmatching images after standardization are shown in Figure 9.

8. GENERAL OBJECTS AND 3D MOMENT TENSORS

The tensor moment method can be generalized to provide a means to identify the orientation and identity of objects with surface features that are not

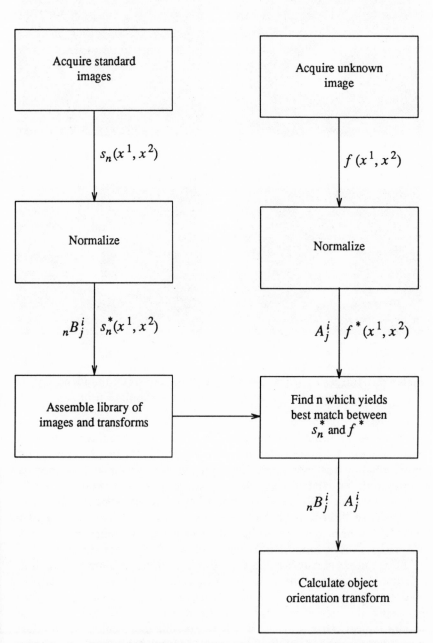

Figure 4. Object identification and orientation estimation algorithm.

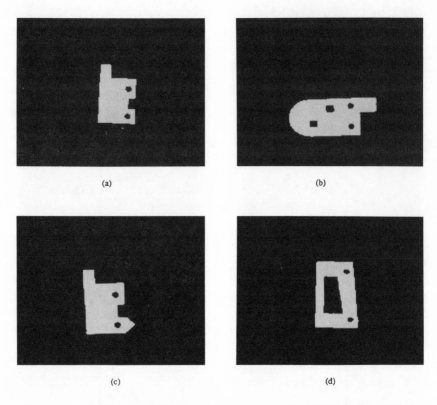

Figure 5. Images of set of four objects to demonstrate the identification
algorithm. Image (a) is chosen as the standard form.

coplanar from a sufficient number of 2D images [19]. For this problem, we
make use of 3D moment tensors and solve directly for the orthogonal
transformation that represents the three-space rotations and three-space
translations that relate the two object observations, rather than solving for
the intermediate affine transformations that relate the object images.

Tensors in three-space behave identically to the 2D tensors so far discussed. One need only recall that all indices will now range from 1 to 3.
We will, however, introduce the special case of the Cartesian tensor. If a
set of quantities transforms like a tensor for all orthogonal transformations
O_j^i, though not necessarily for arbitrary (in general not orthogonal) transformations, we say that this form is a Cartesian tensor. The Cartesian tensor
has a special property: there is no distinction between covariant and contravariant indices. That is to say, it will be possible to execute inner product
operations among any pair of indices with the result being another Cartesian
tensor. The Cartesian tensor is applicable here as we will be dealing with

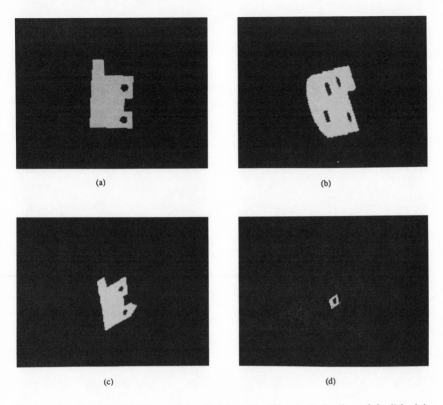

Figure 6. Standardized version of objects in Figure 5. Indices (a), (b), (c), and (d) correspond in Figures 5 and 6.

the orthogonal object transformations in three-space and not more general affine transformations of its image.

Now suppose that a 3D object has some K distinguishable features at locations in three-space given by $_ky^i$. Then we can form an image functional

$$p(x^i) = \sum_{k=1}^{K} \delta(x^i - {_k}y^i),$$

which under orthogonal transformation behaves as

$$\bar{p}(B_j^i x^j) = |J|p(x^i),$$

where as before $J = \det(B^{-1})$. Moments of this function will transform as an absolute tensor,

$$\bar{T}^{i_1 i_2 \cdots i_m} = B_{j_1 j_2 \cdots j_m}^{i_1 i_2 \cdots i_m} T^{j_1 j_2 \cdots j_m}.$$

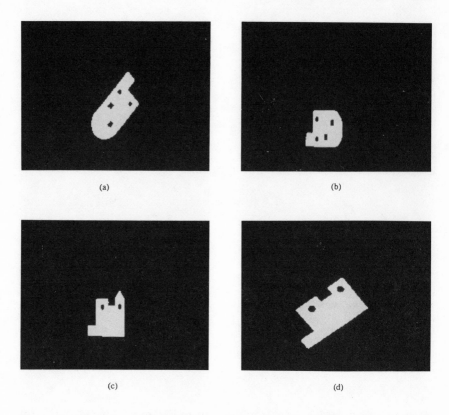

Figure 7.   Images of four arbitrary orientations (including oblique views)
of objects in the library.

If the central moment tensors of an object are known, the transformation
B_j^i may be found by reduction of the tensors to unit rank by inner product
contractions such as

$$u^k = s^{ij}t^{ijk}$$
$$v^j = s^{ij}u^i$$
$$w^k = t^{ijk}u^iv^j.$$

From three such unit-rank tensors, we may find the elements of B_j^i by solving
the associated nine linear equations in the nine unknowns of the linear
transformation. The centers of gravity of the feature sets can be used to
determine the translations of the object in three-space. Choosing arbitrary
forms for standardization we can separate the identity and orientation
problems as before also.

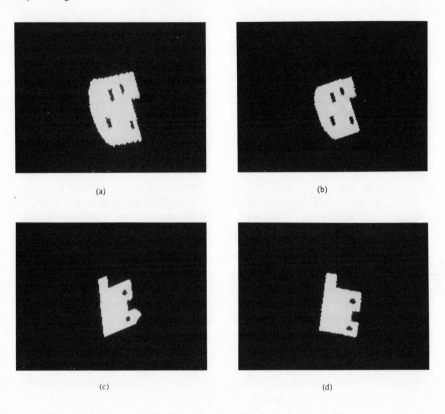

Figure 8. Standardized versions of images in Figure 7.

It may be possible to immediately generate the 3D moment tensors given the proper circumstances. For example, if the features in question are reflective targets on the object and laser ranging is being used, then the three-space location of each feature can be found. In this case the feature moments may be simply calculated and the orientation of the object determined from the transform *B* found as above. Likewise if a complete surface

Table 2. Similarity Value, Object Identification

Unknown Object	Library Object (*Fig. 5*)			
(*Fig. 7*)	(*a*)	(*b*)	(*c*)	(*d*)
(a)	0.600	0.930	0.505	0.126
(b)	0.697	0.757	0.628	0.164
(c)	0.737	0.595	0.823	0.183
(d)	0.904	0.611	0.671	0.172

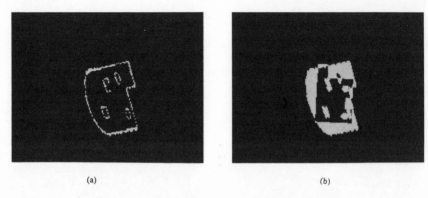

(a)   (b)

Figure 9.   Examples of EXCLUSIVE OR comparison of matching (a) and
non-matching (b) images after standardization.

description were known from some sort of ranging, 3D surface moments
could be found and again the orientation and identity problems could be
solved.

Generally we would like to determine the same orientation information
from just 2D images of the object being examined. One means of accomplish-
ing this is to construct the 3D moment tensors from just the locations of
the projections of some feature points.

It can be shown that all the $M = (m + 1)(m + 2)/2$ independent elements
of a rank m 3D moment tensor can be found from $m + 1$ projections of
the feature set from viewing angles which are not parallel [19]. The basis
for this construction is that the 2D moments of the nth projection, $_nM$ are
exactly some of the components of the 3D moment tensor, T, with respect
to a coordinate system with two of its axes parallel to the nth projection
plane (say x^1 and x^2). That is

$$_nM^{i_1 i_2 \cdots i_m} = {}_nT^{i_1 i_2 \cdots i_m}, 1 \leqslant i_1, i_2, \ldots, i_m \leqslant 2.$$

When the components of T are referred to this special coordinate system
attached to the nth projection plane, we shall refer to it as $_nT$. From the
elementary tensor transformation property we know that

$$_pT^{i_1 i_2 \cdots i_m} = {}_p^q C^{i_1 i_2 \cdots i_m}_{j_1 j_2 \cdots j_m} {}_qT^{j_1 j_2 \cdots j_m}$$

relates the 3D moment tensors with pairs of axes chosen to lie in the p and
qth projection planes, where $_p^q C$ is the transformation that relates these
views. Thus, the 2D moment tensor components of the projections are
linearly related to the 3D moment tensor components of a 3D moment
tensor taken with respect to any view. Hence, with a sufficient number of
projections we can assemble a large enough system of linear equations to

solve for the unknown components of the moment tensor T with respect to some arbitrary coordinate system.

At first glance it would seem that, since each 2D projection provides $m + 1$ independent mth order moments, $\lceil (m + 2)/2 \rceil$ projections would suffice to find the $(m + 1)(m + 2)/2$ independent components of T. However, it can be shown that successive moment sets from projections are not independent.

Let $_p x^i$, $i = 1, 2$, denote a 2D orthogonal coordinate system for the pth projection plane. Consider the moments in this plane as a 2D moment tensor $_p M$. The 2D moment tensor $_p \bar{M}$, for any other coordinate system $_p \bar{x}^i$ in the plane can be determined by applying the familiar tensor transformation rules to $_p M$.

Now consider the fact that two projection planes, taken as passing through the origin of our 3D coordinate system, intersect in a certain line. Then there exists coordinate systems for these two planes, $_p \bar{x}^i$ and $_q \bar{x}^i$ such that the axes $_p \bar{x}^1$ and $_q \bar{x}^1$ are coincident with the line of intersection of the planes. Hence, given the moments, $_p M^{i_1 i_2 \cdots i_m}$, of the object features as projected on the pth plane with respect to coordinates $_p x^i$, we can find a transformation to the $_p \bar{x}^i$ coordinate system such that the moment value

$$_p \bar{M}^{11 \cdots 1} = {}_q \bar{M}^{11 \cdots 1}.$$

This provides one equation toward a system that would enable us to find $_q M^{i_1 i_2 \cdots i_m}$. That this is true between every pair of projection planes immediately follows.

Hence, a rank-m 2D moment tensor provides $m + 1$ independent pieces of information about the desired 3D moment tensor. But only m of the next 2D tensor components are independent of our previous information and so on. Thus, since $1 + 2 + \cdots + m + 1 = (m + 1)(m + 2)/2$, we see that it takes exactly $m + 1$ projections to find all the components of a rank-m 3D moment tensor. So, in light of this and the previous development, at least four projections would be necessary to find the orientation of our object given that second- and third-order moment tensors were used.

This technique allows for the solution of the three rotations in three-space that relate two orientations of an object. Analogously with the 2D tensor case discussed before, normalized feature sets of surface descriptions could be obtained by relating the unit-rank tensor triple u^i, v^i and w^i to an arbitrary set of vectors that are not coplanar. Hence, the same separation of identification and orientation estimation problems can be obtained in the case of 3D objects.

The method can be applied usefully where 3D objects possess identifiable but unlabeled features. This occurs in situations where a fixed number of features may always be extracted from the image but their correspondence between pictures is not immediately obvious. Generalizations of the method could yield additional results of practical importance. Contour features may be more common in some cases than point features. Contour moments appropriately defined might transform as did the point feature moments and hence allow for solution of the three-space transformation.

The large number of views associated with the method as presented is a result of the number of moment tensors needed for the solution by tensor contraction. Recent work has revealed that alternate methods for the solution of the affine transform relating tensors exist [9]. These new decomposition methods work on a single tensor, and do not require several moment tensors for contraction.

While the fact that the 3D moment tensors are Cartesian tensors is useful in developing a simple contraction to unit rank tensors involving a small number of moments, it is not essential. In fact, a general three-dimensional affine transformation could be found instead using contractions that do not involve indices of the same type. Hence, the method would be of use even in the case where the object undergoes a change in shape of a sort that can be expressed by an arbitrary linear transformation. Such a solution may have some interesting applications in metrology and materials mechanics.

9. DIFFERENTIAL TENSORS AND FOURIER DESCRIPTORS

To demonstrate that the usefulness of the tensor representation of image data extends beyond the area of moment methods we will now discuss a considerably different approach to solving the object orientation problem. This development will again illustrate the important role of tensors in making evident certain transformational properties of quantities with geometric origin.

Suppose again that preprocessing of an image has resulted in the extraction of contours from the object projection. As before, assume that each open contour has been closed by a straight line. Now, suppose we wish to find the affine transformation that relates this contour to a projection of that same feature from a different position and orientation of the object.

Exhaustive methods have been proposed for contour matching that are based on the filling of multidimensional accumulation tables with votes for the supporting transform relationship [2]. While robust (especially to missing information), these Hough table methods are computationally burdensome owing to the large number of unknown parameters involved in a general affine transformation.

Other previous works [17, 18, 23] have proposed more direct solution methods. However, these are applicable only to the identification of contour shifts, scaling and image plane rotations and not for dealing with general orientations of an object in three-space. In the following we shall take the

Fourier descriptor method [17] and show how it can be extended to be useful for contour matching under general affine transformation of the contours [10].

We will begin by summarizing the method of Fourier descriptors or elliptic decomposition. Suppose a closed contour is expressed in terms of its parametric equations $x^1(t)$ and $x^2(t)$, where t is the natural arc length measured from an arbitrary starting point on the curve. That is

$$dt = \sqrt{(dx^1)^2 + (dx^2)^2} = \sqrt{dx^i \, dx^i}.$$

Now, suppose we expand the parametric equations of the curve in terms of a Fourier series with the nth harmonic coefficient given by

$$_nE^i = \int_0^1 x^i(t) \, e^{-j2\pi nt} \, dt, \tag{18}$$

where the total arc length is taken as unity with no loss of generality.

If O_j^i is a two-dimensional orthogonal transformation of the image (corresponding to an image plane rotation, that is, rotation of the object on the viewing axis alone) then the new Fourier descriptors will be given by

$$_n\bar{E}^i = O_j^i \, _nE^j \tag{19}$$

if the starting point of the new parameterization and the sense of the parameterization are appropriately transferred to the new curve from the old curve (a simplifying assumption we will maintain for now). This transformational property may be derived from the Fourier integral, (18), and from the invariance of natural arc length under orthogonal transformation. That natural arc length is invariant can be seen from the tensorial expression of the differential arc length, above, recalling that the properties of Cartesian tensors are preserved for inner products across any pair of indices. Unfortunately, a simple transformational property like that of equation (19) no longer holds if the contour is distorted by a more general linear transformation, A, because in general

$$d\bar{t} = \sqrt{A_j^i \, dx^j \, A_k^i \, dx^k} \neq c \, dt.$$

A parameterization of the sort we seek arises in the problem from differential geometry of finding an appropriate moving frame for the description of curves that is invariant under the group of unimodular linear transformations [14]. The classic solution to this problem by Cartan's method for identifying group invariants results in a differential arc measure that is invariant over all affine transforms with unit determinant.

Rather than pursue this solution method, we will use the elementary properties of tensors to find such invariant differentials. Let $x^{i(k:t)}$ denote the unit-rank tensor whose elements are the kth order derivatives of the curve at the point x^i with respect to an arbitrary curve parameterization, t (for example the natural arc length). By the linearity of differentiation we have that

$$\bar{x}^{i(k:t)} = A^i_j x^{j(k:t)},$$

where $\bar{x}$ and x are related by A^i_j. Now, if we were to use a tensor inner product to reduce some number of such derivatives in t to a zero-rank absolute tensor, then by the tensor transformation rules this quantity would be invariant. However, when given the transformed curve, we have no way of differentiating its parametric equations with respect to t since we have no way of knowing the relation that connects t and $\bar{t}$. But on applying the appropriate chain rule substitutions we find for the special cases ($k = 0, l = 1$) and ($k = 1, l = 2$) that

$$\left|\bar{x}^{i(k:\bar{t})}\varepsilon_{ij}\bar{x}^{j(l:\bar{t})}\right|^{1/(k+l)} d\bar{t} = \left|x^{i(k:t)}\varepsilon_{ij}x^{j(l:t)}J^{-1}\right|^{1/(k+l)} dt,$$

where the derivatives on each side are taken with respect to an arbitrary curve parameterization associated with the parametric equations on that side of the equation. (In the following, the variable of differentiation will be assumed to be that associated with the parametric equations that are subject to the operation.) This equation describes a unit rank oriented relative tensor differential, $d\gamma$, with weight $-1/(k + l)$. Since

$$d\bar{\gamma} = |J|^{-1/(k+l)} d\gamma,$$

where J is the Jacobian as defined earlier. Thus, if a curve is a reparameterized on the basis of the evaluation of $d\gamma$ with respect to any initial parameterization, then its total arc length will transform as

$$\bar{\Gamma} = \Gamma|J|^{-1/(k+l)}.$$

Hence,

$$d\tau = d\gamma/\Gamma$$

is an invariant differential with respect to any linear transformation of a curve. Because of its invariance we see that this differential defines a canonical arc length with respect to general linear transformation.

Notice that for $k = 1, l = 2$ the canonical differential defined above is invariant to the general affine transformation since the effects of coordinate translation are removed by the differentiation. However, in the interest of robust behavior given corrupt curves, we have found it useful to use first-order derivative based

$$d\tau = \left|x^i\varepsilon_{ij}x^{j(1)}\right| dt/\Gamma$$

with Γ again being the total arc length derived from use of the differential

$$d\gamma = \left|x^i\varepsilon_{ij}x^{j(1)}\right| dt.$$

To use this form of the differential, however, the effects of translation must be independently removed. This can be accomplished by calculating the center of gravity of the selector function (inside = 1, outside = 0) of the closed contour as done in the case of the contour moment method. Now the simpler parameterization may be applied to the centered curves and the same center of gravity information can be used to determine the object translation.

Now, by the invariance of $d\tau$ we have that if τ is the distance along the curve from a fixed starting point, then we have $\bar{\tau} = \tau$ and

$$\bar{x}^i(\bar{\tau}) = A^i_j x^j(\tau).$$

From this it follows immediately that the nth Fourier harmonic transforms as

$$_n\bar{E}^i = A^i_j \, _nE^j.$$

Thus, a pair of different Fourier components would suffice for the solution of the linear transformation A.

Unfortunately the assumption of a fixed and known starting point and sense of trace on the curve is rarely upheld in practice. In general $\bar{\tau} = \tau + \Delta T$ where ΔT is the unknown value of canonical arc length separating the starting points on the two curves E and $\bar{E}$. If we let $\theta = 2\pi\Delta T$ then we can represent the true relationship between $_nE$ and $_n\bar{E}$ by

$$_n\bar{E}^i = A^i_j \, _nE^j \, e^{jn\theta}.$$

If the sense of the curve tracing has been reversed then

$$_n\bar{E}^i = A^i_j (_nE^j)^* \, e^{jn\theta},$$

where * denotes complex conjugation. Thus, in general, we must find the four linear transformation parameters, the shift angle θ and the proper sense of the trace. Two Fourier harmonics provide us with eight real equations in the five real unknowns. To find the solution least-squares methods can be used to solve the system for fixed θ and sense and then search for the minimum residual over θ and the sense.

In the implementation used to generate the figures to be described, we chose to solve the equations for each possible sense and any given value of θ with the components of A taken to be complex valued. Next, the sum of the squares of the imaginary parts of the A coefficients was minimized with respect to θ. This problem could have been solved analytically as the minimization of a trigonometric polynomial; however, we choose to use an iterative solution technique instead of applying polynomial root finding techniques to high-order polynomials. We used the Powell quadratic search method that found solutions to the desired accuracy in typically just a few iterations. Once solutions were found for each sense; that which minimized the sum-of-squares criterion used above was chosen as the final solution.

In the test cases to be shown, the first and second harmonics were used to find the transformation matrix. This choice yielded the greatest robustness to the errors introduced by spatial quantization. With synthetically generated curves we obtained nearly perfect results by applying the method exactly as described above. However, given contours obtained by camera acquisition of images of real objects, the results were disappointing. The noisiness of the acquired curves significantly disturbed the calculated values of differential arc length. The performance was immensely improved by applying a smoothing operation to the contours before calculation of the invariant arc length. This implementation uses a simple convolutional smoothing operation implemented as a windowing of the DFT of the contour samples. First the curve data was resampled to provide 256 samples equally spaced in natural arc length. The DFT of this data was then truncated at some index value. Finally the inverse DFT of this data was used as the new contour information.

Operation of the differential-tensor method is illustrated using contours extracted from the images of a vehicle model shown in Figures 10a and 10b. The contours of the windows of the vehicle model were extracted using a simple contour following algorithm and are shown in Figures 10c and 10d. Application of the smoothing operation, retaining nine Fourier coefficients, results in the contours depicted in Figures 11a and 11b. The small circles indicate the arbitrarily chosen starting points for parameterization of the curves. The calculated affine transform is given in Table 3, and the result of normalizing the contour in Figure 11b by the inverse of the calculated transform is in Figure 11c. The standard and transformed contours are superimposed in Figure 11d. Good agreement with results obtained using the moment tensor method is evident.

The fact that the smoothing operation was applied before calculation of the canonic parameterization is less than ideal. Because the natural arc length parameterization is applied first, the smoothed-curve description is not closed under general linear transformation. That is, two curves that are exactly related by an affine transformation will not yield smoothed curves that are exactly related by that or any affine transformation. Thus, there is a tradeoff between severity of smoothing and performance of the complete algorithm. This problem would not exist if a canonically parameterized curve were smoothed. Unfortunately, the canonic differential is more sensitive to curve noise than natural arc length because of the involvement of curve derivatives in its computation. Work is under way toward developing smoothing methods that are robust to noise, but also do not distort the affine relationship between curves.

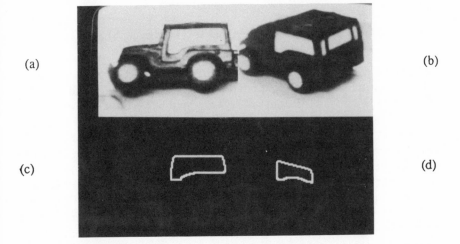

Figure 10. Images of model vehicle in original (a) and reoriented (b) positions. Contours extracted from the windows are illustrated in (c) and (d).

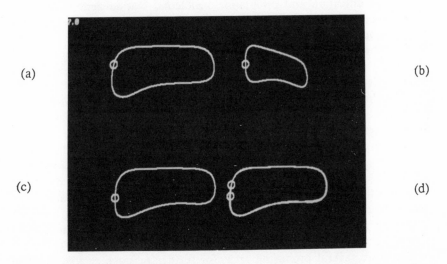

Figure 11. Example of orientation estimation and normalization using differential methods. Parts (a) and (b): contours resulting from Fourier smoothing (with retention of nine Fourier coefficients) of the outlines of the windows in Figure 10. Arbitrarily chosen starting points for curve parameterization are indicated by circles. Part (c): result of normalization of (b) by the estimated transform. Part (d): comparison of Figures 11 (a) and (c).

141

10. CONCLUSIONS AND FUTURE RESEARCH

We have demonstrated the general utility of the tensor representation of image information. This representation makes the invariance and transformational properties of certain image data obvious because of the structure inherent in tensor expressions. All of the derivations above could have been expressed in terms of matrices and matrix Kronecker products. Not only would such a presentation have been difficult to follow because of the complicated and often unobvious relationships among matrix Kronecker forms, but worse, the fact that a solution method existed might never have come to light.

We have seen that the affine transformation relating a single pair of planar objects or coplanar object features could be found in a direct (noniterative) fashion. A pair of such affine transforms leads to a complete specification of the three-space rotations and translations that relate the object's orientations in the imaging instances.

An important feature of this method for finding the affine transformation is that it can also be used as the basis for the derivation of an image normalization. This normalization results in a special decoupling of the object identification and orientation problems. Normalized images of a given object are the same regardless of the object's orientation in three-space at the imaging instant. This allows for the selection of an object prototype from a library of normalized images with great expediency. Subsequently, the object's orientation with respect to a standard position can be estimated from transformations calculated in the normalization process.

The general utility of the tensor representation was further demonstrated by its application to two other problems. First, a generalization of the above method was described for the case of a general object feature set (no coplanarity constraint). The three-space orientation problem could be solved given ranging information about an object's features, or several projections of those features onto images. In addition, the Fourier descriptor, or elliptic decomposition method for matching image contours was generalized. By using an arc differential constructed from tensor reductions we are able to deal with general affine transformations of curves rather than just shifts and rotations on the image plane.

There are several promising areas for further research related to these methods. It should be possible to restate this whole theory in terms of a 4D, homogeneous coordinate system representation. This would lead to a means to deal with the general perspective distortion of images.

In all these realizations, the features in one image of an object must appear completely and exclusively in the others. It would be desirable to borrow the best aspects of the tensor differential theory and the Hough accumulation table methods and generate a method for object recognition that is robust to missing and wrong data while deriving its immunity to image transformation from tensor reductions and not table dimensionality.

A good example of a hybrid method involving a tensor-based method and graph theoretic techniques is that in the work by Bamieh and de Figueiredo [3]. A method was developed to identify the identity and orientation of 3D objects with planar faces given only a single, perhaps partially occluded, view. Here, tensor methods were used to generate invariant values for an attributed graph description of the image. The identification problem in turn becomes a subgraph isomorphism problem. Finally, orientation is determined by means of moment tensor contractions to unit rank.

The tensor-moment methods are well suited to machine implementation because of the simplicity and regularity of the algorithms. We have implemented a working orientation estimation routine on a commercial, industrial vision system that can generate an estimate once a second from camera-acquired data. A machine or coprocessing peripheral specifically designed to implement the algorithm could yield update rates approaching frame-acquisition rates.

REFERENCES

[1] Abu-Mostafa, Y., and D. Psaltis. "Recognitive aspects of moment invariants," *IEEE Trans. Pattern Anal. and Machine Intelligence*, vol. PAMI-6, November 1984, pp. 698–706.

[2] Ballard, D. E., and D. Sabbah. "On shapes," *Proc. IJCAI7*, 1981, pp. 607–612.

[3] Bamieh, B. and R. J. P. de Figueiredo. "A general moment-invariants/attributed graph method for three-dimensional object recognition from a single image," *IEEE Journal of Robotics and Automation*, vol. RA-2, March 1986, pp. 31–41.

[4] Casasent, D., and D. Psaltis. "New optical transforms for pattern recognition," *Proc. IEEE*, vol. 65, January 1977, pp. 77–84.

[5] Dirilten, H., and T. G. Newman. "Pattern matching under affine transformations," *IEEE Trans. Computers*, vol. C-26, March 1977, pp. 314–317.

[6] Dudani, S. A. "An experimental study of moment methods for automatic identification of three-dimensional objects from television images," The Ohio State University, PhD thesis, Computer Science, 1973.

[7] Cyganski, D., and J. A. Orr. "Applications of tensor theory to object recognition and orientation determination," *IEEE Trans. on Pattern Anal. and Machine Intelligence*, vol. PAMI-7, No. 6, November 1985, pp. 662–673.

[8] Cyganski, D., and J. A. Orr. "Object identification and orientation determination in 3-space with no point correspondence information," *Proc. IEEE Intl. Conf. Acoustics, Speech and Signal Processing*, San Diego, CA, 1984, pp. 23.8.1–23.8.4.

[9] Cyganski, D., and J. A. Orr. "The decomposition of image tensors," *Proc. IEEE Conf. Computer Vision and Pattern Recognition*, Miami Beach, FL, June 22–26, 1986.

[10] Cyganski, D., and J. A. Orr. "3-D motion parameters from contours using a canonical differential," *IEEE Intl. Conf. Acoustics, Speech and Signal Processing*, Tampa, FL, March 26–29, 1985, pp. 917–920.

[11] Cyganski, D., J. A. Orr, and Z. Pinjo. "A tensor operator method for identifying the affine transformation relating image pairs," *Proc. IEEE Conf. Computer Vision and Pattern Recognition*, Washington, DC, June 19-23, 1983, pp. 361-363.

[12] Cyganski, D., and J. A. Orr. "Object identification and orientation estimation from point set tensors," *Proc. Seventh International Conf. Pattern Recognition, Montreal, Canada*, July 30-August 2, 1984, pp. 250-253.

[13] Cyganski, D., J. A. Orr, and R. Vaz. "Determination of affine transforms from object contours with no point correspondence information," *Proc. IEEE Intl. Conf. Acoustics, Speech and Signal Processing*, Tampa, FL, March 26-29, 1985, pp. 921-924.

[14] Guggenheimer, H. W. *Differential Geometry*, New York, McGraw-Hill, 1963.

[15] Hu, M. K. "Visual pattern recognition by moment invariants," *IEEE Trans. Inform. Theory*, February 1962, pp. 179-187.

[16] Huang, T. S. *Image Sequence Analysis*, New York, Springer-Verlag, 1981.

[17] Kuhl, F. P. "Elliptic Fourier features of a closed contour," *Computer Graphics and Image Processing*, vol. 18, 1982, pp. 236-258.

[18] Pavlidis, T. *Structural Pattern Recognition*, New York, Springer-Verlag, 1977.

[19] Pinjo, Z., D. Cyganski, and J. A. Orr. "Determination of 3-D object orientation from projections," *Pattern Recognition Letters*, vol. 3, September 1985, pp. 351-356.

[20] Reddi, J. J. "Radial and angular moment invariants for image identification," *IEEE Trans. Pattern Anal. and Machine Intelligence*, vol. PAMI-3, March 1981, pp. 240-242.

[21] Sadjadi, F. A., and E. L. Hall. "Object recognition by three-dimensional moment invariants," *IEEE Trans. Pattern Anal. and Machine Intelligence*, vol. PAMI-6, March 1980, pp. 698-706.

[22] Teague, M. R. "Image analysis via the general theory of moments," *J. Optical Society of America*, vol. 70, August 1980, pp. 920-930.

[23] You, K. C., and K. S. Fu. "A syntactic approach to shape recognition using attributed grammars," *IEEE Trans. Systems Man and Cybernetics*, vol. SMC-9, June 1979, pp. 334-345.

Chapter 5

SOME EXPERIMENTS IN EGO-MOTION COMPLEX LOGARITHMIC MAPPING

R. Jain, S. Bartlett, and N. O'Brien

OUTLINE

Advances in Computer Vision and Image Processing, Vol. 3, pages 145–177.

ABSTRACT

If a dynamic scene is acquired using a translating camera and the camera-motion parameters are known, then the analysis of the scene may be facilitated by Ego-Motion Complex Logarithmic Mapping (ECLM). It is shown in this chapter that by using the Complex Logarithmic Mapping (CLM) with respect to the focus of expansion, the depth of stationary components can be determined easily in the transformed image sequence. An added advantage of the CLM will be the invariances it offers. Here, we discuss different methods of implementing the mapping. Our experiments show that by varying certain parameters in the mapping, we can emphasize different parts of the image.

1. INTRODUCTION

Recently, many researchers have been studying systems that acquire images using a moving camera. Optical flow has been studied with the aim of recovering information about the environment and the motion of the observer. Here, we discuss some characteristics of optical flow that are useful in analyzing dynamic scenes, and then discuss briefly the Ego-Motion Polar (EMP) transformation as described by Jain [9] that is useful in separating stationary and nonstationary components of an image acquired using a translating camera. Next, we present some aspects of the CLM and then introduce the Ego-Motion Complex Logarithmic Mapping (ECLM). We show that the ECLM maintains projection invariance for arbitrary translational motion of the observer and can be used in recovering the depth of stationary objects. We also present aspects of the mapping that are useful in finding the precision of the information that can be recovered using this method. Finally, we discuss our experience in recovering depth in laboratory scenes using different mappings. Our aim in this chapter is to show the effects of different mapping methods on the lines and curves in an image and to study how using the different methods impacts depth determination in real scenes.

2. EGO-MOTION POLAR TRANSFORM

Clocksin [7], Gibson [8], Lee [14], and Prazdny [19] have shown that optical flow carries information about the structure of the environment and the motion of the observer. Optical flow is the instantaneous field of velocity at image points due to the motion of scene points relative to the viewer. When an observer moves through a scene, all points in the scene are in motion relative to him. Points that are close to the observer appear to move relatively faster than points that are further away. The flow vectors due to the stationary components of a scene all intersect at a single point, as shown in Figure 1. This point is called the Focus of Expansion (FOE). Lee [14] and Prazdny [19] have shown that the FOE plays a vital role in the recovery of information from the optical flow field.

The last few years have seen increasing efforts to use optical flow in the analysis of dynamic scenes. Many approaches have been proposed for the computation of optical flow from images of a dynamic scene. Most of these proposed approaches consider only two frames of a scene to compute the flow field. Based on the research of Bruss and Horn [3], it appears that the computation of acceptable quality optical flow for real-world scenes is a very difficult problem. Moreover, the methods for the recovery of the information are sensitive to the noise in the optical flow. Thus, in most realistic applications, the information obtained from the computed flow fields may not be reliable.

In many applications, such as robot vision, either the camera moves under computer control or the camera motion parameters can be obtained by some means. If the camera displacement between two frames is dX, dY, dZ, then the FOE for these frames is

$$F_x = \frac{dX}{dZ} \tag{1}$$

$$F_y = \frac{dY}{dZ}. \tag{2}$$

The information about the camera-motion parameters, and hence about the FOE, may be used in the recovery of information. Jain [9, 10] tried to

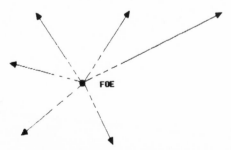

Figure 1. The optical flow field for a moving observer in a stationary environment. The vectors intersect at the focus of expansion.

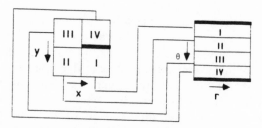

Figure 2. An image $I(x, y)$ is converted to another image $I(r, \theta)$ using the EMP transform.

exploit characteristics of optical flow without actually computing the optical flow field. He used a transformation on images acquired using a moving camera to segment a dynamic scene into its stationary and nonstationary components. This transformation, called the Ego-Motion Polar transform (EMP), is centered around the FOE and converts the original image $I(x, y)$ into an image $I^*(r, \theta)$ using

$$I^*(r, \theta) = I(x, y), \tag{3}$$

where

$$r = \sqrt{(x - F_x)^2 + (y - F_y)^2} \tag{4}$$

and

$$\theta = \arctan \frac{(y - F_y)}{(x - F_x)}. \tag{5}$$

This transformation is shown in Figure 2.

Jain [10] shows that, for a moving observer, all stationary points in a scene will show only horizontal displacement in the EMP-transformed image. This fact can be used to determine whether an object is moving or not. As shown in Figure 3, the apparent motion of stationary points is

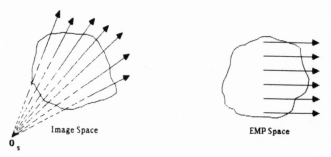

Figure 3. The assorted directions of the velocity vectors for a stationary object are transformed to one direction in the transformed image.

converted from assorted directions, depending on their locations in the image plane, to unidirectional motion in the EMP space. The stationarity of an object is judged by the absence of a θ component for the region corresponding to the object in the EMP space. An algorithm was developed to implement this scheme. Jain [10] reports the results for real world scenes.

3. COMPLEX LOGARITHMIC MAPPING

Schwartz [23] showed that the retino-striate mapping can be approximated using a Complex Logarithmic Mapping (CLM). Retino-striate mapping, a common feature of vertebrate sensory information processing, is a spatial mapping of the peripheral sensory receptive surfaces onto corresponding parts of the central nervous system. Schwartz [23, 24, 25, 26] has also shown that in our own human vision system, as well as those of lower animals, the excitement of the striate cortex can be approximated by a Complex Logarithmic Mapping (CLM) of the eye's retinal image. In other words, what we see as the real world and what is focused on the retinas of our eyes, is reconfigured onto the striate cortex by a process similar to complex logarithmic mapping before it is examined or interpreted in our brain. Schwartz further argued that this mapping is responsible for the scale, rotation and projection invariances in the human visual system. As is well known, these invariances play a vital role in human visual perception. Cavanaugh [4, 5], however, showed that Schwartz's claims about the CLM resulting in the invariances are correct only under certain conditions. The rotation and scale invariances are obtained if the object is in the center of the image and the rotation and scale changes are with respect to the origin. The projection invariance is obtained only if the direction of the observer's gaze and the direction of the motion are the same.

Let us look at the mathematical definition of CLM. Complex log mapping may be written mathematically as

$$w = \log z, \tag{6}$$

where w and z are complex variables:

$$z = x + iy = r(\cos \theta + i \sin \theta) = re^{i\theta} \tag{7}$$

and

$$w = u(z) + iv(z). \tag{8}$$

In this way, a function or image in z-space with coordinates x and y is mapped to w-space with coordinates u and v. The mapping is obtained from the simplified equations:

$$u(r, \theta) = \log r \qquad (9)$$

$$v(r, \theta) = \theta. \qquad (10)$$

Chaikin and Weiman [6, 28], Braccini, Gamberdella, and Tagliasco [2], and Sandini and Tagliasco [22] have pointed out the many attractive features of this mapping. From the psychological viewpoint, it is the only analytic function that maps a circular region, such as an image on the retina, into a rectangular region. This is a desirable feature for the study and modeling of the human visual system. The mappings of two regular patterns are shown in Figure 4 to result in similarly regular patterns. Figure 4a shows concentric circles in an image or the z-plane become vertical lines in the mapped w-plane. This becomes obvious when one examines the CLM definition above. A single circle maps to a single vertical line since the constant radius, r, at all angles, θ, of the circle gives a constant u coordinate for all v coordinates in the mapped space. Similarly in Figure 4b, an image of radial lines which have constant angle but variable radii, result in a map of horizontal lines.

Parallel straight lines in the z-plane become a family of curves with asymptotes π units apart and a reflective line of symmetry halfway between the asymptotes. Consider, for example, the set of lines in the z-plane, $y = m$ for $m = 0, 1, 2, \ldots$, parallel to and including the x axis. These will map into a set of curves asymptotic to the lines $v = 0$ and $v = \pi$ and symmetrical about the line $v = \pi/2$, the axis itself mapping to the asymptotes. The

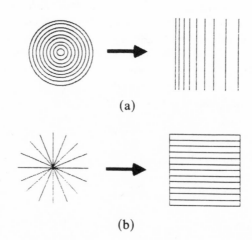

(a)

(b)

Figure 4. The CLM results in the transformation of certain regular patterns in the z-plane into another regular pattern in the u-plane.

spacing between the curves will be logarithmic. To find the mapping for a similar set of lines parallel to the y axis, translate the mapping for the horizontal lines down $\pi/2$. The asymptotes become $v = \pi/2$ and $v = -\pi/2$, and the line of symmetry becomes $v = 0$.

Through these mappings, we can demonstrate some of the invariances of CLM that may be helpful in image understanding. The first such invariance is that of rotation. In Figure 4a, we saw that for a circle, all possible angular orientations of a point at the given radius will map to the same vertical line. Thus, if an object is rotated between successive images, this will result in only a vertical displacement of the mapped image. This same result can be seen in Figure 4b. As a radial line rotates about the origin, its entire horizontal line mapping moves only vertically.

Another characteristic of CLM is size invariance. This also can be seen in Figure 4. As a point moves out from the origin along a radial line in Figure 4b, its mapping stays on the same horizontal line moving only from left to right. The mappings of the concentric circles of Figure 4a remain vertical lines and only move horizontally as the circles change in size.

A third important invariance is that of projection. When an observer translates in space, the images of objects appear to remain unchanged. Thus, though the images of stationary objects do change on the retina, the object perceived on the striate cortex does not change. This is due to the fact that in the CLM space, translation of the observer only causes the object image to be displaced in the horizontal direction; the size and shape of the object image remain unchanged.

These invariances may be useful for object recognition. Reitboeck and Altmann [20] note that size and rotation variations become translations in the complex log space when the object is in the center of the image. They propose applying a translation invariant transform to the mapped images to get templates suitable for matching with templates of known objects for recognition. The Fourier transform is dismissed as a candidate since there is no evidence that it is used anywhere in the visual system. The authors propose a C-transform, which is more consistent with operations that neurons can do. The Laplacian of the Gaussian operator is applied to the images before they are mapped into the complex log space. All the operations the authors do on the images can be performed with special hardware.

Massone, Sandini, and Tagliasco [17] study some of the characteristics of the CLM. They present a sampling algorithm based on the human visual system. A template matching approach is used for object recognition, where the center of gravity of a binary image of the object is used for the origin around which the object is mapped. Templates of the known object are created in this manner, as are maps of unknown objects.

Messner and Szu [15] propose an architecture to perform an algorithm that simulates the CLM. A nonuniform sampling grid similar to the sampling algorithm of Massone et al. is hardwired into a uniform grid. They show that this mechanism duplicates the properties of the CLM.

Reeves, Prokop, Andrews, and Kuhl [21] compare the performance of several shape recognition methods based on moments and Fourier descriptors. Each of these methods requires a large library (hundreds) of views to compare with the transformed image. This, along with the fact that these methods have no analogue in the human visual system, makes them less attractive than a complex log-based approach.

Arsenault, Hsu, and Chalasinska-Macukow [1] present a rotation and space invariant pattern recognition system based on matched filters. The various order circular harmonic components are used to differentiate between similar objects. However, there is no way to tell, a priori, what order component will be needed in a given situation. More work will have to be done before the performance of this method can be compared with the CLM.

Chaikin and Weiman [6, 28] have pointed out several advantages of the CLM in computer vision systems. In particular, they show that the CLM space may allow iconic processing and can be implemented in hardware. They [6] and Schenker, Wong, and Cande [27] suggest other advantages of the CLM for industrial applications. Thus, we see that efforts have been made by several researchers to use features of CLM for object recognition. According to Kent [13], some efforts are in progress to have a hardware device that can transform an image from cartesian space to its CLM representation in real time. One very attractive feature of Complex Logarithmic Mapping is that it is conformal and, hence, unlike most other commonly used transformations in image processing, does not lose spatial connectivity of points. An important property for information recovery from images is that a surface in the real world is mapped into a single region in an image. This surface coherence is used in recovering the structure of surfaces from the corresponding regions in images. The CLM preserves regions and hence also allows recovery of surface structure.

4. EGO-MOTION COMPLEX LOG MAPPING

To achieve the invariances, which are so important, the images must be obtained under certain constraints. The scale and rotation invariances are present only if the object is centered in the image, and the scale and rotation changes are with respect to the origin. In other cases, these invariances are not obtained. The projection invariance is only obtained by a camera translating along its optical axis. In this case the direction of the gaze and the direction of the motion are the same. This is a serious constraint. Indeed, in this case the FOE is $(0, 0)$ and hence the projection invariance really is the same as the scale invariance. If the observer motion is translational and is known, then the FOE is also known. The CLM is then taken so that all radii, r, and angles, θ, are in reference to this calculated FOE. This transformation is called Ego-Motion Complex Logarithmic Mapping (ECLM), since the mapping is performed with regard to the motion of the camera/observer as described by Jain, O'Brien, and Bartlett [12, 18]. Let us consider this transformation for a point in the 3D space.

When the observer moves in the direction of his gaze, the (X, Y, Z) coordinates of objects that are stationary relative to the observer, change only in the Z coordinate. With the perspective projection, the invariance resulting from the ECLM gives only a horizontal displacement between images for corresponding points. This is very similar to the size invariance and can be compared to it and visualized with a little thought.

For a stationary point in the environment, with real world coordinates (X, Y, Z) relative to the observer at a time instant, the perspective projection, (x, y), of this point onto the image plane, is given by

$$x = \frac{X}{Z} \tag{11}$$

$$y = \frac{Y}{Z} \tag{12}$$

assuming that the projection plane is parallel to the XY plane at $Z = 1$. For a translational motion along the direction of the gaze of the observer, the relationship between the distance, r, of the projection of the point from the FOE, and the distance, Z, of the point from the observer is

$$\frac{dr}{dZ} = \frac{d\sqrt{x^2 + y^2}}{dZ} = -\frac{r}{Z}. \tag{13}$$

By the chain rule

$$\frac{du}{dZ} = \frac{du}{dr} \cdot \frac{dr}{dZ} \tag{14}$$

and from (9),

$$\frac{du}{dr} = \frac{1}{r}. \tag{15}$$

Therefore, we have

$$\frac{du}{dZ} = -\frac{1}{Z}. \tag{16}$$

Similarly, to find dv/dz,

$$\frac{d\theta}{dZ} = \frac{d(\tan^{-1} y/x)}{dZ} = 0 \tag{17}$$

and

$$\frac{dv}{dZ} = \frac{dv}{d\theta} \cdot \frac{d\theta}{dZ} = 0. \tag{18}$$

In (16) we see that the depth, Z, of a point can be determined from the horizontal displacement, du, in the ECLM for that point, and from the velocity, dZ, of the observer. Furthermore, the axial movement of the observer will result in only a horizontal change in the mapping of the image points since $dv/dZ = 0$. There will be no vertical movement of the mapped points and thus correspondence of points between the two stereo pictures will become easier. Note that this is similar to the epi-polar constraint used in the lateral stereo. Now, assuming that there is sufficient control of the camera to be able to determine the amount of its movement, both variables necessary to determine image depths are readily available. Thus, it is possible to recover depth, in principle, if the camera motion is along its optical axis.

What is more interesting is that the depth can be recovered using the above technique even if the camera motion is not along its optical axis. To see that the depth can be recovered for an arbitrary translatory motion of the camera, let us assume that the polar transform is taken with respect to the point (a, b) in the image plane. Then

$$r = \sqrt{(x - a)^2 + (y - b)^2}$$
$$u = \log r = \log(\sqrt{(x - a)^2 + (y - b)^2}). \tag{19}$$

Now

$$\frac{du}{dZ} = \frac{d}{dZ} \log r = \frac{1}{r} \frac{dr}{dZ}. \tag{20}$$

Let us substitute for x and y from (11) and (12), and evaluate dr/dZ.

$$\frac{dr}{dZ} = \frac{d\sqrt{\left(\frac{X}{Z} - a\right)^2 + \left(\frac{Y}{Z} - b\right)^2}}{dZ}$$

$$= \frac{1}{2\sqrt{\left(\frac{X}{Z} - a\right)^2 + \left(\frac{Y}{Z} - b\right)^2}} \left[2\left(\frac{X}{Z} - a\right)\frac{Z\frac{dX}{dZ} - X}{Z^2} \right.$$

$$\left. + 2\left(\frac{Y}{Z} - b\right)\frac{Z\frac{dY}{dZ} - Y}{Z^2} \right] \tag{21}$$

$$= \frac{1}{\sqrt{\left(\frac{X}{Z} - a\right)^2 + \left(\frac{Y}{Z} - b\right)^2}} \cdot \frac{1}{Z} \cdot \left[\left(\frac{X}{Z} - a\right)\left(\frac{dX}{dZ} - \frac{X}{Z}\right) + \left(\frac{Y}{Z} - b\right) \right]$$

$$\times \left(\frac{dY}{dZ} - \frac{Y}{Z} \right) \bigg].$$

Hence

$$\frac{du}{dZ} = \frac{1}{\left(\frac{X}{Z} - a \right)^2 + \left(\frac{Y}{Z} - b \right)^2} \cdot \frac{1}{Z}$$

$$\cdot \left[\left(\frac{X}{Z} - a \right) \left(\frac{dX}{dZ} - \frac{X}{Z} \right) + \left(\frac{Y}{Z} - b \right) \left(\frac{dY}{dZ} - \frac{Y}{Z} \right) \right].$$

Now suppose that we let (a, b) be the FOE, i.e.,

$$a = \frac{dX}{dZ} \quad \text{and} \quad b = \frac{dY}{dZ}.$$

Then, substituting for dX/dZ and dY/dZ

$$\frac{du}{dZ} = \frac{1}{\left(\frac{X}{Z} - a \right)^2 + \left(\frac{Y}{Z} - b \right)^2} \cdot \frac{1}{Z} \cdot \left[-\left(\frac{X}{Z} - a \right)^2 - \left(\frac{Y}{Z} - b \right)^2 \right]$$

$$= -\frac{1}{Z}.$$

Now let us examine dv/dZ, when v is calculated with respect to any FOE (a, b).

$$v = \theta = \tan^{-1} \frac{(y - b)}{(x - a)}$$

$$\frac{dv}{dZ} = 1 + \frac{1/(y - b)^2}{(x - a)^2} \frac{d}{dZ} \frac{(y - b)}{(x - a)}.$$

Considering only the second factor of this equation, and substituting for x and y

$$\frac{d}{dZ} \frac{(y - b)}{(x - a)} = \frac{d}{dZ} \frac{\left(\frac{Y}{Z} - b \right)}{\left(\frac{X}{Z} - a \right)}$$

$$= \frac{\left(\frac{X}{Z} - a \right) \left(Z \frac{dY}{dZ} - Y \right) \bigg/ Z^2 - \left(\frac{Y}{Z} - b \right) \left(Z \frac{dX}{dZ} - X \right) \bigg/ Z^2}{\left(\frac{X}{Z} - a \right)^2}$$

$$= \frac{\left(\dfrac{X}{Z} - a\right)\left(\dfrac{dY}{dZ} - \dfrac{Y}{Z}\right) - \left(b - \dfrac{Y}{Z}\right)\left(\dfrac{X}{Z} - \dfrac{dX}{dZ}\right)}{Z\left(\dfrac{X}{Z} - a\right)^2}.$$

Remembering that $dX/dZ = a$ and $dY/dZ = b$

$$\frac{d}{dZ} \frac{(y - b)}{(x - a)} = \frac{\left(\dfrac{X}{Z} - a\right)\left(b - \dfrac{Y}{Z}\right) - \left(\dfrac{X}{Z} - a\right)\left(b - \dfrac{Y}{Z}\right)}{Z\left(\dfrac{X}{Z} - a\right)^2}$$

$$= 0.$$

Therefore,

$$\frac{dv}{dZ} = 0.$$

Note that when the complex log coordinates are obtained with respect to the FOE, the displacement in the u direction depends only on the Z coordinate of the point. For other values of (a, b) the above property will not be true.

Another interesting feature of this stereo approach is that, if required, we can obtain many frames for solving ambiguities that cannot be resolved based only on two frames. Moravec [16] developed a technique for interpolating over nine frames which he used with common stereo. This technique may be even more applicable to motion stereo, because the series of frames can be naturally extended each time the observer moves. The frame sequence can be constantly updated by merely pushing back the current series by one time instant and adding a new frame to the front of the sequence.

5. THE MAPPING

Mathematically, each point in the image space corresponds to exactly one point in the space transformed through the CLM. However, in computer vision systems where only a finite amount of memory space and computation time is available, an image can only be stored as a finite number of pixels and only a finite number of intensities are representable. This quantization of the image leads to ambiguity in the mapping, since an image pixel can map to a range of pixels in the transformed space. For example, for a pixel in the first quadrant with coordinates (x, y) at the lower-left corner, the u coordinate in the transformed space will range from $\log\sqrt{x^2 + y^2}$ to

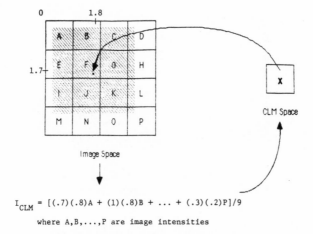

$$I_{CLM} = [(.7)(.8)A + (1)(.8)B + \ldots + (.3)(.2)P]/9$$

where A,B,...,P are image intensities

Figure 5. The interpolation scheme used for the ECLM mapping uses the area of pixels that contribute to the intensity at the point in the ECLM space.

$\log\sqrt{(x+1)^2 + (y+1)^2}$ and the v-coordinate will range from $\tan^{-1} y/(x+1)$ to $\tan^{-1}(y+1)/x$. These ranges can be quite wide for points close to the origin, or practically negligible for points far from the origin. For this reason, pixels closer to the FOE will contribute to a much larger area of the mapping than pixels farther away.

We considered several different interpolations of the image pixels to produce the CLM. One very simple method that we examined involved merely computing the range of each image pixel in the mapped space and setting each map pixel in this range to the corresponding image intensity. This procedure resulted in a very broken, choppy mapping. We also tried working inversely from the mapped space. The image point corresponding to each pixel in the CLM space was determined, and then various interpolations of the intensities of the image pixels around this point were tested This method of inverse mapping resulted in a much smoother CLM.

Figure 6. An image and its ECLM are shown in this figure.

Figure 7.   The increase in the size of the blindspot results in an increase
in the details of the peripheral areas.

The combination of image pixels we found that resulted in the most
continuous and pleasing mapping was surprisingly simple. It involved
merely adding the intensities of the portions of the image covered by a
three-pixel square centered at the point found from the inverse mapping.
An indication of how this worked is shown in Figure 5. The results of such
a mapping are shown in Figure 6. This method may be refined by assigning

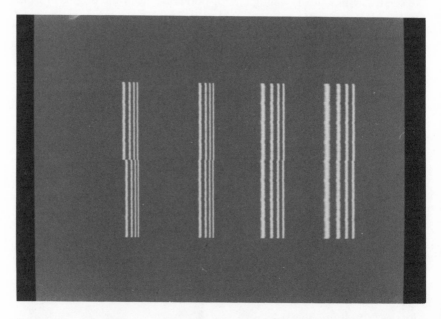

Figure 8.   Comparison of the mapping of concentric circles by O'Brien
and Jain [18] (top) and the adaptation of Massone [17] (bottom). Parameters
are 0.5, 1.0, 5.0, and 10.0 (from left to right).

weights to the various areas of the square. In the future, if the CLM indeed becomes useful, it can easily be implemented in hardware.

6. AVAILABLE RESOLUTION AND THE BLINDSPOT

6.1 Available Resolution

The degree of resolution available for the determination of depth in motion stereo depends directly on the amount of resolution used for the images and the mappings. The resolution determines how large the pieces of information are that must be squeezed into each pixel. As the resolution increases, the information can be kept more exactly. With infinite resolution we could determine depths exactly. Unfortunately infinite resolution requires infinite memory and computation, which we cannot provide.

We must distribute the entire image onto a mapping. The factor that we use to distribute the u coordinate over the mapping will determine what depths can be recovered, since it will tell what increments of du are possible. The u scale factor was found in the following way: The resolution for both

Figure 9. Mapping of concentric circles (upper left) using O'Brien and Jain [18] with no blindspot (upper right), the adaptation of Massone [17] with minimum eccentricity of 0.5 (lower right), and $\log(z + a)$ with $a = 0.5$ (lower left).

the images and the mappings was the same and shall be called ρ. We produced images so that the FOE was at the center of the image, therefore the x and y coordinates in an image could range from $-\rho/2$ to $+\rho/2$. The maximum possible value for u, then, is

$$u_{max} = \log\sqrt{\left(\frac{\rho}{2}\right)^2 + \left(\frac{\rho}{2}\right)^2} = \log\left(\frac{\rho}{2}\sqrt{2}\right).$$

Thus, the u-axis of the CLM will range from 0 to u_{max} over ρ pixels, and every u in the CLM determined from the image pixel locations is multiplied by ρ/u_{max} so that they are distributed over the entire CLM. We do not consider that u may have negative values since all mapping is done in reverse from the map to the image and there are only four pixels directly adjacent to the FOE that can have distance less than one and result in a negative u. These pixels will be interpolated into the map by their neighbors.

The smallest du that can be detected, for the camera displacement of one pixel, is u_{max}/ρ and, therefore, the greatest distance that is recoverable is ρ/u_{max}. No u displacement between mappings for corresponding points in the CLM indicates that the depth of that point is too much greater than

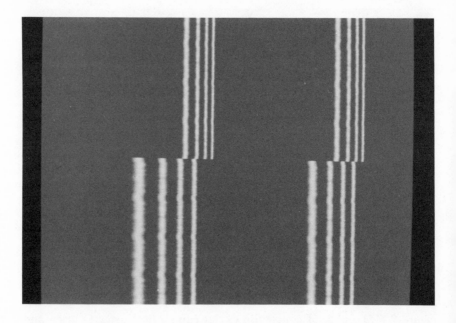

Figure 10. Mapping of concentric circles using O'Brien and Jain [18] with blind spot of 0.0, 1.0, 5.0, and 10.0 (starting in upper-left corner and going clockwise).

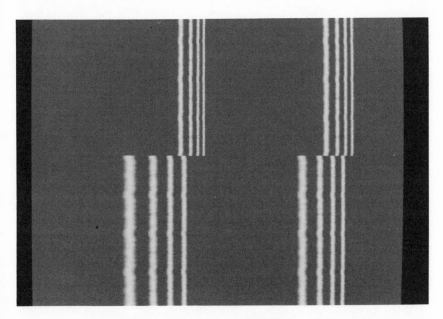

Figure 11.   Mapping of concentric circles using the adaptation of Massone
[17] with minimum eccentricity of 0.5, 1.0, 5.0, and 10.0 (starting in upper-left
corner and going clockwise).

this to be determined. Other du's can be found in integer multiples of
u_{max}/ρ, i.e.,

$$du = n \times \frac{u_{max}}{\rho} \quad \text{for } n = 1, 2, 3, \ldots$$

and the depths which can be determined will be

$$Z = \frac{1}{n} \times \frac{\rho}{u_{max}} \quad \text{for } n = 1, 2, 3, \ldots.$$

See Table 1 for depths recoverable with different resolutions.

It is interesting to note that as n increases, the depth Z decreases and
there is increasing accuracy available. In other words, the depth of points
that are closer to the observer can be more precisely determined than points
that are further away. This is similar to what we observe in our own vision,
that we can perceive depth best for objects that are close to us.

The numbers in Table 1 tell us some of the limitations of axial motion
stereo. At a very low resolution of 128×128, the greatest distance that can
be recovered is about 28 units (where 1 unit is the distance dZ traveled
between images). All points that are much further away than this will have

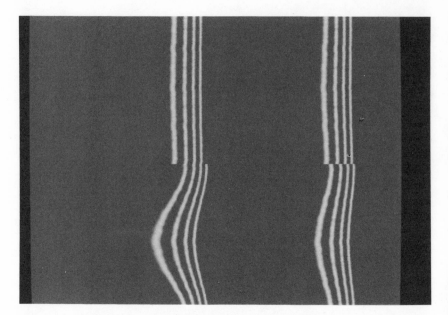

Figure 12. Mapping of concentric circles using $\log(z + a)$ with a having values of 0.5, 1.0, 5.0, and 10.0 (starting in upper-left corner and going clockwise).

no u displacement. Also, for small u displacements of very few pixels in the map, there are large intervals between the depths that can be recovered. Specifically, the second-furthest depth that can be determined is exactly half of the furthest depth! This is quite a large distance, especially relatively.

6.2 The Blindspot

That closer points can be more precisely gauged makes good practical sense. For objects that are close to us, usually a decision must be made

Table 1. Recoverable Depths at Various Resolutions

ρ	1	2	3	4	5	6
64	16.8	8.4	5.6	4.2	3.4	2.8
128	28.4	14.2	9.5	7.1	5.7	4.7
256	49.2	24.6	16.4	12.3	9.8	8.2
512	86.9	43.5	29.0	21.7	17.4	14.5
1024	155.5	77.8	51.8	38.9	31.1	25.9

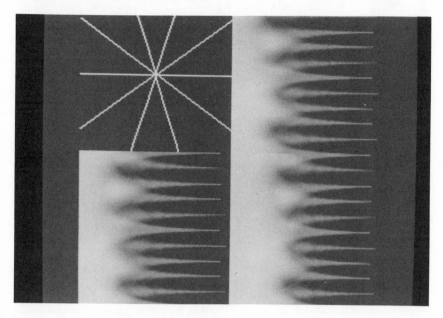

Figure 13. Mapping of radial lines (upper left) using O'Brien and Jain [18] with no blindspot (upper right), the adaptation of Massone [17] with minimum eccentricity of 0.5 (lower right), and $\log(z + a)$ with $a = 0.5$ (lower left).

about how to treat or avoid that object before a similar decision is made for more distant objects. It would be advantageous, however, to have more precision available.

As was shown above, the available resolution depends on u_{max}. In fact, the resolution depends on the range of u values for the mapping. In the above discussion, the lower bound, u_{min}, was assumed to be 0. The resolution at the periphery can be improved by sacrificing some vision along the line of sight. We can introduce a blind spot at the FOE in the image, and thus increase u_{min}. Depending on the size of the blindspot, the range $[u_{min}, u_{max}]$ will change and hence the resolution will also change. The resolution at the periphery will improve with increasing size of the blindspot. This can be seen from Figure 7.

7. EXPERIMENTS

7.1 Mapping Using Different Methods

Working inversely from the mapped space is very time consuming. The sampling algorithm of Massone, Sandini, and Tagliasco [17] requires fewer

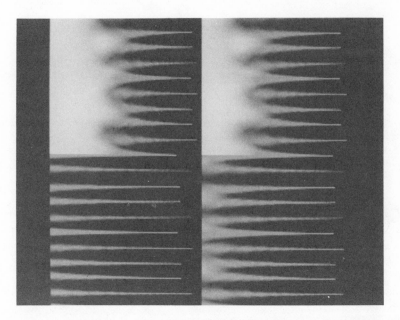

Figure 14. Mapping of radial lines using O'Brien and Jain [18] with blindspot of 0.0, 1.0, 5.0, and 10.0 (starting in upper-left corner and going clockwise).

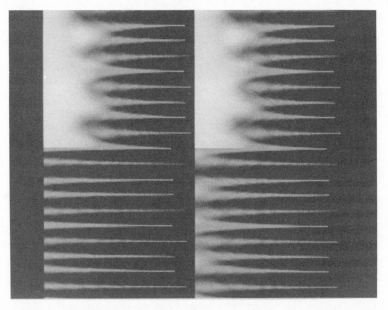

Figure 15. Mapping of radial lines using the adaptation of Massone with minimum eccentricity of 0.5, 1.0, 5.0, and 10.0 (starting in upper corner and going clockwise).

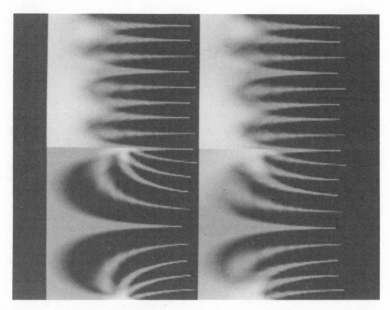

Figure 16. Mapping of radial lines using $\log(z + a)$ with a having values of 0.5, 1.0, 5.0, and 10.0 (starting in upper-left corner and going clockwise).

computations and could be built into a camera. They use a triangular tessellation and a sampling grid formed by concentric circles with logarithmic spacing. The number of pixels sampled over each circle is constant and determines the resolution of the v axis. The number of concentric circles determines the resolution of the u axis. These parameters are chosen on the basis of the physical limitations of the technology and the spatial frequency content of the object. A version of the method using a rectangular tessellation of the z-plane was implemented. The number of concentric circles and the number of samples per circle were determined to produce a mapping that could be compared to the one described by O'Brien and Jain [18] rather than a mapping based on the spatial frequency content of the objects to be mapped, since the purpose is to compare the mapping methods rather than optimize the performance of an object recognition or depth perception algorithm that uses the map. The minimum sampled eccentricity, which determines the radius of the smallest circle, is a parameter that can be arbitrarily specified. The intensities of the pixels in the mapped image were determined as shown in Figure 5.

The results of this mapping algorithm are very similar to those obtained using the method described by O'Brien and Jain [18]. Only by rapidly alternating images produced by the two systems can the differences be noted (see Figure 8). The minimum sampled eccentricity corresponds, in a very rough sense, to the blind spot. Both cut a circle out of the center of the image and portion out the total resolution available in the mapped image to the remainder of the original image. The result is less information from the center of the image with increased resolution of peripheral details. With the blind spot, the extra resolution is redistributed linearly, whereas the other does it nonlinearly.

The retinotopic mappings in primates are more closely approximated by using $\log(z + a)$, where a is a real number that is characteristic of the species as shown by Schwartz [25]. The results of adding an arbitrary constant are very interesting, as can be seen in Figures 12, 16, and 20. Why this should give the animal an evolutionary advantage is an interesting question.

These three mapping methods were applied to three images to study the differences that resulted. The first image used was a set of concentric circles. In Figure 9 the synthetic image and three maps using very small parameters are shown. The differences between the maps are very subtle, but can be observed if the images are rapidly alternated on a screen. The results of using larger parameters are shown in Figures 10–12. Note that the images

Figure 17. Mapping of USC GIRL (upper left) using O'Brien and Jain [18] with no blindspot (upper right), the adaptation of Massone [17] with minimum eccentricity of 0.5 (lower right), and $\log(z + a)$ with $a = 0.5$ (lower left).

Figure 18. Mapping of USC GIRL using O'Brien and Jain [18] with blindspot of 0.0, 1.0, 5.0, and 10.0 (starting in upper-left corner and going clockwise).

in Figures 10 and 11 are very similar. Again, the results for each parameter value appear slightly different if the images are alternated on a screen. The warping produced by adding a real number to z before mapping is most evident at higher values of a. (See Figure 12.)

A synthetic image of radial lines was also mapped using the three methods. Figure 13 shows the synthetic image and the three maps, again using small parameters. The results are very similar. Note the increase in blurring as the radius decreases. This is because the pixels closest to the center are mapped more than once. The results of using larger parameters are shown in Figures 14–16. Note that the resolution of the periphery of the synthetic image improves as the blind spot and the minimum eccentricity are increased. (See Figures 14 and 15.) The "cutting out" of the center removes the blurred portion of the mapping. However, the lines become very warped using $\log(z + a)$ for large a and the center of the mapped image becomes more blurred, as shown in Figure 16.

The USC GIRL was also mapped, just to show the results on a real image. Figure 17 shows the mappings made using small parameters. Careful inspection will show that the algorithm described in Massone [17] allocates slightly more of the mapped image to the center of the original image than O'Brien and Jain [18]. (The area of blurring is larger and the observable

Figure 19. Mapping of USC GIRL using the adaptation of Massone [17] with minimum eccentricity of 0.5, 1.0, 5.0, and 10.0 (starting in upper-left corner and going clockwise).

details like the flower are slightly more compressed.) Images mapped using larger parameters are shown in Figures 18–20. With large parameters it is impossible to differentiate the results shown in Figures 18 and 19. If they are alternated rapidly on a screen, the subtle differences become apparent. Using $\log(z + a)$ results in much more loss of detail. (See Figure 20.)

There is a fundamental difference between the mapping performed by living systems and that done by computer systems using TV camera images. Computers try to simulate the biological spatial sampling system by performing mathematical operations on a uniform sampling of the intensity information in the Cartesian plane. In the fovea of the eye, the cones are dense so the center of the image is frequently sampled. In digitized images that computers use, the center of the image is sampled the least! The center of the image, which is the origin of the mapping, is a singularity of the log function, so its information is conceptually lost. To calculate the values for the column $u = 0$ in the mapped image, only 8 pixels have their neighborhoods sampled. If the resolution of both the computer system and the biological system is 128×128, then the computer has 8 pieces of information for $u = 0$, whereas the biological system has 128. The results of this can be seen in the mapped images produced by the computer. (See Figures 13 and

Figure 20. Mapping of USC GIRL using $\log(z + a)$ with a having values of 0.5, 1.0, 5.0, and 10.0 (starting in upper-left corner and going clockwise).

17.) When the distance from the origin is small, that is when u is small, the mapped image is very blurry. The detail of the periphery of the image is more easily discerned. This is the opposite of what is known about human image processing. For this reason special cameras are needed to obtain biologically equivalent results.

7.2 Depths Using Real Images

To study the efficacy of the proposed approach for determining depths of objects in real scenes, we performed several experiments in our laboratory. We mounted a camera on a PUMA robot. This set up allowed us to move the camera in a desired direction by a desired amount. The objects used were wooden blocks with dimensions less than 6 inches. Three frames of the sequence obtained are shown in Figure 21.

Corners were found and the coordinates in complex log space of these points were calculated. The corner detector used simple masks to find corners, so the corner images produced were noisy. No effort was made to remedy this since it served to make the problem more challenging. The corners obtained using our algorithms are shown in Figure 22. Note that the corner locations are noisy and many false corners are detected.

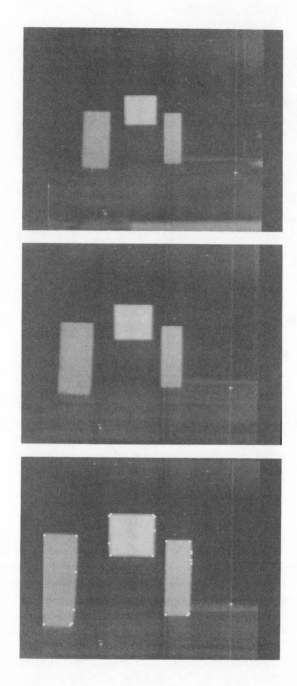

Figure 21. Three frames of the laboratory sequence used in our experiments.

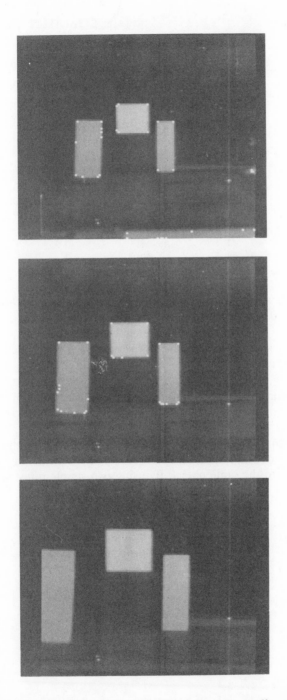

Figure 22. Corners detected in the frames. Note the poor quality of the corners.

Table 2.   Depths of Objects

Threshold	Frame-pair	obj 1 (65)	obj 2 (83)	obj 3 (75)
.01	1–3	50	74	57
.01	2–4	58	79	77
.01	1–4	53	72	56
.01	1–5	52	71	51
.02	1–3	50	67	54
.02	2–4	59	78	71
.02	1–4	49	72	56
.02	1–5	50	71	51
.05	1–3	50	67	61
.05	2–4	57	78	70
.05	1–4	49	72	56
.05	1–5	50	71	52

The corners were mapped to the ECLM space using the method described by O'Brien and Jain [18]. Figure 23 shows the corners of Figure 22 mapped in the ECLM space. The correspondence between corners was established in the ECLM space. Theoretically, two matching points should have the same θ value (v coordinate). Due to digitization error, blurring in the images from shrinking, and errors in corner detection, matching points do not have the same θ value. So a threshold for dv (the difference between the θ values) is used. A point from one image matches every point in the second image whose v value differs by less than the threshold.

The algorithm was run on every pair of images using three different thresholds for dv: 0.01, 0.02, and 0.05. A match is considered correct if the points belong to the same object. By using two simple rules, all errors are

Table 3.   Depths of Objects Using $a = 0.5$

Threshold	Frame-pair	obj 1 (65)	obj 2 (83)	obj 3 (75)
.01	1–3	51	76	55
.01	2–4	59	80	64
.01	1–4	53	73	55
.01	1–5	53	72	51
.02	1–3	50	68	53
.02	2–4	59	79	76
.02	1–4	53	73	55
.02	1–5	50	72	51
.05	1–3	50	68	62
.05	2–4	57	79	71
.05	1–4	49	73	56
.05	1–5	60	72	51

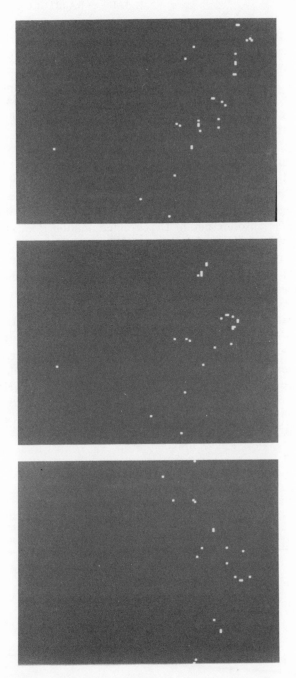

Figure 23. The corners of Figure 22 in the ECLM space.

detected by the system. The rules are: a camera cannot see behind itself and if you pass an object, it will not be in the second image. This eliminates all matches with a distance less than the amount the camera moved. By including an upper bound on the depth, the system always matched points of an object in one frame with points in the same object in the second frame. Figure 24 shows some examples of matches and the results of applying the rules to the matches.

The depth of an object was obtained by averaging the depth obtained for its corners. The calculated depths tended to be lower than the real depths. We did not use the focal length of the camera in our depth computation, since for the camera we used, the focal length is not known. Without the focal length, the depth values should indicate the relative depth values, rather than the absolute depth. Depth determination from images where the camera was closer to the objects was more accurate. Larger camera movement gave better results when the camera was far from the objects, but not from closer positions. Some results are shown in Table 2. We ran the experiments for several other frame pairs. In some cases the results indicated wrong depth order for the objects.

Noting that primates use a mapping more closely approximated by $\log(z + a)$, the depths were determined using values of 0.5, 1.0, 2.0, and 3.0 for a. For this set of images, performance was poorer for relative depth determination. Small values of a improved absolute depth determination when the depths were largest, but this improvement was outweighed by the poor values obtained in all other cases. Many more matching errors were made as well, though these were corrected by the system in all but a few cases. Tables 3 and 4 show depths determined using large and small values of a.

Table 4.   Depths of Objects Using $a = 3.0$

Threshold	Frame-pair	obj 1 (65)	obj 2 (83)	obj 3 (75)
.01	1–3	52	86	—
.01	2–4	58	75	54
.01	1–4	24	77	49
.01	1–5	29	77	—
.02	1–3	50	86	46
.02	2–4	56	78	59
.02	1–4	43	77	49
.02	1–5	43	77	45
.05	1–3	47	73	65
.05	2–4	55	86	79
.05	1–4	46	78	52
.05	1–5	56	77	47

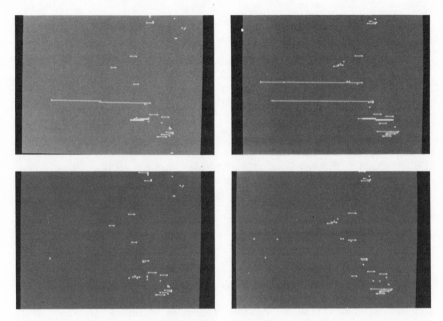

Figure 24. Match found by the algorithm. Images on the left are for frames 1 and 3. Images on the right are for frames 2 and 4. The top images show all the matches found. The bottom images show the corrected matches.

8. CONCLUSION

ECLM is a very promising computer vision tool. Its rotation and scale invariances have important implications for object recognition and graphics applications. The reliability and speed of its point correspondence determinations make it a candidate for relative depth calculations in autonomous vehicle navigation and dynamic scene analysis. By varying the relevant parameter, such as the blind spot or the minimum eccentricity, different portions of the image can be emphasized for more detailed study. Simulations of the human visual system can be built and studied using ECLM, giving further insight into how we see. These preliminary experiments have brought to light more questions than they have answered and have pointed out many exciting directions for further study.

ACKNOWLEDGMENT

This work was partially supported by National Science Foundation Grant no. MCS8219739 and AFOSR contract no. F49620-82-C-0089.

REFERENCES

[1] Arsenault, H. H., Y. N. Hsu, and K. Chalasinska-Macukow. "Rotation-Invariant Pattern Recognition," *Optical Engineering*, vol. 23, pp. 705-709, November/December 1984.

[2] Braccini, C., Gamberdella, G., and V. Tagliasco. "A model of the early stages of human visual system," *Biological Cybernetics*, vol. 44, 1982, pp. 47-88.

[3] Bruss, A. R., and B. K. P. Horn. "Passive Navigation," *Computer Vision, Graphics, and Image Processing*, vol. 21, 1983.

[4] Cavanaugh, P. "Size and position invariance in the visual system," *Perception*, vol. 7, pp. 167-177, 1978.

[5] Cavanaugh, P. "Size invariance: reply to Schwartz," *Perception*, vol. 10, pp. 469-474, 1981.

[6] Chaikin, G., and C. Weiman. "Log spiral grids in computer pattern recognition," *Computer Graphics and Pattern Recognition*, vol. 4, pp. 197-226, 1979.

[7] Clocksin, W. F. "Perception of surface slant and edge labels from optical flow: A computational approach," *Perception*, vol. 9, 1980, pp. 253-269.

[8] Gibson, J. J. *The Ecological Approach to Visual Perception*, Boston, Houghton Mifflen, 1979.

[9] Jain, R. "Complex Logarithmic Mapping and the Focus of Expansion," SIG-GRAPH/SIGART Workshop on MOTION: Representation and Perception, Toronto, April 1983.

[10] Jain, R. "Segmentation of frame sequences obtained by a moving observer," *IEEE Trans. PAMI*, pp. 624-629, September 1984.

[11] Jain, R., and N. O'Brien. "Ego-Motion Complex Logarithmic Mapping," *SPIE*, November 1984.

[12] Jain, R., S. L. Bartlett, and N. O'Brien. "Motion Stereo Using Ego-Motion Complex Logarithmic Mapping," *RSD-TR-3-86*, Center for Robotics and Integrated Manufacturing, Robot Systems Division, University of Michigan, Ann Arbor, February 1986.

[13] Kent, E., Personal Communication.

[14] Lee, D. N. "The optic flow field: The foundation of vision," *Phil. Trans. R. Soc. of London*, vol. B290, 1980, pp. 169-179.

[15] Messner, R. A., and H. H. Szu. "An Image Processing Architecture for Real Time Generation of Scale and Rotation Invariant Patterns," *Computer Vision, Graphics, and Image Processing*, vol. 31, pp. 50-66, 1985.

[16] Moravec, H. P. *Robot Rover Visual Navigation*, Ann. Arbor, MI, UMI Research Press, 1981.

[17] Massone, L., G. Sandini, and V. Tagliasco. " 'Form-Invariant' Topological Mapping Strategy for 2D Shape Recognition," *Computer Vision, Graphics, and Image Processing*, vol. 30, pp. 169-188, 1985.

[18] O'Brien, N., and R. Jain. "Axial Motion Stereo," *Proc. of Workshop on Computer Vision*, pp. 88-92, Anapolis, MD, April, 1984.

[19] Prazdny, K. "Egomotion and relative depth map from optical flow," *Biological Cybernetics*, vol. 36, 1980, pp. 87-102.

[20] Reitboeck, H. J., and J. Altmann. "A Model for Size- and Rotation-Invariant Pattern Processing in the Visual System," *Biological Cybernetics*, vol. 51, pp. 113-121, 1984.

[21] Reeves, A. P., R. J. Prokop, S. E. Andrews, and F. P. Kuhl. "Three Dimensional Shape Analysis Using Moments and Fourier Descriptors," *Seventh International Conference on Pattern Recognition*, vol. 1, pp. 447-450, Montreal, July 1984.

[22] Sandini, G., and V. Tagliasco. "An anthromomorphic retin-like structure for scene analysis," *Computer Graphics and Image Processing*, vol. 14, pp. 365-372, 1980.

[23] Schwartz, E. L. "The development of specific visual connections in the monkey and goldfish: Outline of a geometric theory of receptotopic structure," *J. Theoretical Biology*, vol. 69, pp. 655-683.

[24] Schwartz, E. L. "Computational anatomy and functional architecture of striate cortex: a spatial mapping approach to coding," *Vision Research*, 20, pp. 645-669, 1980.

[25] Schwartz, E. L. "Cortical anatomy, size invariance, and spatial frequency analysis," *Perception*, vol. 10, pp. 455-468, 1981.

[26] Schwartz, E. L. "Columnar architecture and computational anatomy in primate visual cortex; Segmentation and feature extraction via spatial frequency coded difference mapping," *Biological Cybernetics*, vol. 42, pp. 157-168, 1982.

[27] Schenker, P. S., K. M. Wong, and E. G. Cande. "Fast adaptive algorithms for low-level scene analysis: Application of polar exponential grid (PEG) representation to high-speed, scale-and-rotation invariant target segmentation," *Proc. SPIE*, vol. 281, Techniques and Applications of Image Understanding, pp. 47-57, 1981.

[28] Weiman, C. F. R., and G. Chaikin. "Logarithmic Spiral Grids for Image Processing and Display," *Computer Graphics and Image Processing*, vol. 11, pp. 197-226, November 1979.

Chapter 6

MOTION ANALYSIS OF DEFORMABLE OBJECTS

Su-shing Chen and Michael Penna

OUTLINE

Advances in Computer Vision and Image Processing, Vol. 3, pages 179–220.
Copyright © 1988 JAI Press Inc.
All rights of reproduction in any form reserved
ISBN: 0–89232–635–2

ABSTRACT

In computer vision and image-understanding research, rigidity of bodies and their motions has long been a key assumption in obtaining information about the motion of 3-dimensional (3D) bodies from information provided by 2-dimensional (2D) images. Here, the rigidity assumption is relaxed in the study of motion analysis.

Assume that images of an object before and after a generalized motion are given. (A deformation is a generalized motion.) We present three approaches to recovery of the generalized motion. The infinitesimal approach is concerned with determining the linear approximation (the Jacobian matrix) of the generalized motion. This approach is based on the study of the local surface geometry of the object. To illustrate this approach, we show how the linear approximation of a generalized motion can be obtained in closed form for a special class of generalized motions. The global approach is concerned with completely determining the generalized motion. To illustrate this approach, we use projective geometry to recover generalized motion parameters from point pair correspondences. The third approach is a hybrid of the infinitesimal approach and the global approach. This approach provides insight to the ultimate goal of understanding human perception. With this approach, correspondence and motion analysis are treated in a unified fashion. The hybrid approach is based on a new vision model, the spherical perspective model. The orthographic model is a limit of spherical models as the viewer moves to infinity; there is no similar relationship between orthographic projection and planar perspective projection.

1. INTRODUCTION

In computer vision and image-understanding research, rigidity of bodies and their motions has long been a key assumption in obtaining information about the motion of 3-dimensional (3D) bodies from information provided by 2-dimensional (2D) images. This chapter is a survey of recent work in which the rigidity assumption is relaxed in the study of motion analysis. More specifically, this chapter surveys the motion results of [7], [8], [9], [10], [11], [12], [13], [25] and [26].

Here, we consider nonrigid, elastic bodies under orthographic projection, and under planar and spherical perspective projection. In the case of static elasticity, we use Hooke's Law and the Fundamental Theorem of Statics to show that deformations of such bodies are diffeomorphisms of the bodies. In the case of dynamic elasticity, we use Hooke's Law and Newton's Law to show that generalized motions (generalized motions include deformations) are 1-parameter families of diffeomorphisms. For simplicity, we consider a single diffeomorphism of bodies; a 1-parameter family of diffeomorphisms of bodies can be viewed as a sequence of single diffeomorphisms of intermediate bodies.

The primary goal of this chapter is to determine a generalized motion (a diffeomorphism) of a known nonrigid, elastic body given images of the body before and after the generalized motion. We present three approaches—the infinitesimal approach, the global approach, and a hybrid approach. These three approaches are all important for a number of reasons. On one hand, all of them have both theoretical and practical strengths and weaknesses; in a given situation, one may be more useful than another. On the other hand, more than one approach may apply, and redundant approaches can be used to provide more robust information.

The infinitesimal approach is concerned with determining the linear approximation (the Jacobian matrix) of the generalized motion. The image transformation between two images is recovered by point correspondences and least squares. The Jacobian of the image transformation (its linear approximation) is then coupled with the Jacobian of orthographic or planar perspective projection to recover the Jacobian of the generalized motion. In general, a generalized motion cannot be uniquely recovered from an image transformation (see [6]). To obtain an essentially unique solution in closed form, we restrict our attention to a class of isometric generalized motions (diffeomorphisms of R^3 that are isometric on the body surface). This class includes rigid motions and bendings, as well as locally rigid motions and bendings, but not shearing. The results of this approach include the results [20] and [34] (see [20] and [34] for further references).

The global approach deals with completely determining a generalized motion. To illustrate this approach, we show how projective geometry can be used to recover generalized motion parameters from point pair-correspondences in images. For simplicity, we restrict attention to affine motions—motions whose constant component represents an arbitrary translation, whose linear component represents an arbitrary (nonsingular) linear transformation, and which has no higher-order components; this type of motion includes rigid motions as well as shearings. This approach can be extended to transformations that contain arbitrarily higher-order terms (see [8] and [13]). Just as with the infinitesimal approach, unique solutions in closed form can only be obtained for rigid motions and other special transformations. Our results include those on rigid motions presented in [20] and related work. (Again, see [20] for further references.)

The hybrid approach is a fusion of the above two approaches. This approach provides insight to the understanding of human perception. Using local shading analysis (see [25] and [26]), correspondence and motion analysis are treated in a unified fashion. The hybrid approach is based on a new vision model, the spherical perspective model. The orthographic model is a limit of spherical models as the viewer moves to infinity (the viewing sphere remaining fixed), thus providing a unification of orthographic projection and spherical perspective projection; there is no similar relationship between orthographic projection and planar perspective projection. Motion analysis using spherical perspective is a reasonable model for both computer and human motion analysis.

This chapter is organized as follows: In section 2, we discuss some basic concepts related to differential calculus in R^n and parametrized surfaces, and some of the concepts in 3D elasticity that motivate the motion analysis of deformed objects. In section 3, we discuss motion analysis using the infinitesimal approach, focusing in particular on information that can be obtained from orthographic and planar perspective images. In section 4, we discuss the global approach, again focusing in particular on information that can be obtained from orthographic and planar perspective images. In section 5, we discuss the hybrid approach. We present the spherical model, discuss the limitations of planar perspective projection, and discuss how this vision model overcomes obstacles encountered in motion analysis with the infinitesimal and global approaches. Finally, in section 6, we summarize our results.

2. DIFFERENTIAL CALCULUS AND ELASTICITY

Here we discuss some basic concepts, including some of the concepts that motivate the motion analysis of deformable objects.

2.1   Differential Calculus in R^n

As usual, R^n is the set of all real ordered n-tuples $\mathbf{x} = (x_1, \ldots, x_n)$. Our primary concern is with $n = 2$ or $n = 3$. The scalar product $\langle \mathbf{x}, \mathbf{y} \rangle$ of two elements $\mathbf{x}$ and $\mathbf{y}$ in R^n is given by $\langle \mathbf{x}, \mathbf{y} \rangle = \Sigma_i x_i y_i$, the norm $|\mathbf{x}|$ of $\mathbf{x}$ is given by $|\mathbf{x}| = \langle \mathbf{x}, \mathbf{x} \rangle^{1/2}$, and the Euclidean distance $d(\mathbf{x}, \mathbf{y})$ between two points $\mathbf{x}$ and $\mathbf{y}$ is given by $d(\mathbf{x}, \mathbf{y}) = |\mathbf{x} - \mathbf{y}|$.

The tangent space $T_{x_0}R^n$ of R^n at $x_0 \in R^n$ is the n-dimensional vector space whose elements consist of all ordered pairs $(x_0, v) \in \{x_0\} \times R^n$. A vector space structure is defined on $T_{x_0}R^n$ by identifying it with R^n as follows (see Figure 1):

$$T_{x_0}R^n \leftrightarrow R^n$$

$$(x_0, v) \leftrightarrow v.$$

The transformations $F: R^n \to R^n$ of R^n that preserve the Euclidean structure of R^n, that is, the length and angle preserving transformations of R^n, are isometries. For example, translation $t_{x_0}(x) = x + x_0$, x_0 fixed, is an isometry. Any isometry F of R^n may be written $F = r \circ t_{x_0}$, where r is an orthogonal transformation of R^n and t_{x_0} is a translation of R^n; r is the orthogonal component of F, and t_{x_0} is the translational component of F. An orthogonal transformation is a linear transformation $F(x) = A*x$ for which

$$\langle F(x), F(y) \rangle = \langle x, y \rangle$$

for all $x, y \in R^n$. The basic types of orthogonal transformations are rotations (orientation preserving orthogonal transformations), and reflections (such as $\rho(x) = -x$). An orthogonal transformation is represented by an orthogonal matrix A, a matrix whose row and column vectors are mutually perpendicular unit vectors, or, equivalently, a matrix for which $A^T = A^{-1}$. If r is a rotation, then F is a congruence or rigid motion; if r is a combination of rotation and reflection, then F is a symmetry.

A continuous map

$$F(x_1, \ldots, x_n) = (F_1(x_1, \ldots, x_n), \ldots, F_m(x_1, \ldots, x_n)): U \to R^m$$

defined on an open subset $U \subseteq R^n$ is differentiable if all partial derivatives $\partial F_i/\partial x_j$, for $i = 1, \ldots, m$ and $j = 1, \ldots, n$ are continuous. The Jacobian matrix dF of a differentiable map $F: R^n \to R^m$ at x_0 is the $m \times n$ matrix $((\partial F_i/\partial x_j)(x_0))$. The Jacobian matrix dF defines a map (see Figure 2) called the Jacobian

$$dF: T_{x_0}R^n \to T_{F(x_0)}R^m$$

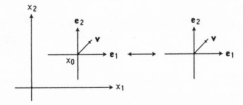

Figure 1.

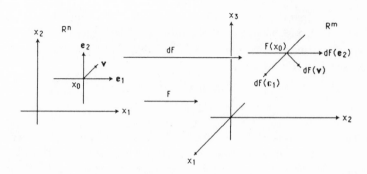

Figure 2.

by

$$dF(\mathbf{v}) = ((\partial F_i/\partial x_j)(\mathbf{x}_0))\mathbf{v}.$$

One of the basic results related to differentiable mappings is the Chain Rule.

THEOREM (Chain Rule). If $F: R^m \to R^n$ and $G: R^n \to R^p$, then $d(G \circ F) = dG * dF$.

A one-to-one, differentiable map $F: U \to U'$ from the open subset $U \subseteq R^n$ to the open subset $U' \subseteq R^n$ is a diffeomorphism if $F^{-1}: U' \to U$ is also differentiable. A diffeomorphism $F: U \to U'$ may be written

$$x_1' = F_1(x_1, x_2, x_3), \qquad x_2' = F_2(x_1, x_2, x_3), \qquad x_3' = F_3(x_1, x_2, x_3),$$

where F_1, F_2, and F_3 are differentiable.

2.2   Parametrized Surfaces

Planes and graphs of functions (see Figure 3) are simple surfaces. Roughly speaking, a simple surface is a surface that can faithfully be described by

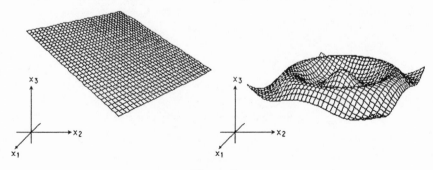

Figure 3.

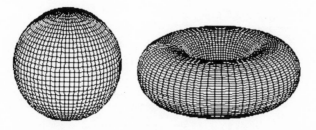

Figure 4.

a one page (geographical) map. Spheres and tori (see Figure 4) are surfaces that are not simple—a sphere, for example, cannot be faithfully described by a one page (geographical) map; at least two pages are necessary to describe it (see Figure 5). Surfaces that are not simple are described in the same way the surface of the earth is described: by an atlas. A world atlas is a book consisting of pages. Each page is a simple surface description of part of the earth's surface. These pages cover the earth's surface. These pages may or may not overlap; if they do overlap, they do so in a consistent fashion.

To be specific, a parametrized surface is a differentiable mapping $\mathbf{x} : U \to R^3$ from an open subset U of R^2 to R^3, such that the Jacobian

$$d\mathbf{x} : T_{(u_1, u_2)} R^2 \to T_{\mathbf{x}(u_1, u_2)} R^3$$

is one-to-one for all $(u_1, u_2) \in U$ (see Figure 6). (The condition that the Jacobian $d\mathbf{x}$ is one-to-one at all points of U plays a role in saying what it means for two simple surfaces to overlap in a consistent fashion.) For example, if $U = R^2$ and $\mathbf{v}_1$ and $\mathbf{v}_2$ are two linearly independent vectors in

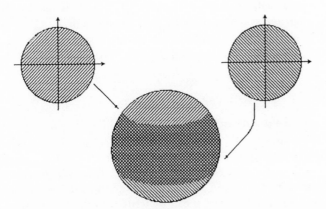

Figure 5.

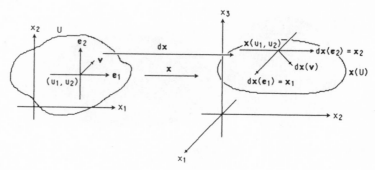

Figure 6.

R^3, then

$$\mathbf{x}(u_1, u_2) = \mathbf{x}_0 + u_1\mathbf{v}_1 + u_2\mathbf{v}_2$$

is a parametrization of the plane in R^3 that passes through the terminal point of the position vector $\mathbf{x}_0$, and whose unit normal vector is $\mathbf{v}_1 \times \mathbf{v}_2 / |\mathbf{v}_1 \times \mathbf{v}_2|$.

Two simple surfaces overlap in a consistent fashion if they are differentiably related. The simple surfaces $\mathbf{x}: U \to R^3$ and $\mathbf{y}: V \to R^3$ are differentiably related if the transformations

$$\mathbf{x}^{-1} \circ \mathbf{y} : \mathbf{y}^{-1}(\mathbf{x}(U) \cap \mathbf{y}(V)) \to \mathbf{x}^{-1}(\mathbf{x}(U) \cap \mathbf{y}(V))$$

and

$$\mathbf{y}^{-1} \circ \mathbf{x} : \mathbf{x}^{-1}(\mathbf{x}(U) \cap \mathbf{y}(V)) \to \mathbf{y}^{-1}(\mathbf{x}(U) \cap \mathbf{y}(V))$$

are differentiable transformations of subsets of R^2 whenever $\mathbf{x}(U) \cap \mathbf{y}(V)$ is nonempty (see Figure 7).

The 2D linear subspace $d\mathbf{x}(T_{(u_1, u_2)}R^2) \subseteq T_{\mathbf{x}(u_1, u_2)}R^3$ is the tangent space to $\mathbf{x}$ at (u_1, u_2), and is denoted by $T_{(u_1, u_2)}\mathbf{x}$. Elements of $T_{(u_1, u_2)}\mathbf{x}$ are tangent vectors to $\mathbf{x}$ at (u_1, u_2). If $\mathbf{x}: U \to R^3$ is a simple surface, $\mathbf{x}_1 = \partial \mathbf{x}/\partial u_1$ and $\mathbf{x}_2 = \partial \mathbf{x}/\partial u_2$, then $d\mathbf{x} = (\mathbf{x}_1, \mathbf{x}_2)$, and $T_{(u_1, u_2)}\mathbf{x}$ is parametrized by the map

$$R^2 \to T_{(u_1, u_2)}\mathbf{x} \subseteq T_{\mathbf{x}(u_1, u_2)}R^3 = R^3$$

$$(v_1, v_2) \to (u_1, u_2) + v_1\mathbf{x}_1 + v_2\mathbf{x}_2.$$

A vector field along a surface $\mathbf{x}: U \to R^3$ is a differentiable map $\mathbf{v}: U \to R^3$ that associates to each $(u_1, u_2) \in U$ a vector $\mathbf{v}(u_1, u_2) \in T_{\mathbf{x}(u_1, u_2)}R^3$. A vector field $\mathbf{v}$ along $\mathbf{x}$ is tangential if $\mathbf{v}(u_1, u_2) \in T_{(u_1, u_2)}\mathbf{x}$ for each $(u_1, u_2) \in U$, and normal if $\mathbf{v}(u_1, u_2)$ is perpendicular to $T_{(u_1, u_2)}\mathbf{x}$ for each $(u_1, u_2) \in U$. The vector fields $\mathbf{x}_1 = \partial \mathbf{x}/\partial u_1$ and $\mathbf{x}_2 = \partial \mathbf{x}/\partial u_2$ are tangential vector fields, and any tangent vector field along $\mathbf{x}$ can be written in the form $\mathbf{v} = a\mathbf{x}_1 + b\mathbf{x}_2$, where a and b are real valued differentiable functions on U. The vector

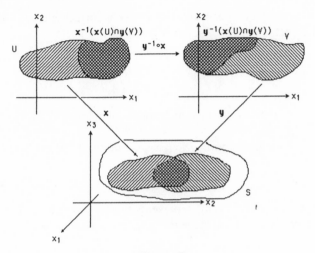

Figure 7.

field $x_1 \times x_2$ along x is a normal vector field along x, and $n = x_1 \times x_2 / |x_1 \times x_2|$ is the Gauss unit normal vector field along x. The map

$$n : U \to S^2 = \{(x_1, x_2, x_3) \in R^3 | x_1^2 + x_2^2 + x_3^2 = 1\} \subseteq R^3$$

that associates to each point $(u_1, u_2) \in U$ the vector $n(u_1, u_2)$, is the Gauss map.

2.3 The Mechanics of 3D Elasticity

If a 3D elastic body is put under external forces or stresses, the body becomes deformed or strained. In this section we investigate the stress, strain, and governing laws of 3D elasticity. For further reference see [1], [30], and [31].

The external forces acting on a 3D body may be divided into two classes: body forces and surface forces. Body forces (forces such as electrostatic, gravitational, magnetic, and inertial forces) are forces that act on each volume element of the body. Surface forces (forces such as pressure, surface tension, shearing, and friction) are forces that act on each surface element of a body. (Such a surface element can lie on the boundary of the body or within the body.)

Surface forces are specified by a stress tensor T_{ij}, $i, j = 1, 2, 3$. Each T_{ij} can be thought of as a pressure (force per unit area). The tensor T_{ij} acts on vectors like the matrix

$$(T_{ij}) = \begin{pmatrix} T_{11} & T_{12} & T_{13} \\ T_{21} & T_{22} & T_{23} \\ T_{31} & T_{32} & T_{33} \end{pmatrix}.$$

For example, the force per unit area across a surface element dA whose unit normal vector $\mathbf{n} = (n_1, n_2, n_3)$ is given by the vector

$$\begin{pmatrix} T_{11} & T_{12} & T_{13} \\ T_{21} & T_{22} & T_{23} \\ T_{31} & T_{32} & T_{33} \end{pmatrix} \begin{pmatrix} n_1 \\ n_2 \\ n_3 \end{pmatrix}.$$

In the absence of body torques on volume elements dV, T_{ij} (and (T_{ij})) is symmetric: $T_{ij} = T_{ji}$.

Under deformation, a point $P(x_1, x_2, x_3)$ of an elastic body is displaced to the point

$$Q[x_1 + v_1(x_1, x_2, x_3), x_2 + v_2(x_1, x_2, x_3), x_3 + v_3(x_1, x_2, x_3)].$$

The vector field $\mathbf{v} = (v_1, v_2, v_3)$ represents the (relative) change in position of P. The first-order 3D Taylor series approximation for v_i about P, is

$$v_i \approx \Sigma_j \frac{\partial v_j}{\partial x_j} dx_j$$

$$= \Sigma_j \left(\frac{1}{2} \left(\frac{\partial v_i}{\partial x_j} + \frac{\partial v_j}{\partial x_i} \right) dx_j - \frac{1}{2} \left(\frac{\partial v_j}{\partial x_i} - \frac{\partial v_i}{\partial x_j} \right) dx_j \right)$$

$$= \Sigma_j(\eta_{ij} \, dx_j - \xi_{ij} \, dx_j).$$

The functions $\partial v_i/\partial x_j$ define a tensor. The antisymmetric part ξ_{ij} of $\partial v_i/\partial x_j$ may be identified as a rotation (or couple) about an axis through P in the direction of $\nabla \times \mathbf{v}$ through $|\nabla \times \mathbf{v}|$ radians. The symmetric part η_{ij} of $\partial h_i/\partial x_j$ is the strain tensor. The diagonal elements η_{11}, η_{22}, and η_{33} of η_{ij} represent stretches, and the off-diagonal elements of η_{ij} represent shear strains.

Stress and strain are related by Hooke's Law, which states that as long as stress and strain are small, the stress is linearly related to the strain

$$T_{ij} = \Sigma_{kl} c_{ijkl} \eta_{kl}$$

for constants c_{ijkl}, where i, j, k, and $l = 1, 2, 3$.

The governing laws of static elasticity are Hooke's Law and the Fundamental Theorem of Statics, which states that the total force acting on a body must be zero if the body is at rest with no acceleration. The total force is the sum of all the surface forces as computed from the stresses plus any body forces that may be present. If the total force acting on a body is known, the displacement $\mathbf{v} = (v_1, v_2, v_3)$ can be found. Under suitable differentiability, this solution yields a diffeomorphism F of Euclidean three-space

$$F(x_1, x_2, x_3) = (x_1 + v_1(x_1, x_2, x_3), x_2 + v_2(x_1, x_2, x_3), x_3 + v_3(x_1, x_2, x_3)).$$

Conversely, if the displacement $\mathbf{v}$ is known, information about the total force acting on the body can be found.

The governing laws of dynamic elasticity are Hooke's Law and Newton's Law of Motion, which states that total force is equal to the mass times the acceleration:

$$\Sigma_j(\partial T_{ij}/\partial x_j)\, dA = \rho\, \partial^2 v_i/\partial t^2\, dA$$

or

$$\Sigma_j(\partial T_{ij}/\partial x_j) = \rho\, \partial^2 v_i/\partial t^2,$$

where $i = 1, 2, 3$, where ρ is density, where dA is a surface element, and where $\partial^2 v_i/\partial t^2$ is acceleration. Using Hooke's Law, we can substitute for the stresses in terms of the strains to find the equations of motion

$$\rho\, \partial^2 v_i/\partial t^2 = \Sigma_j[(a + b)\, \partial^2 v_j/\partial x_i\, \partial x_j + b\, \partial^2 v_i/\partial x_j^2],$$

where $i = 1, 2, 3$. This system of partial differential equations illustrates the complicated nature of 3D elasticity. If the total force acting on a body is known, a 1-parameter family of displacements $v_t = (v_1, v_2, v_3)$ can be found. Under suitable differentiability, this solution yields a 1-parameter family of diffeomorphisms F_t of Euclidean three-space

$$F_t(x_1, x_2, x_3)$$
$$= (x_1 + v_1(t, x_1, x_2, x_3), x_2 + v_2(t, x_1, x_2, x_3), x_3 + v_3(t, x_1, x_2, x_3))$$

(see section 2.4). Conversely, if the 1-parameter family of displacements v_t is known, information about the total force acting on the body can be found.

2.4 Motions of Surfaces

A diffeomorphism from the surface S to the surface S' is a map $F: S \to S'$, which can be extended to a diffeomorphism $F: U \to U'$ of R^3, where U is an open set containing S and U' is an open set containing S'. The surfaces S and S' are isometric if and only if there is a diffeomorphism $F: U \to U'$ of R^3 taking S to S' that preserves the length of curves and the angles between the intersections of curves. The surfaces S and S' are rigidly equivalent if and only if there is a rigid motion $F: U \to U'$ of R^3 taking S to S'.

Under an isometry, a surface S may be bent like a piece of paper (see Figure 8). If there is an isometry $F: U \to U'$ of R^3 taking S to S', then S

Figure 8.

Figure 9.

and S' are isometric; but if S and S' are isometric, there need not be an isometry $F: U \to U'$ of R^3 taking S to S'. Bending a piece of paper (see Figure 9), for example, is an isometry on the piece of paper that does not extend to an isometry $F: U \to U'$ of R^3 (the length of curves is not preserved). If two simple surfaces are rigidly equivalent, they are isometric; but if they are isometric, they need not be rigidly equivalent. For example, a flat piece of paper and a bent piece of paper are isometric but not rigidly equivalent; also the helicoid and the catenoid (see Figure 10) are isometric but not rigidly equivalent.

A 1-parameter family of diffeomorphisms of a surface S is a family of functions $F_t: U \to R^3$, where U is an open set containing S and $t \in R$, that is differentiable in both $\mathbf{x}$ and t, and such that

1. $F_t: U \to F_t(U)$ is a diffeomorphism for each $t \in R$,
2. $F_t \circ F_s = F_{t+s}$, and
3. $F_0 = id$.

For example (see [12]), Figure 11 illustrates a 1-parameter family of diffeomorphisms taking the helicoid (at $t = 0$) to the catenoid (at $t = 1$).

Here, we consider nonrigid, elastic bodies. As indicated in section 2.3, in the case of static elasticity (the body is displaced), Hooke's Law and the Fundamental Theorem of Statics can be used to show that generalized

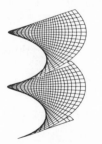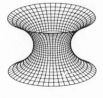

Figure 10.

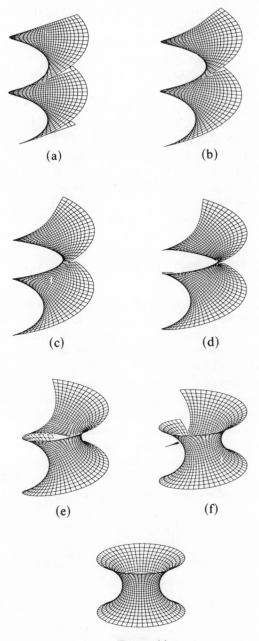

(a)

(b)

(c)

(d)

(e)

(f)

Figure 11.

motions of such bodies are diffeomorphisms, and in the case of dynamic elasticity (the body is displaced and deformed), Hooke's Law and Newton's Law can be used to show that generalized motions of such bodies are 1-parameter families of diffeomorphisms.

The primary goal of this chapter is to determine a generalized motion of a known nonrigid, elastic body given images of the body before and after the generalized motion. We assume that the surface S of the body is the graph of an equation $H(x_1, x_2, x_3) = 0$, where H is differentiable. For us, a generalized motion of S is a diffeomorphism $F: R^3 \to R^3$. A generalized motion F transforms the graph S of the equation $H(x_1, x_2, x_3) = 0$ into the graph S' of the equation $H'(x_1', x_2', x_3') = 0$, where $H = H' \circ F$. For simplicity, we consider only a single diffeomorphism throughout the remainder of this chapter. (A 1-parameter family of diffeomorphisms of two bodies can be viewed as a sequence of single diffeomorphisms of intermediate bodies.)

3. THE INFINITESIMAL APPROACH

In this section, we discuss an approach to recovery of a generalized motion of an object that is based on the study of the local-surface geometry of the object. This approach is concerned with determining the linear approximation (the Jacobian matrix) of the generalized motion. The image transformation between two images is recovered by point correspondences and least squares. The Jacobian of the image transformation (its linear approximation) is then coupled with the Jacobian of orthographic or planar perspective projection to recover the Jacobian of the generalized motion. In general, a generalized motion cannot be uniquely recovered from an image transformation. To obtain an essentially unique solution in closed form, we restrict our attention to a class of isometric generalized motions (diffeomorphisms of R^3 which are isometric on the body surface). This class includes rigid motions and bendings, as well as locally rigid motions and bendings, but not shearing.

3.1   Assumptions

We let $\pi: R^3 \to R^2$ denote either orthographic projection

$$\pi(x_1, x_2, x_3) = (x_1, x_2)$$

or planar perspective projection

$$\pi(x_1, x_2, x_3) = (x_1/x_3, x_2/x_3)$$

and we let I, respectively I', denote the image of S, respectively, S' under π. Restricted to a visible surface, π is a one-to-one differentiable transformation whose Jacobian matrix $d\pi$ has rank 2.

If F is a generalized motion from S to S', and f is the corresponding image transformation, then as long as $P(x_1, x_2, x_3)$ and the image $P'(x_1', x_2', x_3')$ of P under F are visible, we have the following commutative diagram

$$
\begin{array}{ccc}
(x_1, x_2, x_3) & \xrightarrow{\ F\ } & (x_1', x_2', x_3') \\
{\scriptstyle \pi}\downarrow & & \downarrow{\scriptstyle \pi} \\
(X_1, X_2) & \xrightarrow{\ f\ } & (X_1', X_2').
\end{array}
$$

That is, $\pi \circ F = f \circ \pi$. We assume that the image of $P(p_1, p_2, p_3)$ under π is $Q(q_1, q_2)$, that the image of P under F is $P'(p_1', p_2', p_3')$, and that the image of Q under f (or the image of P' under π) is $Q'(q_1', q_2')$.

If dF and df denote the Jacobian matrices of F and f, respectively,

$$
dF = \begin{pmatrix} \partial F_1/\partial x_1 & \partial F_1/\partial x_2 & \partial F_1/\partial x_3 \\ \partial F_2/\partial x_1 & \partial F_2/\partial x_2 & \partial F_2/\partial x_3 \\ \partial F_3/\partial x_1 & \partial F_3/\partial x_2 & \partial F_3/\partial x_3 \end{pmatrix} \quad \text{and} \quad df = \begin{pmatrix} \partial f_1/\partial X_1 & \partial f_1/\partial X_2 \\ \partial f_2/\partial X_1 & \partial f_2/\partial X_2 \end{pmatrix}
$$

then the above commutative diagram induces another commutative diagram $d\pi * dF = df * d\pi$ on tangent vector spaces; that is, $(d\pi * dF)\mathbf{v} = (df * d\pi)\mathbf{v}$ for all tangent vectors $\mathbf{v}$ to S at P.

We assume that we are given points $Q(q_1, q_2)$ in I and $Q'(q_1', q_2')$ in I' for which $Q' = f(Q)$; Q is the projection of a point $P(p_1, p_2, p_3)$ of S, and Q' is the projection at point $P'(p_1', p_2', p_3')$ of S'. Typically, we would know S, and hence also P, but S', and also P' would be unknown. We assume that we know the Jacobian $df_{|Q} = (a_{ij})$ of f at Q, and we compute the Jacobian

$$
dF_{|P} = A = (A_{ij}) = \begin{pmatrix} A_{11} & A_{12} & A_{13} \\ A_{21} & A_{22} & A_{23} \\ A_{31} & A_{32} & A_{33} \end{pmatrix}
$$

of F at P. This allows us to recover the first-order Taylor series approximation for F about P:

$$
F(x_1, x_2, x_3) \approx F(p_1, p_2, p_3) + (x_1 - p_1, x_2 - p_2, x_3 - p_3)A^T
$$
$$
= (p_1', p_2', p_3') + (x_1 - p_1, x_2 - p_2, x_3 - p_3)A^T.
$$

(From the dynamic point of view, what we are doing is assuming we know the original surface—initial conditions for the system of partial differential equations described in section 2.3—and incrementally solving the system. That is, we represent a solution to this system as a sequence of solutions: we know the first solution—the initial conditions—and we compute each successive solution from the previous one.)

We use the Lambertian intensity function $i(X_1, X_2)$, which is defined for points $Q = \pi(P)$, P on S, by

$$i(X_1, X_2) = \begin{cases} r(x_1, x_2, x_3)\langle \mathbf{n}_p, \mathbf{s} \rangle & \text{if } \langle \mathbf{n}_p, \mathbf{s} \rangle \geq 0 \\ 0 & \text{if } \langle \mathbf{n}_p, \mathbf{s} \rangle < 0. \end{cases}$$

Here $\langle \ , \ \rangle$ is the Euclidean inner product, $\mathbf{n}_p$ is the unit normal vector to S at P, $\mathbf{s}$ is the unit vector in the direction of the light source (which we assume is at infinity), and $r = r(x_1, x_2, x_3)$ is the reflectance of S at $P(x_1, x_2, x_3)$.

We assume that the part of S visible under orthographic projection to Π is the graph of an equation $x_3 = h(x_1, x_2)$, where $h: I \to R$. Although h is not, in general, continuous along curves of occlusion (in I), it is differentiable at all other points. If $\mathbf{u} = (1, 0, -\alpha)$ and $\mathbf{v} = (0, 1, -\beta)$ are tangent vectors to S at P ($\alpha = -h_1(P)$ and $\beta = -h_2(P)$), then $\mathbf{u} \times \mathbf{v} = (\alpha, \beta, 1)$ so

$$\mathbf{n}_p = (n_1, n_2, n_3) = \frac{\mathbf{u} \times \mathbf{v}}{|\mathbf{u} \times \mathbf{v}|}$$

$$= \left(\frac{\alpha}{(\alpha^2 + \beta^2 + 1)^{1/2}}, \frac{\beta}{(\alpha^2 + \beta^2 + 1)^{1/2}}, \frac{1}{(\alpha^2 + \beta^2 + 1)^{1/2}} \right).$$

Thus if $\boldsymbol{\sigma} = (\sigma_1, \sigma_2, \sigma_3)$, then

$$i(Q) = \frac{r\alpha\sigma_1 + r\beta\sigma_2 + r\sigma_3}{(\alpha^2 + \beta^2 + 1)^{1/2}}$$

so α, β, and r can be recovered if the intensities i are known for three light sources whose directions $\boldsymbol{\sigma}_1$, $\boldsymbol{\sigma}_2$, and $\boldsymbol{\sigma}_3$ are linearly independent.

Assume that three images of S are recorded using three light sources whose directions $\boldsymbol{\sigma}_1 = (\sigma_{11}, \sigma_{12}, \sigma_{13})$, $\boldsymbol{\sigma}_2 = (\sigma_{21}, \sigma_{22}, \sigma_{23})$, $\boldsymbol{\sigma}_3 = (\sigma_{31}, \sigma_{32}, \sigma_{33})$ are linearly independent (see Figure 12). The direction $\boldsymbol{\sigma}$ of

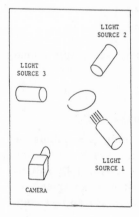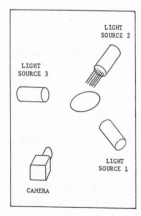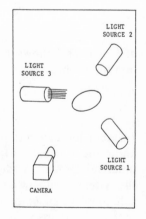

Figure 12.

one light source and the corresponding intensity $i(Q)$ at Q determine a (single) linear equation

$$(\sigma_1, \sigma_2, \sigma_3) \begin{pmatrix} r\alpha/(\alpha^2 + \beta^2 + 1)^{1/2} \\ r\beta/(\alpha^2 + \beta^2 + 1)^{1/2} \\ r/(\alpha^2 + \beta^2 + 1)^{1/2} \end{pmatrix} = i(Q)$$

in

$$r\alpha/(\alpha^2 + \beta^2 + 1)^{1/2}, r\beta/(\alpha^2 + \beta^2 + 1)^{1/2}, r/(\alpha^2 + \beta^2 + 1)^{1/2}.$$

If we are given three such equations

$$\begin{pmatrix} \sigma_{11} & \sigma_{12} & \sigma_{13} \\ \sigma_{21} & \sigma_{22} & \sigma_{23} \\ \sigma_{31} & \sigma_{32} & \sigma_{33} \end{pmatrix} \begin{pmatrix} r\alpha/(\alpha^2 + \beta^2 + 1)^{1/2} \\ r\beta/(\alpha^2 + \beta^2 + 1)^{1/2} \\ r/(\alpha^2 + \beta^2 + 1)^{1/2} \end{pmatrix} = \begin{pmatrix} i_1(Q) \\ i_2(Q) \\ i_3(Q) \end{pmatrix}$$

and the directions of the three light sources are linearly independent, then

$$\begin{pmatrix} r\alpha/(\alpha^2 + \beta^2 + 1)^{1/2} \\ r\beta/(\alpha^2 + \beta^2 + 1)^{1/2} \\ r/(\alpha^2 + \beta^2 + 1)^{1/2} \end{pmatrix} = \begin{pmatrix} \sigma_{11} & \sigma_{12} & \sigma_{13} \\ \sigma_{21} & \sigma_{22} & \sigma_{23} \\ \sigma_{31} & \sigma_{32} & \sigma_{33} \end{pmatrix}^{-1} \begin{pmatrix} i_1(Q) \\ i_2(Q) \\ i_3(Q) \end{pmatrix}.$$

Consequently we can find α, β, and r at P: if

$$\begin{pmatrix} r\alpha/(\alpha^2 + \beta^2 + 1)^{1/2} \\ r\beta/(\alpha^2 + \beta^2 + 1)^{1/2} \\ r/(\alpha^2 + \beta^2 + 1)^{1/2} \end{pmatrix} = \begin{pmatrix} k_1 \\ k_2 \\ k_3 \end{pmatrix}$$

then $\alpha = k_1/k_3$, $\beta = k_2/k_3$ and $r = (k_1^2 + k_2^2 + k_3^2)^{1/2}$. (In practice, for greater accuracy, we use more than three light sources whose directions are in general position, and least squares to find α, β, and r.)

3.2 Recovery of the Image Transformation

Assume that $f = (f_1, f_2)$. Given n points Q_i in I and n points Q'_i in I', $n \geqslant 6$, for which $f(Q_i) = Q'_i$, we can determine the coefficients of the second-order Taylor series approximations for f_1 and f_2 about $Q(q_1, q_2)$

$$f_1(X_1, X_2) \approx q'_1 + a_{11}(X_1 - q_1) + a_{12}(X_2 - q_2) + b_1(X_1 - q_1)^2 + c_1(X_1 - q_1) \times (X_2 - q_2) + d_1(X_2 - q_2)^2$$

$$f_2(X_1, X_2) \approx q'_2 + a_{21}(X_1 - q_1) + a_{22}(X_2 - q_2) + b_2(X_1 - q_1)^2 + c_2(X_1 - q_1) \times (X_2 - q_2) + d_2(X_2 - q_2)^2$$

and thus the Jacobian

$$df_{|Q} = \begin{pmatrix} a_{11} & a_{12} \\ a_{21} & a_{22} \end{pmatrix}$$

of f at Q, by applying least squares to the system of $2n$ linear equations in 12 unknowns that arises when we evaluate the second-order Taylor series approximation to f at Q_i.

We use a second-order approximation instead of a first-order approximation since f is nonlinear. To obtain a better approximation, we could use higher-order Taylor series approximations to f; but to account for the nonlinearity of f, we must use at least a second-order approximation.

3.3   Recovery of the Surface Transformation

Here, we show how the Jacobian of an isometric generalized motion for which

$$dF(\mathbf{u}) \times dF(\mathbf{v}) = dF(\mathbf{u} \times \mathbf{v})$$

can be recovered from images generated by orthographic projection and by planar perspective projection.

3.3.1   Orthographic Projection

We use the vision model illustrated in Figure 13. The direction of projection is along the x_3-axis of an $x_1 x_2 x_3$-coordinate system, and the viewplane is the plane Π whose equation is $x_3 = 1$. Orthographic projection π from $P(x_1, x_2, x_3)$ to $Q(X_1, X_2)$ is given by

$$\pi(x_1, x_2, x_3) = (x_1, x_2).$$

The Jacobian matrix $d\pi$ of π is given by

$$d\pi = \begin{pmatrix} \partial X_1/\partial x_1 & \partial X_1/\partial x_2 & \partial X_1/\partial x_3 \\ \partial X_2/\partial x_1 & \partial X_2/\partial x_2 & \partial X_2/\partial x_3 \end{pmatrix} = \begin{pmatrix} 1 & 0 & 0 \\ 0 & 1 & 0 \end{pmatrix}.$$

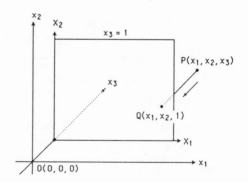

Figure 13.

The equation $(d\pi * dF)\mathbf{v} = (df * d\pi)\mathbf{v}$ for all tangent vectors $\mathbf{v}$ to S at P can be written

$$\begin{pmatrix} 1 & 0 & 0 \\ 0 & 1 & 0 \end{pmatrix} A \begin{pmatrix} 1 & 0 \\ 0 & 1 \\ -\alpha & -\beta \end{pmatrix} = \begin{pmatrix} a_{11} & a_{12} \\ a_{21} & a_{22} \end{pmatrix} \begin{pmatrix} 1 & 0 & 0 \\ 0 & 1 & 0 \end{pmatrix} \begin{pmatrix} 1 & 0 \\ 0 & 1 \\ -\alpha & -\beta \end{pmatrix}$$

or

$$\begin{pmatrix} 1 & 0 & 0 \\ 0 & 1 & 0 \end{pmatrix} A \begin{pmatrix} 1 & 0 \\ 0 & 1 \\ -\alpha & -\beta \end{pmatrix} = \begin{pmatrix} a_{11} & a_{12} \\ a_{21} & a_{22} \end{pmatrix}.$$

Now define the vector (a_{13}, a_{23}) by

$$\begin{pmatrix} a_{13} \\ a_{23} \end{pmatrix} = \begin{pmatrix} 1 & 0 & 0 \\ 0 & 1 & 0 \end{pmatrix} \begin{pmatrix} n'_1 \\ n'_2 \\ n'_3 \end{pmatrix} = \begin{pmatrix} 1 & 0 & 0 \\ 0 & 1 & 0 \end{pmatrix} A \begin{pmatrix} n_1 \\ n_2 \\ n_3 \end{pmatrix},$$

where

$$A \, \mathbf{n}_p = A \begin{pmatrix} n_1 \\ n_2 \\ n_3 \end{pmatrix} = \begin{pmatrix} n'_1 \\ n'_2 \\ n'_3 \end{pmatrix} = \mathbf{n}_{p'}.$$

Then

$$\begin{pmatrix} 1 & 0 & 0 \\ 0 & 1 & 0 \end{pmatrix} AM = \begin{pmatrix} a_{11} & a_{12} & a_{13} \\ a_{21} & a_{22} & a_{23} \end{pmatrix},$$

where

$$M = \begin{pmatrix} 1 & 0 & n_1 \\ 0 & 1 & n_2 \\ -\alpha & -\beta & n_3 \end{pmatrix}.$$

Thus

$$\begin{pmatrix} 1 & 0 & 0 \\ 0 & 1 & 0 \end{pmatrix} A = \begin{pmatrix} a_{11} & a_{12} & a_{13} \\ a_{21} & a_{22} & a_{23} \end{pmatrix} M^{-1}.$$

If F is an isometric generalized motion for which

$$dF(\mathbf{u}) \times dF(\mathbf{v}) = dF(\mathbf{u} \times \mathbf{v})$$

for all tangent vectors $\mathbf{u}$ and $\mathbf{v}$ to S at P (in other words, an isometric generalized motion that preserves normal vectors), then A is orthogonal (see [12]); that is $A^T = A^{-1}$. Thus

$$\begin{pmatrix} 1 & 0 & 0 \\ 0 & 1 & 0 \end{pmatrix} = \begin{pmatrix} a_{11} & a_{12} & a_{13} \\ a_{21} & a_{22} & a_{23} \end{pmatrix} M^{-1} A^T.$$

Transposing this equation, we obtain

$$A(M^T)^{-1}\begin{pmatrix} a_{11} & a_{21} \\ a_{12} & a_{22} \\ a_{13} & a_{23} \end{pmatrix} = \begin{pmatrix} 1 & 0 \\ 0 & 1 \\ 0 & 0 \end{pmatrix}.$$

Now define the vector (a_{31}, a_{32}, a_{33}) by

$$\begin{pmatrix} a_{31} \\ a_{32} \\ a_{33} \end{pmatrix} = M^T\left((M^T)^{-1}\begin{pmatrix} a_{11} \\ a_{12} \\ a_{13} \end{pmatrix} \times (N^T)^{-1}\begin{pmatrix} a_{21} \\ a_{22} \\ a_{23} \end{pmatrix}\right).$$

Since A is orthogonal (A represents a rotation of Euclidean three-space)

$$A(M^T)^{-1}\begin{pmatrix} a_{31} \\ a_{32} \\ a_{33} \end{pmatrix} = A\left((M^T)^{-1}\begin{pmatrix} a_{11} \\ a_{12} \\ a_{13} \end{pmatrix} \times (M^T)^{-1}\begin{pmatrix} a_{21} \\ a_{22} \\ a_{23} \end{pmatrix}\right)$$

$$= A(M^T)^{-1}\begin{pmatrix} a_{11} \\ a_{12} \\ a_{13} \end{pmatrix} \times A(M^T)^{-1}\begin{pmatrix} a_{21} \\ a_{22} \\ a_{23} \end{pmatrix} = \begin{pmatrix} 1 \\ 0 \\ 0 \end{pmatrix} \times \begin{pmatrix} 0 \\ 1 \\ 0 \end{pmatrix}$$

$$= \begin{pmatrix} 0 \\ 0 \\ 1 \end{pmatrix}.$$

Thus

$$A(M^T)^{-1}\begin{pmatrix} a_{11} & a_{21} & a_{31} \\ a_{12} & a_{22} & a_{32} \\ a_{13} & a_{23} & a_{33} \end{pmatrix} = \begin{pmatrix} 1 & 0 & 0 \\ 0 & 1 & 0 \\ 0 & 0 & 1 \end{pmatrix}$$

and consequently

$$A = \begin{pmatrix} a_{11} & a_{21} & a_{31} \\ a_{12} & a_{22} & a_{32} \\ a_{13} & a_{23} & a_{33} \end{pmatrix}^{-1} M^T = \begin{pmatrix} a_{11} & a_{21} & a_{31} \\ a_{12} & a_{22} & a_{32} \\ a_{13} & a_{23} & a_{33} \end{pmatrix}^{-1} \begin{pmatrix} 1 & 0 & -\alpha \\ 0 & 1 & -\beta \\ n_1 & n_2 & n_3 \end{pmatrix}.$$

Since all quantities in this expression for the Jacobian of F are either observable (from images of S) or computable from observable quantities, the Jacobian $A = dF|_P$ of dF at P is computable from observable quantities.

3.3.2 Planar Perspective Projection

In this section, we show how the Jacobian of an isometric generalized motion for which

$$dF(\mathbf{u}) \times dF(\mathbf{v}) = dF(\mathbf{u} \times \mathbf{v})$$

can be recovered from images generated by planar perspective projection.

We use the vision model illustrated in Figure 14. The viewer is at the origin $0(0, 0, 0)$, and the image plane Π is the plane whose equation is $x_3 = 1$; the X_1 and X_2 coordinate axes of Π are the lines of intersection of Π with the $x_1 x_3$- and $x_2 x_3$-coordinate planes. We let $P'(x'_1, x'_2, x'_3)$ be the image of $P(x_1, x_2, x_3)$ under F. Planar perspective projection π from $P(x_1, x_2, x_3)$ to $Q(X_1, X_2)$ is defined by intersecting the ray from 0 to P with Π; thus

$$\pi(x_1, x_2, x_3) = (X_1, X_2),$$

where $X_1 = x_1/x_3$ and $X_2 = x_2/x_3$. We let $Q'(X'_1, X'_2)$ be the image in Π of $P' = F(P)$ under π; thus $X'_1 = x'_1/x'_3$ and $X'_2 = x'_2/x'_3$. The Jacobian matrix $d\pi$ of π is given by

$$d\pi = \begin{pmatrix} \partial X_1/\partial x_1 & \partial X_1/\partial x_2 & \partial X_1/\partial x_3 \\ \partial X_2/\partial x_1 & \partial X_2/\partial x_2 & \partial X_2/\partial x_3 \end{pmatrix} = \begin{pmatrix} 1/x_3 & 0 & -x_1/x_3^2 \\ 0 & 1/x_3 & -x_2/x_3^2 \end{pmatrix}.$$

Observe that $d\pi$ varies with $P(x_1, x_2, x_3)$.

Now,

$$d\pi = \begin{pmatrix} 1/p_3 & 0 & -p_1/p_3^2 \\ 0 & 1/p_3 & -p_2/p_3^2 \end{pmatrix} \text{ at } P,$$

and

$$d\pi = \begin{pmatrix} 1/p'_3 & 0 & -p'_1/p'^2_3 \\ 0 & 1/p'_3 & -p'_2/p'^2_3 \end{pmatrix} \text{ at } P'$$

so that the equation $(d\pi * dF)v = (df * d\pi)v$ for all tangent vectors v to S at P, can be written

$$\begin{pmatrix} 1/p'_3 & 0 & -p'_1/p'^2_3 \\ 0 & 1/p'_3 & -p'_2/p'^2_3 \end{pmatrix} A \begin{pmatrix} 1 & 0 \\ 0 & 1 \\ -\alpha & -\beta \end{pmatrix}$$

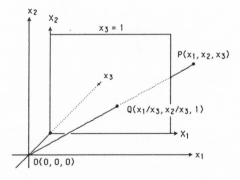

Figure 14.

$$= \begin{pmatrix} a_{11} & a_{12} \\ a_{21} & a_{22} \end{pmatrix} \begin{pmatrix} 1/p_3 & 0 & -p_1/p_3^2 \\ 0 & 1/p_3 & -p_2/p_3^2 \end{pmatrix} \begin{pmatrix} 1 & 0 \\ 0 & 1 \\ -\alpha & -\beta \end{pmatrix}$$

or

$$\frac{p_3}{p_3'} \begin{pmatrix} 1 & 0 & -q_1' \\ 0 & 1 & -q_2' \end{pmatrix} A \begin{pmatrix} 1 & 0 \\ 0 & 1 \\ -\alpha & -\beta \end{pmatrix} = \begin{pmatrix} b_{11} & b_{12} \\ b_{12} & b_{22} \end{pmatrix},$$

where

$$\begin{pmatrix} b_{11} & b_{12} \\ b_{21} & b_{22} \end{pmatrix} = \begin{pmatrix} a_{11} & a_{12} \\ a_{21} & a_{22} \end{pmatrix} \begin{pmatrix} 1 & 0 & -q_1 \\ 0 & 1 & -q_2 \end{pmatrix} \begin{pmatrix} 1 & 0 \\ 0 & 1 \\ -\alpha & -\beta \end{pmatrix}.$$

Since

$$A \mathbf{n}_p = A \begin{pmatrix} n_1 \\ n_2 \\ n_3 \end{pmatrix} = \begin{pmatrix} n_1' \\ n_2' \\ n_3' \end{pmatrix} = \mathbf{n}_{p'}$$

can be recovered from the intensities of images of S' associated to three light sources whose directions are linearly independent, we define b_{13} and b_{23} by

$$\frac{p_3}{p_3'} \begin{pmatrix} 1 & \dot{0} & -q_1' \\ 0 & 1 & -q_2' \end{pmatrix} \begin{pmatrix} n_1' \\ n_2' \\ n_3' \end{pmatrix} = \begin{pmatrix} b_{13} \\ b_{23} \end{pmatrix}.$$

Thus

$$\frac{p_3}{p_3'} \begin{pmatrix} 1 & 0 & -q_1' \\ 0 & 1 & -q_2' \end{pmatrix} AM = \frac{p_3}{p_3'} \begin{pmatrix} 1 & 0 & -q_1' \\ 0 & 1 & -q_2' \end{pmatrix} A \begin{pmatrix} 1 & 0 & n_1 \\ 0 & 1 & n_2 \\ -\alpha & -\beta & n_3 \end{pmatrix}$$

$$= \begin{pmatrix} b_{11} & b_{12} & b_{13} \\ b_{21} & b_{22} & b_{23} \end{pmatrix}.$$

Now

$$\frac{p_3}{p_3'} \begin{pmatrix} 1 & 0 & -q_1' \\ 0 & 1 & -q_2' \end{pmatrix} A = \begin{pmatrix} b_{11} & b_{12} & b_{13} \\ b_{21} & b_{22} & b_{23} \end{pmatrix} M^{-1}$$

and since $A^T = A^{-1}$,

$$\begin{pmatrix} b_{11} & b_{12} & b_{13} \\ b_{21} & b_{22} & b_{23} \end{pmatrix} M^{-1} A^T = \frac{p_3}{p_3'} \begin{pmatrix} 1 & 0 & -q_1' \\ 0 & 1 & -q_2' \end{pmatrix}.$$

Transposing this equation, we obtain

$$A(M^T)^{-1}\begin{pmatrix} b_{11} & b_{21} \\ b_{12} & b_{22} \\ b_{13} & b_{23} \end{pmatrix} = \frac{p_3}{p_3'}\begin{pmatrix} 1 & 0 \\ 0 & 1 \\ -q_1' & -q_2' \end{pmatrix}.$$

Now define b_{31}, b_{32}, and b_{33} by

$$\begin{pmatrix} b_{31} \\ b_{32} \\ b_{33} \end{pmatrix} = M^T\left((M^T)^{-1}\begin{pmatrix} b_{11} \\ b_{12} \\ b_{13} \end{pmatrix} \times (M^T)^{-1}\begin{pmatrix} b_{21} \\ b_{22} \\ b_{13} \end{pmatrix}\right).$$

Since A is orthogonal (A represents a rotation of Euclidean three-space),

$$A(M^T)^{-1}\begin{pmatrix} b_{31} \\ b_{32} \\ b_{33} \end{pmatrix} = A\left((M^T)^{-1}\begin{pmatrix} b_{11} \\ b_{12} \\ b_{13} \end{pmatrix} \times (M^T)^{-1}\begin{pmatrix} b_{21} \\ b_{22} \\ b_{23} \end{pmatrix}\right)$$

$$= A(M^T)^{-1}\begin{pmatrix} b_{11} \\ b_{12} \\ b_{13} \end{pmatrix} \times A(M^T)^{-1}\begin{pmatrix} b_{21} \\ b_{22} \\ b_{23} \end{pmatrix}$$

$$= \frac{p_3}{p_3'}\begin{pmatrix} 1 \\ 0 \\ -q_1' \end{pmatrix} \times \frac{p_3}{p_3'}\begin{pmatrix} 0 \\ 1 \\ -q_2' \end{pmatrix}$$

$$= \frac{p_3}{p_3'}\begin{pmatrix} (p_3/p_3')q_1' \\ (p_3/p_3')q_2' \\ (p_3/p_3') \end{pmatrix}.$$

Thus

$$A(M^T)^{-1}\begin{pmatrix} b_{11} & b_{21} & b_{31} \\ b_{12} & b_{22} & b_{32} \\ b_{13} & b_{23} & b_{33} \end{pmatrix} = \frac{p_3}{p_3'}\begin{pmatrix} 1 & 0 & (p_3/p_3')q_1' \\ 0 & 1 & (p_3/p_3')q_2' \\ -q_1' & -q_2' & (p_3/p_3') \end{pmatrix}.$$

Consequently

$$A = \frac{p_3}{p_3'}\begin{pmatrix} 1 & 0 & (p_3/p_3')q_1' \\ 0 & 1 & (p_3/p_3')q_2' \\ -q_1' & -q_2' & (p_3/p_3') \end{pmatrix}\begin{pmatrix} b_{11} & b_{21} & b_{31} \\ b_{12} & b_{22} & b_{32} \\ b_{13} & b_{23} & b_{33} \end{pmatrix}^{-1} M^T.$$

Observe that A is written in terms of p_3/p_3', which we can compute using any of the relations on A that arise since A is orthogonal. Even though we do not know p_1', p_2', or p_3', we do know $q_1' = p_1'/p_3'$ and $q_2' = p_2'/p_3'$. Thus, we can couple knowing p_3 and p_3/p_3' with knowing q_1' and q_2' to find p_1', p_2', and p_3'; if $p_3/p_3' = k$ then $p_3' = p_3/k$, $p_1' = p_3q_1'/k$, and $p_2' = p_3q_2'/k$. This allows us to recover the first-order Taylor series approximation for F about P:

$$F(x_1, x_2, x_3) \approx F(p_1, p_2, p_3) + (x_1 - p_1, x_2 - p_2, x_3 - p_3)A^T$$
$$= (p_1', p_2', p_3') + (x_1 - p_1, x_2 - p_2, x_3 - p_3)A^T.$$

4. THE GLOBAL APPROACH

In this section, we consider the complete determination of a generalized motion given images of before and after the generalized motion. To illustrate this approach, we show how projective geometry can be used to recover generalized motion parameters from point-pair correspondences in images. For simplicity, we restrict attention to affine motions—motions whose constant component represents an arbitrary translation, whose linear component represents an arbitrary (nonsingular) linear transformation, and that has no higher-order components; this type of motion includes rigid motions as well as shearings. This approach can be extended to transformations that contain arbitrarily higher-order terms. Just as with the infinitesimal approach, unique solutions in closed form can only be obtained for rigid motions and other special transformations.

4.1 Assumptions

As indicated in section 2.4, a diffeomorphism F from a surface S to a surface S' is a map $F: S \to S'$ which can be extended to a diffeomorphism $F: U \to U'$ of R^3, where U is an open set containing S and U' is an open set containing S'. A diffeomorphism $F: U \to U'$ may be written

$$x_1' = F_1(x_1, x_2, x_3), x_2' = F_2(x_1, x_2, x_3), x_3' = F_3(x_1, x_2, x_3),$$

where $F_1, F_2,$ and F_3 are differentiable. If $F_1, F_2,$ and F_3 are analytic (that is, if they have convergent power series expansions), they can be expanded into power series and approximated by polynomials in $x_1, x_2,$ and x_3.

One global approach to recovery of a generalized motion $F: S \to S'$ is to recover power series expansions of $F_1, F_2,$ and F_3 given point-pair correspondences in images. Here we present an efficient algorithm for determining the first order affine approximation

$$x_1' = h + m_{11}x_1 + m_{12}x_2 + m_{13}x_3$$
$$x_2' = k + m_{21}x_1 + m_{22}x_2 + m_{23}x_3$$
$$x_3' = l + m_{31}x_1 + m_{32}x_2 + m_{33}x_3$$

of a generalized motion $F: S \to S'$.

The surfaces S and S' may be replaced by any two-point sets $\mathscr{S}$ and $\mathscr{S}'$ which have no local geometric structure. In [20] and other related works, algorithms are developed for recovery of rigid motions of arbitrary point sets given images before and after the rigid motion. We extend these results by considering transformations of the form

$$x_1' = F_1(x_1, x_2, x_3),\ x_2' = F_2(x_1, x_2, x_3),\ x_3' = F_3(x_1, x_2, x_3),$$

where F_1, F_2, and F_3 are polynomials in x_1, x_2, and x_3.

Instead of working with the commutative diagram $(d\pi * dF)v = (df * d\pi)v$, for all tangent vectors v to S at a point P, we use the commutative diagram $(\pi \circ F)P = (f \circ \pi)P$

$$
\begin{array}{ccc}
(x_1, x_2, x_3) & \xrightarrow{\ F\ } & (x_1', x_2', x_3') \\
\ \downarrow{\scriptstyle \pi} & & \ \downarrow{\scriptstyle \pi} \\
(X_1, X_2) & \xrightarrow{\ f\ } & (X_1', X_2'),
\end{array}
$$

where $P(x_1, x_2, x_3)$ is any point in $\mathscr{S}$.

4.2   The Affine Case

We use both Cartesian and homogeneous coordinates in R^2 and R^3. The Cartesian coordinates of a point P in R^n are denoted by curved brackets $(x_1, \ldots, x_n)$, and the homogeneous coordinates of P are denoted by square brackets $[x_1, \ldots, x_n, 1]$. We assume that the affine transformation $F: R^3 \to R^3$ is given by

$$
F\begin{pmatrix} a_1 \\ a_2 \\ a_3 \\ 1 \end{pmatrix} = \begin{bmatrix} \begin{pmatrix} m_{11} & m_{12} & m_{13} & h \\ m_{21} & m_{22} & m_{23} & k \\ m_{31} & m_{32} & m_{33} & l \\ 0 & 0 & 0 & 1 \end{pmatrix} \begin{pmatrix} a_1 \\ a_2 \\ a_3 \\ 1 \end{pmatrix} \end{bmatrix}.
$$

4.2.1   *Orthographic Projection*

If Π denotes the plane whose equation is $x_3 = 1$, then orthographic projection $\pi: R^3 \to \Pi$ is given by

$$
\pi\begin{pmatrix} a_1 \\ a_2 \\ a_3 \\ 1 \end{pmatrix} = \begin{bmatrix} \begin{pmatrix} 1 & 0 & 0 & 0 \\ 0 & 1 & 0 & 0 \\ 0 & 0 & 0 & 1 \end{pmatrix} \begin{pmatrix} a_1 \\ a_2 \\ a_3 \\ 1 \end{pmatrix} \end{bmatrix} = \begin{bmatrix} a_1 \\ a_2 \\ 1 \end{bmatrix}.
$$

Thus

$$
(\pi \circ F)\begin{pmatrix} a_1 \\ a_2 \\ a_3 \\ 1 \end{pmatrix} = \begin{bmatrix} \begin{pmatrix} m_{11} & m_{12} & m_{13} & h \\ m_{21} & m_{22} & m_{23} & k \\ 0 & 0 & 0 & 1 \end{pmatrix} \begin{pmatrix} a_1 \\ a_2 \\ a_3 \\ 1 \end{pmatrix} \end{bmatrix}.
$$

Now suppose that $(\pi \circ F)([a_1, a_2, a_3, 1]) = [B_1, B_2, 1]$. Then

$$\begin{pmatrix} m_{11} & m_{12} & m_{13} & h \\ m_{21} & m_{22} & m_{23} & k \\ 0 & 0 & 0 & 1 \end{pmatrix} \begin{pmatrix} a_1 \\ a_2 \\ a_3 \\ 1 \end{pmatrix} = b_3 \begin{pmatrix} B_1 \\ B_2 \\ 1 \end{pmatrix},$$

where $[B_1, B_2, 1] = [b_3(B_1, B_2, 1)]$. Equating third entries on the left- and right-hand sides of this equation, we find that $b_3 = 1$. Thus, we may rewrite this equation

$$\begin{pmatrix} m_{11} & m_{12} & m_{13} & h \\ m_{21} & m_{22} & m_{23} & k \\ 0 & 0 & 0 & 1 \end{pmatrix} \begin{pmatrix} a_1 \\ a_2 \\ a_3 \\ 1 \end{pmatrix} = \begin{pmatrix} B_1 \\ B_2 \\ 1 \end{pmatrix}$$

or

$$\begin{pmatrix} m_{11} & m_{12} & m_{13} & h \\ m_{21} & m_{22} & m_{23} & k \end{pmatrix} \begin{pmatrix} a_1 \\ a_2 \\ a_3 \\ 1 \end{pmatrix} = \begin{pmatrix} B_1 \\ B_2 \end{pmatrix}$$

or

$$\begin{pmatrix} m_{11} & m_{12} & m_{13} & h \\ m_{21} & m_{22} & m_{23} & k \\ 0 & 0 & 0 & 0 \end{pmatrix} \begin{pmatrix} a_1 \\ a_2 \\ a_3 \\ 1 \end{pmatrix} = (\mathbf{c}_1 \quad \mathbf{c}_2 \quad \mathbf{c}_3 \quad \mathbf{c}_4) \begin{pmatrix} a_1 \\ a_2 \\ a_3 \\ 1 \end{pmatrix} = \begin{pmatrix} B_1 \\ B_2 \\ 0 \end{pmatrix},$$

where $\mathbf{c}_1, \mathbf{c}_2, \mathbf{c}_3$, and $\mathbf{c}_4$ are column vectors.

If $(A_1, A_2) = (a_1, a_2)$ are the Cartesian coordinates of the orthographic projection onto Π of the point whose homogeneous coordinates are $[a_1, a_2, a_3, 1]$, then this equation becomes

$$\begin{pmatrix} m_{11} & m_{12} & m_{13} & h \\ m_{21} & m_{22} & m_{23} & k \\ 0 & 0 & 0 & 0 \end{pmatrix} \begin{pmatrix} A_1 \\ A_2 \\ a_3 \\ 1 \end{pmatrix} = (\mathbf{c}_1 \quad \mathbf{c}_2 \quad \mathbf{c}_3 \quad \mathbf{c}_4) \begin{pmatrix} A_1 \\ A_2 \\ a_3 \\ 1 \end{pmatrix} = \begin{pmatrix} B_1 \\ B_2 \\ 0 \end{pmatrix}$$

or

$$A_1\mathbf{c}_1 + A_2\mathbf{c}_2 + a_3\mathbf{c}_3 + \mathbf{c}_4 = (B_1, B_2, 0). \tag{1}$$

In practice, we know (A_1, A_2) for several points $P(a_1, a_2, a_3)$ in world space, and (B_1, B_2) for the corresponding points $F(P)$. Our goal is to deduce from this information the vectors $\mathbf{c}_1, \mathbf{c}_2, \mathbf{c}_3$, and $\mathbf{c}_4$ (or, even more ambitiously, the rows of the matrix representing F). Many things can be said about c_1, c_2, c_3, and c_4 on the basis of Eq. 1; this equation is more of a framework within which questions may be answered than an answer to all questions.

In general, for example, taking the cross product of both sides of Eq. (1) with c_3, we obtain the equation

$$A_1 c_1 \times c_3 + A_2 c_2 \times c_3 + c_4 \times c_3 = (B_1, B_2, 0) \times c_3.$$

Since c_1, c_2, c_3, c_4, and $(B_1, B_2, 0)$ are all vectors in the $x_1 x_2$-coordinate plane, each of the cross products in this equation is a multiple of $e_3 = (0, 0, 1)$, so we may rewrite this equation as

$$A_1 c_1 + A_2 c_2 + c_4 = B_1 m_{23} - B_2 m_{13}.$$

This is a homogeneous equation in the five unknowns $c_1 = c_1 \times c_3 \cdot e_3$, $c_2 = c_2 \times c_3 \cdot e_3$, $c_4 = c_4 \times c_3 \cdot e_3$, m_{13} and m_{23}. If we are given four independent point-pair correspondences in the images, we can use this equation to generate a system of four homogeneous linear equations in five unknowns which can be solved for c_1, c_2, c_4, m_{13} and m_{23}. Once we know $c_3 = (m_{13}, m_{23}, 0)$, we return to Eq. (1). If we are given six independent point-pair correspondences in the images, we can use this equation to generate a system of twelve inhomogeneous linear equations in twelve unknowns (six of these unknowns are the nonzero components of the vectors c_1, c_2, and c_4, and the other six of these unknowns are the a_3 values for the six world space points used to generate the system of equations) that can be solved for c_1, c_2, and c_4. In general, it is impossible to retrieve the third column of the 4×3 matrix representing F.

If we know that F is a rigid motion, we can obtain more information about the 4×3 matrix representing F. In this case, the matrix

$$\begin{pmatrix} m_{11} & m_{12} & m_{13} \\ m_{21} & m_{22} & m_{23} \\ m_{31} & m_{32} & m_{33} \end{pmatrix}$$

is orthogonal, so once we have determined the first and second columns, we can determine the third column since it is the cross product of the first two columns. (This technique requires that we use six independent point-pair correspondences in the images. Actually, however, we can obtain comparable results with fewer: Once four independent point-pair correspondences in the images have been used to determine $c_1 = c_1 \times c_3 \cdot e_3$, $c_2 = c_2 \times c_3 \cdot e_3$, $c_4 = c_4 \times c_3 \cdot e_3$, m_{13} and m_{23}, we can use orthogonality of this matrix to determine all other entries. Although arguments that are directed at determining the fewest point-pair correspondences in the images necessary to determine F are certainly of importance, it is, in general, practically more natural to use a large number of point-pair correspondences in the images and least squares to determine F.) In general, however, it is impossible to retrieve the translational component l.

4.2.2 Planar Perspective Projection

If Π denotes the plane whose equation is $x_3 = 1$, then planar perspective projection $\pi : R^3 \to \Pi$ is given by

$$\pi \begin{pmatrix} a_1 \\ a_2 \\ a_3 \\ 1 \end{pmatrix} = \begin{pmatrix} 1 & 0 & 0 & 0 \\ 0 & 1 & 0 & 0 \\ 0 & 0 & 1 & 0 \end{pmatrix} \begin{pmatrix} a_1 \\ a_2 \\ a_3 \\ 1 \end{pmatrix} = \begin{pmatrix} a_1 \\ a_2 \\ a_3 \end{pmatrix}.$$

Thus

$$(\pi \circ F) \begin{pmatrix} a_1 \\ a_2 \\ a_3 \\ 1 \end{pmatrix} = \left[\begin{pmatrix} m_{11} & m_{12} & m_{13} & h \\ m_{21} & m_{22} & m_{23} & k \\ m_{31} & m_{32} & m_{33} & l \end{pmatrix} \begin{pmatrix} a_1 \\ a_2 \\ a_3 \\ 1 \end{pmatrix} \right].$$

Now suppose that $(\pi \circ F)([a_1, a_2, a_3, 1]) = [B_1, B_2, 1]$. Then

$$\begin{pmatrix} m_{11} & m_{12} & m_{13} & h \\ m_{21} & m_{22} & m_{23} & k \\ m_{31} & m_{32} & m_{33} & l \end{pmatrix} \begin{pmatrix} a_1 \\ a_2 \\ a_3 \\ 1 \end{pmatrix} = (\mathbf{c}_1 \quad \mathbf{c}_2 \quad \mathbf{c}_3 \quad \mathbf{c}_4) \begin{pmatrix} a_1 \\ a_2 \\ a_3 \\ 1 \end{pmatrix} = b_3 \begin{pmatrix} B_1 \\ B_2 \\ 1 \end{pmatrix},$$

where $\mathbf{c}_1, \mathbf{c}_2, \mathbf{c}_3,$ and $\mathbf{c}_4$ are column vectors and $[B_1, B_2, 1] = [b_3(B_1, B_2, 1)]$. If $(A_1, A_2) = (a_1/a_3, a_2/a_3)$ are the Cartesian coordinates of the planar perspective projection onto Π of the point whose homogeneous coordinates are $[a_1, a_2, a_3, 1]$, and $\mathbf{B} = (B_1, B_2, 1)$, then we may rewrite this equation

$$(\mathbf{c}_1 \quad \mathbf{c}_2 \quad \mathbf{c}_3 \quad \mathbf{c}_4) \begin{pmatrix} a_3 A_1 \\ a_3 A_2 \\ a_3 \\ 1 \end{pmatrix} = b_3 \mathbf{B}$$

or

$$a_3 A_1 \mathbf{c}_1 + a_3 A_2 \mathbf{c}_2 + a_3 \mathbf{c}_3 + \mathbf{c}_4 = b_3 \mathbf{B}$$

or

$$A_1 \mathbf{c}_1 + A_2 \mathbf{c}_2 + \mathbf{c}_3 + (1/a_3)\mathbf{c}_4 = (b_3/a_3)\mathbf{B}. \qquad (2)$$

In practice, we again know (A_1, A_2) for several points $P(a_1, a_2, a_3)$ in world space, and (B_1, B_2) for the corresponding points $F(P)$. Our goal is to deduce from this information the vectors $\mathbf{c}_1, \mathbf{c}_2, \mathbf{c}_3,$ and $\mathbf{c}_4$ (or, even more ambitiously, the rows of the matrix representing F). Many things can be said about c_1, c_2, c_3, and c_4 on the basis of Eq. (2); this equation is, again, more of a framework within which questions may be answered than an answer to all questions.

For example, assume we know that $c_4 \neq 0$. Taking the cross product of both sides of Eq. (2) with c_4 we obtain

$$A_1 c_1 \times c_4 + A_2 c_2 \times c_4 + c_3 \times c_4 = (b_3/a_3)B \times c_4$$

and dotting both sides of this equation with B, we obtain (the scalar equation)

$$A_1 B \cdot c_1 \times c_4 + A_2 B \cdot c_2 \times c_4 + B \cdot c_3 \times c_4 = 0.$$

If we treat the vectors $v_1 = c_1 \times c_4$, $v_2 = c_2 \times c_4$, and $v_3 = c_3 \times c_4$ as unknown, this is a single homogeneous linear equation in nine unknowns (namely the components of v_1, v_2, and v_3). If we are given eight independent point-pair correspondences in the images, we can use this equation to generate a system of eight homogeneous linear equations in nine unknowns which can be solved for v_1, v_2, and v_3.

Having found v_1, v_2, and v_3, observe that since v_1 and v_2 are both perpendicular to c_4, $v_1 \times v_2$ has the same or opposite direction of c_4, so we can determine the direction of c_4; that is, $c_4 = cv$, where v is a known unit vector and c is an unknown constant. (If $v_1 \times v_2 = 0$, we can use $v_2 \times v_3$ to determine the direction of c_4; and if $v_1 \times v_2 = 0$ and $v_2 \times v_3 = 0$, then we can use $v_1 \times v_3$.) Thus we may rewrite the equations

$$c_1 \times c_4 = v_1, \qquad c_2 \times c_4 = v_2, \qquad c_3 \times c_4 = v_3$$

as

$$cc_1 \times v = v_1, \qquad cc_2 \times v = v_2, \qquad cc_3 \times v = v_3$$

or, letting $c' = 1/c$,

$$c_1 \times v = c'v_1, \qquad c_2 \times v = c'v_2, \qquad c_3 \times v = c'v_3,$$

where v_1, v_2, v_3, and v are known, and where c_1, c_2, c_3, and c are unknown. Again, we have a homogeneous, linear system of nine equations in ten unknowns (namely, the components of c_1, c_2, and c_3, and c), which can be solved for c_1, c_1, c_3, and c'.

If we know that $c_4 = 0$, then, taking the cross product of both sides of Eq. 2 with B, we find

$$A_1 B \times c_1 + A_2 B \times c_2 + B \times c_3 = 0.$$

This equation represents three real homogeneous linear equations in nine unknowns (namely, the components of c_1, c_2, and c_3). If we are given three independent point-pair correspondences in the images, we can use this equation to generate a system of eight homogeneous linear equations in nine unknowns that can be solved for c_1, c_2, and c_3.

5. A HYBRID APPROACH

Here we present an approach that is a fusion of the infinitesimal approach
and the global approach. This approach provides insight into the understanding of human perception. Using local shading analysis, correspondence
and motion analysis are treated in a unified fashion. The hybrid approach
is based on the spherical perspective model. The orthographic model is a
limit of spherical models as the viewer moves to infinity (the viewing sphere
remaining fixed), thus providing a unification of orthographic projection
and spherical perspective projection; there is no similar relationship between
orthographic projection and planar perspective projection. Motion analysis
using spherical perspective is a reasonable model for both computer and
human motion analysis.

5.1   Spherical Perspective Projection

A spherical coordinate surface S is a parametrized surface of the form

$$\mathbf{x}(\theta, \phi) = (\rho(\theta, \phi) \sin \phi \cos \theta, \rho(\theta, \phi) \sin \phi \sin \theta, \rho(\theta, \phi) \cos \phi),$$

where $\rho(\theta, \phi)$ is a nonzero, real-valued differentiable function.

We use the spherical-perspective vision model illustrated in Figure 15.
The viewer is located at the origin $0(0, 0, 0)$. The image sphere of the model
is the 2D unit sphere S^2. Spherical perspective projection π from a point
P on S to a point Q on S^2 is defined by intersecting the ray from 0 to P
with S^2; it follows that

$$\pi(\rho \sin \phi \cos \theta, \rho \sin \phi \sin \theta, \rho \cos \phi) = (\sin \phi \cos \theta, \sin \phi \sin \theta, \cos \phi).$$

Typically, image intensity is determined from a flat image; that is, from
an image obtained by projecting an object onto a flat recording surface

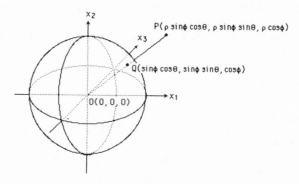

Figure 15.

(such as the film of a camera). The Lambertian intensity function of spherical perspective is related to the Lambertian intensity function of planar perspective (see Figure 16), by the (θ, ϕ) to (X_1, X_2) transformation

$$X_1 = k(p_2 \sin \phi \cos \theta - p_1 \sin \phi \sin \theta)$$

$$X_2 = k(-Fp_1p_3 \sin \phi \cos \theta - Fp_2p_3 \sin \phi \sin \theta$$
$$+ F\sqrt{p_1^2 + p_2^2} \cos \phi),$$

where F is focal length, $P(p_1, p_2, p_3)$ is the viewplane reference point of the image plane, and $k = F^{-2}(p_1 \sin \phi \cos \theta + p_2 \sin \phi \sin \theta + p_3 \cos \phi)^{-1}$. To determine the image intensity $i(\theta, \phi)$ from a flat image of S we first compute the X_1- and X_2-coordinates corresponding to (θ, ϕ), and then we compute i; that is, $i(\theta, \phi) = i(X_1(\theta, \phi), X_2(\theta, \phi))$.

We now use multiple light sources to determine simultaneously the depth value ρ as well as the variations $\rho_1 = \partial\rho/\partial\theta$ and $\rho_2 = \partial\rho/\partial\phi$ of ρ with respect to θ and ϕ. Our computation of ρ, ρ_1, and ρ_2 avoids numerical differentiation. (Numerical integration is subject to unstability in the presence of noise, so avoiding numerical integration is desirable. Our computation of ρ, ρ_1, and ρ_2 is by linear algebra, and thus practically quite useful.) Knowing ρ, ρ_1, and ρ_2 is enough to determine completely the geometric invariants of S (see sections 5.3 and 5.4). Computation of the geometric invariants of S also involves the computation of s, s_1, and s_2. Since s, s_1, and s_2 are functions only of θ and ϕ, however, they can be computed from images of S without differentiating; they can be computed simply by using the inverse of the (θ, ϕ) to (X_1, X_2) transformation described above.

For spherical perspective, the Lambertian intensity function

$$i(Q) = \frac{-\rho\rho_1 \sin \phi \langle s_1, \sigma \rangle - \rho\rho_2 csc\phi \langle s_2, \sigma \rangle + \rho^2 \sin \phi \langle s, \sigma \rangle}{(\rho_1^2 \sin^2\phi + \rho_2^2 + \rho^2 \sin^2 \phi)^{1/2}}$$

is a linear equation in the three unknowns

$$\rho\rho_1/(\rho_1^2 \sin^2 \phi + \rho_2^2 + \rho^2 \sin^2 \phi)^{1/2}$$

$$\rho\rho_2/(\rho_1^2 \sin^2 \phi + \rho_2^2 + \rho^2 \sin^2 \phi)^{1/2}$$

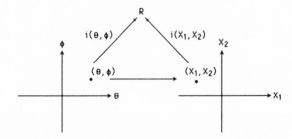

Figure 16.

$$\rho^2/(\rho_1^2 \sin^2 \phi + \rho_2^2 + \rho^2 \sin^2 \phi)^{1/2}.$$

Given the image intensities i_1, i_2, and i_3 of a surface under three light sources whose directions $\boldsymbol{\sigma}^1$, $\boldsymbol{\sigma}^2$, and $\boldsymbol{\sigma}^3$ are linearly independent, we have three such equations that can be solved for ρ, ρ_1, and ρ_2; we find that

$$\rho = \pm k_3(k_1^2 \sin^2 \phi + k_2^2 + \sin^2 \phi)^{1/2}, \qquad \rho_1 = \rho k_1/k_3, \quad \text{and} \quad \rho_2 = \rho k_2/k_3,$$

where

$$\begin{pmatrix} k_1 \\ k_2 \\ k_3 \end{pmatrix} = \begin{pmatrix} -\sin \phi \langle s_1, \boldsymbol{\sigma}_1 \rangle & -\csc \phi \langle s_2, \boldsymbol{\sigma}_1 \rangle & \sin \phi \langle s, \boldsymbol{\sigma}_1 \rangle \\ -\sin \phi \langle s_1, \boldsymbol{\sigma}_2 \rangle & -\csc \phi \langle s_2, \boldsymbol{\sigma}_2 \rangle & \sin \phi \langle s, \boldsymbol{\sigma}_2 \rangle \\ -\sin \phi \langle s_1, \boldsymbol{\sigma}_3 \rangle & -\csc \phi \langle s_2, \boldsymbol{\sigma}_3 \rangle & \sin \phi \langle s, \boldsymbol{\sigma}_3 \rangle \end{pmatrix}^{-1} \begin{pmatrix} i_1(Q) \\ i_2(Q) \\ i_3(Q) \end{pmatrix}.$$

(Using spherical coordinates in R^3, $(\pi \circ x)(\theta, \phi) = (\theta, \phi)$, so we can again compute $i_1(Q)$, $i_2(Q)$, and $i_3(Q)$.)

5.2   Limitations of Planar Perspective Projection

We now describe some of the limitations of planar perspective projection in the context of human vision. Although our objective is to describe 2D surfaces in 3D space, we draw analogies to the description of 1D curves in 2D space in this section to simplify our exposition.

First, planar perspective projection does not model human vision, although spherical perspective projection does. To illustrate this, consider the sequence of planar-perspective images of a cube as the cube is translated parallel to the viewplane away from the observer illustrated in Figure 17(a). Note the distortion that occurs as the cube moves farther and farther away

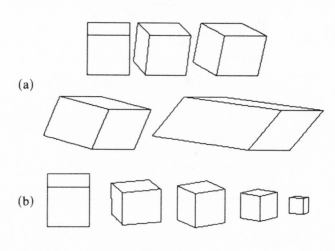

Figure 17.

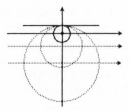

Figure 18.

from the observer. With human vision, objects do not become distorted like this as they move away from an observer. Figure 17(b), on the other hand, is a corresponding sequence of spherical perspective images of the same cube. Note the lack of distortion as the cube moves farther and farther away from the observer.

Second, orthographic projection is the limit of spherical perspective projection just as viewing distant objects is the limit of viewing nearby objects for humans (see Figure 18), but there is no comparable relationship between orthographic projection and planar perspective projection.

Third, although Monge surfaces are the correct type of surfaces to use in the study of orthographic projection, the correct type of surfaces to use in the study of perspective projection are spherical coordinate surfaces, not Monge surfaces. This is because there is, in general, no natural relationship between Monge surfaces and perspective projection, but a natural relationship between spherical coordinate surfaces and perspective projection. In a situation such as the one illustrated in Figure 19(a), for example, part of the Monge surface is not visible under perspective projection to an observer at the origin. In a situation such as the one illustrated in Figure 19(b), on the other hand, the surface visible to an observer at the origin under perspective projection is not a Monge surface (a vertical line intersects the graph of a function in at most one point).

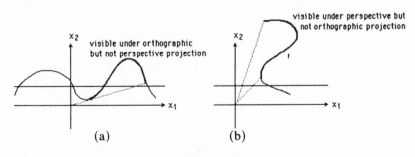

Figure 19.

This is just the first of a number of artificial and unnatural problems that arise in the study of perspective using planar perspective projection. Another problem is illustrated in Figure 20: although P is visible, any Monge patch describing S will fail to be differentiable at P; indeed, computation of the normal vector to S at P must avoid the Monge patch description of S. (A normal vector to the graph of a differentiable function $x_3 = h(x_1, x_2)$ at an arbitrary point is given by

$$(-\partial h/\partial x_1, -\partial h/\partial x_2, 1)$$

and since the third component of this vector is always 1, a normal vector can never be parallel to the $x_1 x_2$-coordinate plane.)

Fourth, we will later see that if we know the reflectance of a surface then we can completely determine the geometry of the surface given images of the surface generated from two different light sources. Since using images of the surface generated from two different light sources is equivalent to stereoscopic vision, this effectively means that the spherical perspective vision model can accomplish what human vision can accomplish. On the other hand, we will also later see that we cannot completely determine the geometry of a surface using images of the surface generated from multiple light sources and the planar perspective model.

Finally, if we study the relationship between generalized motions of a surface and changes in images of the surface using the planar perspective model, then there are three maps that must be considered [see Figure 21(a)]: the motion $F: S \to S'$ of the surface, the change $f_I: I \to I'$ in the images of the surface, and the motion $f_U: U \to U'$ of the domains of the parametrized surfaces that describe S and S'. Using the orthographic and spherical perspective models, there are only two maps to be considered [see Figures 21(b) and (c)]: the motion $F: S \to S'$ of the surface, and the motion $f_I: I \to I'$ in the images of the surface (which is now the same as the motion $f_U: U \to U'$ of the domains of the parametrized surfaces that describe S and S'). Our problem is simplified by using the orthographic and spherical perspective models since there is a natural inverse relationship between Monge surfaces

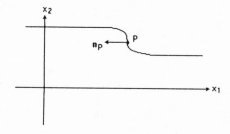

Figure 20.

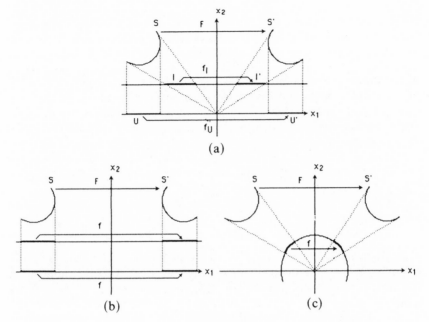

Figure 21.

and orthographic projection, and between spherical coordinate surfaces and spherical perspective.

5.3 The Local Geometric Invariants of Surfaces

The hybrid approach to the recovery of information about the motion of 3D bodies from information provided by 2D images is based on the identification of the local geometric invariants of a surface. Here, we present a brief discussion of these invariants.

Let $\mathbf{x}: U \to R^3$ be a simple surface, and $(u_1, u_2) \in U$. The inner product on $T_{\mathbf{x}(u_1, u_2)}R^3$ induces a quadratic form $\mathbf{I}(\mathbf{v}_1, \mathbf{v}_2)$, the first fundamental form, on $T_{(u_1, u_2)}\mathbf{x} \subseteq T_{\mathbf{x}(u_1, u_2)}R^3$. The first fundamental form is an inner product on $T_{(u_1, u_2)}\mathbf{x}$; it associates to each pair $(\mathbf{v}_1, \mathbf{v}_2)$ of vectors the scalar $\mathbf{I}(\mathbf{v}_1, \mathbf{v}_2)$. If $\mathbf{v}_1 = v_{11}\mathbf{x}_1 + v_{22}\mathbf{x}_2$ and $\mathbf{v}_2 = v_{21}\mathbf{x}_1 + v_{22}\mathbf{x}_2$, then

$$\mathbf{I}(\mathbf{v}_1, \mathbf{v}_2) = (v_{11}v_{12})(g_{ij})\begin{pmatrix} v_{21} \\ v_{22} \end{pmatrix} = (v_{11}v_{12})\begin{pmatrix} g_{11} & g_{12} \\ g_{21} & g_{22} \end{pmatrix}\begin{pmatrix} v_{21} \\ v_{22} \end{pmatrix},$$

where the symmetric matrix $(g_{ij}) = d\mathbf{x}^T * d\mathbf{x} = (\langle \mathbf{x}_i, \mathbf{x}_j \rangle)$. If two simple surfaces $\mathbf{x}: U \to R^3$ and $\mathbf{y}: V \to R^3$ are defined consistently and $\mathbf{x}(U) \cap \mathbf{y}(Y)$ is nonempty, then the (g_{ij}) matrices of $\mathbf{x}$ and $\mathbf{y}$ are defined consistently at corresponding points of U and V: if

$$f = \mathbf{y}^{-1} \circ \mathbf{x}: \mathbf{x}^{-1}(\mathbf{x}(U) \cap \mathbf{y}(Y)) \to \mathbf{y}^{-1}(\mathbf{x}(U) \cap \mathbf{y}(Y))$$

then

$$(g_{ij})_y = df^T * (g_{ij})_x * df.$$

Because of the way the (g_{ij}) matrices transform, the (g_{ij}) matrices depend on the parametrization with respect to which they are computed; hence they are not (component by component) surface invariants themselves. From the (g_{ij}) matrices, however, surface invariants (quantities that do not depend on a given parametrization, but rather only on the surface geometry) can be computed.

The second fundamental form $\mathbf{II}(\mathbf{v}_1, \mathbf{v}_2)$ of $\mathbf{x}: U \to R^3$ associates to each pair $(\mathbf{v}_1, \mathbf{v}_2)$ of vectors the scalar $\mathbf{II}(\mathbf{v}_1, \mathbf{v}_2)$. If $\mathbf{v}_1 = v_{11}\mathbf{x}_1 + v_{12}\mathbf{x}_2$ and $\mathbf{v}_2 = v_{21}\mathbf{x}_1 + v_{22}\mathbf{x}_2$, then

$$\mathbf{II}(\mathbf{v}_1, \mathbf{v}_2) = (v_{11}v_{12})(L_{ij}) \begin{pmatrix} v_{21} \\ v_{22} \end{pmatrix} = (v_{11}v_{12}) \begin{pmatrix} L_{11} & L_{12} \\ L_{21} & L_{22} \end{pmatrix} \begin{pmatrix} v_{21} \\ v_{22} \end{pmatrix},$$

where the symmetric matrix $(L_{ij}) = -d\mathbf{n}^T * d\mathbf{x}$. If two simple surfaces $\mathbf{x}: U \to R^3$ and $\mathbf{y}: Y \to R^3$ are defined consistently and $\mathbf{x}(U) \cap \mathbf{y}(Y)$ is nonempty, then the (L_{ij}) mtrices of $\mathbf{x}$ and $\mathbf{y}$ are defined consistently at corresponding points of U and Y: if

$$f = \mathbf{y}^{-1} \circ \mathbf{x}: \mathbf{x}^{-1}(\mathbf{x}(U) \cap \mathbf{y}(Y)) \to \mathbf{y}^{-1}(\mathbf{x}(U) \cap \mathbf{y}(Y))$$

then

$$(L_{ij})_y = df^T * (L_{ij})_x * df.$$

Again, because of the way the (L_{ij}) matrices transform, the (L_{ij}) matrices depend on the parametrization with respect to which they are computed; hence they are not (component by component) surface invariants themselves. From the (L_{ij}) matrices, however, surface invariants can be computed.

If we think of using U as a geographic map of $\mathbf{x}(U) \subseteq R^3$, then we can think of (L_{ij}) as information we can use when looking at U to tell us about the curvature of $\mathbf{x}(U)$: For example, for each $\mathbf{v}$ in the unit circle

$$\{\mathbf{v} \in T_{(u_1, u_2)}\mathbf{x} | \mathbf{I}(\mathbf{v}, \mathbf{v}) = 1\}$$

in $T_{(u_1, u_2)}\mathbf{x}$, $k(\mathbf{v}) = \mathbf{II}(\mathbf{v}, \mathbf{v})$ represents the curvature of the curve of intersection of $\mathbf{x}(U)$ and the plane passing through $\mathbf{x}(u_1, u_2)$ that is perpendicular to $T_{(u_1, u_2)}\mathbf{x}$ and that contains $\mathbf{v}$ (see Figure 22); $k(\mathbf{v})$ is the sectional curvature of $\mathbf{x}(U)$ at $\mathbf{x}(u_1, u_2)$ in the direction of $\mathbf{v}$. A vector $\mathbf{v}_0$ is a principal direction if $\mathbf{v}_0$ is a critical point of $k(\mathbf{v})$, and if $\mathbf{v}_0$ is a principal direction then $k(\mathbf{v}_0)$ is a principal curvature of $\mathbf{x}(U)$ at $\mathbf{x}(u_1, u_2)$. If $\mathbf{v}_0$ is a principal direction, then so is $-\mathbf{v}_0$. There are (up to a $\pm$ sign) exactly two mutually perpendicular principal directions (the directions in which $k(\mathbf{v})$ takes on its maximum and minimum values, k_1 and k_2), unless $\mathbf{II} = k\mathbf{I}$, in which case every direction is a principal direction ($\mathbf{x}(u_1, u_2)$ is an umbilic point).

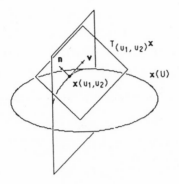

Figure 22.

Let $(L_i^j) = (L_{ij})(g_{ij})^{-1}$. The principal curvatures are the eigenvalues of (L_i^j), and the corresponding (unit) eigenvectors $\mathbf{v}_1$ and $\mathbf{v}_2$ (in $T_{(u_1, u_2)}\mathbf{x}$) are the principal directions of $\mathbf{x}$ at (u_1, u_2). Further, the determinant of (L_i^j) is the Gaussian curvature

$$K = \det(L_i^j) = \frac{\det(L_{ij})}{\det(g_{ij})} = k_1 k_2$$

of $\mathbf{x}(U)$ at $\mathbf{x}(u_1, u_2)$, and half the trace of (L_i^j) is the mean curvature

$$H = \tfrac{1}{2}\operatorname{trace}(L_i^j) = \tfrac{1}{2}(k_1 + k_2)$$

of $\mathbf{x}(U)$ at $\mathbf{x}(u_1, u_2)$.

A geometric invariant of a surface S is any quantity that only depends on S, and not on the way in which S is parametrized. The geometric invariants of S include the principal directions and principal curvatures, and the Gaussian and mean curvatures.

5.4 Computation of the Local Geometric Invariants of a Spherical Surface

In this section we show how to compute the geometric invariants of a spherical surface.

If

$$\mathbf{s} = (\sin \phi \cos \theta, \sin \phi \sin \theta, \cos \phi)$$

then

$$\mathbf{s}_1 = (\cos \phi \cos \theta, \cos \phi \sin \theta, -\sin \phi)$$

and

$$\mathbf{s}_2 = (-\sin \phi \sin \theta, \sin \phi \cos \theta, 0).$$

Thus

$$\langle \mathbf{s}, \mathbf{s} \rangle = 1 \qquad \langle \mathbf{s}_1, \mathbf{s}_1 \rangle = 1 \qquad \langle \mathbf{s}_2, \mathbf{s}_2 \rangle = \sin^2 \phi$$
$$\langle \mathbf{s}, \mathbf{s}_1 \rangle = 0 \qquad \langle \mathbf{s}, \mathbf{s}_2 \rangle = 0 \qquad \langle \mathbf{s}_1, \mathbf{s}_2 \rangle = 0$$
$$\mathbf{s} \times \mathbf{s}_1 = \csc \phi \mathbf{s}_2 \quad \mathbf{s}_1 \times \mathbf{s}_2 = \sin \phi \mathbf{s} \quad \mathbf{s}_2 \times \mathbf{s} = \sin \phi \mathbf{s}_1.$$

To compute the first fundamental form of $\mathbf{x}$, observe that

$$\langle \mathbf{x}_1, \mathbf{x}_1 \rangle = \langle \rho_1 \mathbf{s} + \rho \mathbf{s}_1, \rho_1 \mathbf{s} + \rho \mathbf{s}_1 \rangle = \rho_1^2 + \rho^2$$

$$\langle \mathbf{x}_1, \mathbf{x}_2 \rangle = \langle \rho_1 \mathbf{s} + \rho \mathbf{s}_1, \rho_2 \mathbf{s} + \rho \mathbf{s}_2 \rangle = \rho_1 \rho_2$$

$$\langle \mathbf{x}_2, \mathbf{x}_2 \rangle = \langle \rho_2 \mathbf{s} + \rho \mathbf{s}_2, \rho_2 \mathbf{s} + \rho \mathbf{s}_2 \rangle = \rho_2^2 + \rho^2 \sin^2 \phi.$$

Thus

$$(g_{ij}) = \begin{pmatrix} \rho_1^2 + \rho^2 & \rho_1 \rho_2 \\ \rho_1 \rho_2 & \rho_2^2 + \rho^2 \sin^2 \phi \end{pmatrix}.$$

To compute the unit normal vector $\mathbf{n}$, observe that

$$\mathbf{x}_1 \times \mathbf{x}_2 = -\rho \rho_1 \sin \phi \mathbf{s}_1 - \rho \rho^2 \csc \phi \mathbf{s}_2 + \rho^2 \sin \phi \mathbf{s}$$

so that

$$\mathbf{n} = \frac{\mathbf{x}_1 \times \mathbf{x}_2}{|\mathbf{x}_1 \times \mathbf{x}_2|} = \frac{-\rho \rho_1 \sin \phi \mathbf{s}_1 - \rho \rho_2 \csc \phi \mathbf{s}_2 + \rho^2 \sin \phi \mathbf{s}}{(\rho_1^2 \sin^2 \phi + \rho_2^2 + \rho^2 \sin^2 \phi)^{1/2}}.$$

As indicated above, once we know $\mathbf{n}$, we can theoretically compute $(L_{ij}) = -d\mathbf{n}^T * d\mathbf{x}$. Practically, however, computation of $d\mathbf{n}$ involves the numerical differentiation of ρ, ρ_1, and ρ_2. Since this type of computation is unstable in the presence of noise, we use the following technique for determining $d\mathbf{n}$ to avoid numerical differentiation.

If the reflectance r of S is constant in a neighborhood of P, then for a single light source

$$i(Q) = r\langle \mathbf{n}_p, \boldsymbol{\sigma} \rangle$$

so that

$$di = r\langle d\mathbf{n}, \boldsymbol{\sigma} \rangle$$

or

$$(\partial i / \partial \theta \; \partial i / \partial \phi) = r(\sigma_1 \sigma_2 \sigma_3) * d\mathbf{n}.$$

Since the intensities i_1, i_2, and i_3 are known for three light sources $\boldsymbol{\sigma}_1$, $\boldsymbol{\sigma}_2$, and $\boldsymbol{\sigma}_3$, we obtain three such equations

$$\begin{pmatrix} \partial i_1 / \partial \theta & \partial i_1 / \partial \phi \\ \partial i_2 / \partial \theta & \partial i_2 / \partial \phi \\ \partial i_3 / \partial \theta & \partial i_3 / \partial \phi \end{pmatrix} = r \begin{pmatrix} \sigma_1^1 & \sigma_2^1 & \sigma_3^1 \\ \sigma_1^2 & \sigma_2^2 & \sigma_3^2 \\ \sigma_1^3 & \sigma_2^3 & \sigma_3^3 \end{pmatrix} d\mathbf{n}$$

that can be solved for **dn**

$$\mathbf{dn} = \frac{1}{r}\begin{pmatrix} \sigma_1^1 & \sigma_2^1 & \sigma_3^1 \\ \sigma_1^2 & \sigma_2^2 & \sigma_3^2 \\ \sigma_1^3 & \sigma_2^3 & \sigma_3^3 \end{pmatrix}^{-1}\begin{pmatrix} \partial i_1/\partial\theta & \partial i_1/\partial\phi \\ \partial i_2/\partial\theta & \partial i_2/\partial\phi \\ \partial i_3/\partial\theta & \partial i_3/\partial\phi \end{pmatrix}.$$

Since we can directly compute

$$\mathbf{dx} = (\rho_1\mathbf{s} + rs_1\rho_2\mathbf{s} + rs_2)$$

we can compute $(L_{ij}) = -\mathbf{dn}^T * \mathbf{dx}$, $(L_i^j) = (L_{ij})(g_{ij})^{-1}$, the principal directions and principal curvatures, the Gaussian and mean curvatures at any visible point P.

5.5 Motion Analysis and Correspondence

If a body undergoes a generalized motion F and we are given images of the body under multiple light sources before and after F as well as a correspondence between image points before and after F, then F can be approximated as follows: Using images before the motion and images after the motion, we first reconstruct the surface of the body before the motion and after the motion. Using the correspondence between points of the image, we then establish a correspondence between points of the surface. If

$$x_i' = \sum c_{ijkl}x_1^j x_2^k x_3^l$$

is a degree n polynomial approximation of F, then each correspondence between points of the surface determines three linear equations in c_{ijkl}. Given enough such equations (the precise number depends on n), the constants c_{ijkl} can be determined.

If F is an isometric generalized motion, then, since Gaussian curvature is invariant under isometric generalized motions (see [26]), we can use Gaussian curvature as a feature with which we establish a correspondence between image points. If F is a rigid motion, then we can use principal directions and principal curvatures, as well as Gaussian and mean curvatures, to establish a correspondence between image points. Since a rigid motion is a degree-one polynomial transformation, we can thus completely determine F from images of the body under multiple light sources before and after F.

This method for establishing image-point correspondence works, of course, only if the surface of the body is adequately nonregular. In a case of extreme regularity (when the surface is a plane or sphere, for example), no information can be obtained from the local surface geometry. In this case, other information (such as boundary contour information) must be used to establish correspondence.

6. SUMMARY

We have presented three different approaches to obtaining information about generalized motions of 3D objects given 2D image information—an infinitesimal approach, a global approach, and a hybrid approach.

With the infinitesimal approach, we assume that we are given multiple images of the object under either orthographic projection or planar perspective projection before and after the generalized motion, that image-point correspondences can be established, that we know the initial object, and that the isometric generalized motions preserve normal vectors (this includes rigid motions and bendings, as well as locally rigid motions and bendings, but not shearing). We can then determine the first-order Taylor series approximation of the generalized motion; we can completely determine a rigid motion. (We can also determine the geometric invariants of the surface after the generalized motion if the images were generated through orthographic projection, although we can determine only partial geometric information if the images were generated through planar perspective projection. See [26].)

With the global approach, we again assume that image-point correspondences can be established, but we make no further assumptions about the generalized motion (in particular, the generalized motion can involve shearing). If we are working with orthographic projections, we can obtain partial information about the first-order Taylor series approximation of the generalized motion. If we know that the transformation is a rigid motion we can obtain more information: in particular, we can completely determine the rotational component. In general, however, it is impossible to recover all information from images generated by orthographic projection. If we are working with perspective projections, we can completely determine the first-order Taylor series approximation of the generalized motion. This approach also applies to arbitrary-point sets in world space that are under a generalized motion; in this case, establishing image-point correspondences has the potential to be easier.

With the hybrid approach, we assume that we are given multiple images of the object under spherical perspective projection before and after the generalized motion. If image-point correspondences can be established, we can determine Taylor series approximations of arbitrary degree, of the generalized motion; we can completely determine a rigid motion. In addition, if the surface of the object is adequately nonregular and the generalized motion is either isometric or a rigid motion, we can use geometric features to help establish image-point correspondences: for an isometric generalized motion we use Gaussian curvature, and for a rigid motion we use principal directions and principal curvatures, Gaussian and mean curvatures.

ACKNOWLEDGMENT

The authors are grateful to Professor T. S. Huang for his assistance and constant encouragement.

REFERENCES

[1] Arfken, G. *Mathematical Methods for Physicists*, Third Edition, Academic Press, NY, 1985.

[2] Barnard, S., and W. B. Thompson. "Disparity Analysis of Images," *IEEE Transactions on Pattern Analy. and Machine Intelligence*, PAMI-2, 1980, pp. 333–340.

[3] Bruss, A. "Shape from Shading and Boundary Contour," Ph.D. Dissertation, Department of Electrical Engineering and Computer Science, Massachusetts Institute of Technology, 1981.

[4] Chen, S. "An Intelligent Computer Vision System," *International Journal of Intelligent Systems*, John Wiley & Sons, vol. 1, 1986, pp. 15–28.

[5] Chen, S. "A New Vision System and the Fourier Descriptor Method by Group Representation Theory," *Proceedings of the IEEE Computer Society Conference on Computer Vision and Pattern Recognition*, June 9–13, San Francisco, CA, 1985.

[6] Chen S. "Optical Flow Fields and Generalized Motions of Nonrigid Objects," *Applied Artificial Intelligence Laboratory Publications*, no. 2, December 1985.

[7] Chen, S. "Structure-from-Motion without the Rigidity Assumption," *Proceedings of The Third Workshop on Computer Vision: Representation and Control*, October 13–16, 1985, Bellaire, MI, pp. 105–112.

[8] Chen, S., and M. Penna. "An Algebraic Geometric Approach to Computer Vision," Technical Report, University of North Carolina, Charlotte, 1986.

[9] Chen, S., and M. Penna. "A Geometric Approach to Motion Analysis, *Proceedings of the Conference on Intelligent Systems and Machines*, 1986, Oakland University, Rochester, MI.

[10] Chen, S., and M. Penna. "Recognizing Deformations of Nonrigid Bodies," *Proceedings of the IEEE Computer Society Conference on Computer Vision and Pattern Recognition*, 1986, Miami, FL, pp. 452–455.

[11] Chen, S., and M. Penna. "Shape and Correspondence," *Proceedings of the SPIE— Advances in Intelligent Robotics Systems Symposium.* October 28–31, 1986, Cambridge, MA, pp. 115–119.

[12] Chen, S., and M. Penna. "Shape and Motion of Nonrigid Bodies," *Computer Vision, Graphics, and Image Processing*, 36 (1986), pp. 175–207.

[13] Chen, S., and M. Penna. "Spherical Analysis in Computer Vision and Image Understanding," Technical Report, University of North Carolina, Charlotte, 1987.

[14] do Carmo, M. "Differential Geometry of Curves and Surfaces," Englewood Cliffs, NJ, Prentice-Hall, 1976.

[15] Dreschler, L., and H. H. Nagel. "Volumetric Model and 3-D-Trajectory of a Moving Car Derived from Monocular TV-Frame Sequences of a Street Scene," *7th International Joint Conference of Artificial Intelligence, Vancouver, BC, Canada*, August 1981, pp. 692–697.

[16] Fennema, C. L., and W. B. Thompson. "Velocity Determination in Scenes Containing Several Moving Objects," *Computer Graphics and Image Processing*, 9 (1979), pp. 301–315.

[17] Gauss, K. F. "General Investigations of Curved Surfaces," tr. A. Hiltebertel and J. Morehead, Raven Press, Hewlett, NY, 1965.

[18] Horn, B. K. P. "Understanding Image Intensities," *Artificial Intelligence*, 8 (1977), pp. 201–231.

[19] Horn, B. K. P., and B. G. Schunck. "Determining Optical Flow," *Artificial Intelligence*, 17 (1981), pp. 185–204.

[20] Huang, T. S. "Determining Three-Dimensional Motion/Structure from Two Perspective Views," *Pattern Recognition and Image Processing Handbook*, edited by T. Y. Young and K. S. Fu, New York, Academic Press, 1986.

[21] Kanade, T., and J. R. Kender. "Mapping Image Properties into Shape Constraints: Skewer Symmetry and Affine-Transformable Patterns," *Proceedings of the IEEE Workshop on Picture Data Description and Management, NY*, August 1980, pp. 130–135.

[22] Lucas, B. D., and T. Kanade. "An Iterative Image Registration Technique with an Application to Stereo Vision," *7th International Joint Conference on Artificial Intelligence, Vancouver, BC, Canada*, August 1981, pp. 674–679.

[23] Nagel, H. H. "On the Derivation of 3-D Rigid Point Configurations from Image Sequences," *Proceedings of the IEEE Conference on Pattern Recognition and Imaging Processes, Dallas, TX*, August 1981, pp. 103–108.

[24] Penna, M. "Lecture Notes on Elementary Differential Geometry," mimeographed notes, IUPUI, 1984.

[25] Penna, M., and S. Chen. "Spherical analysis of optical flow," *Proceedings of the SPIE— Advances in Intelligent Robotics Systems Symposium*, Cambridge, MA, 1987.

[26] Penna, M, and S. Chen. "Shape-from-Shading Using Multiple Light Sources," *International Journal of Intelligent Systems*, 1 (1986).

[27] Penna, M., and R. Patterson. *Projective Geometry and its Applications to Computer Graphics*, Englewood Cliffs, NJ, Prentice-Hall, 1986.

[28] Pentland, A. "Local Shading Analysis," *IEEE Transactions on Pattern Anal. and Machine Intelligence*, PAMI-6, No. 2, March 1984, pp. 170–187.

[29] Roach, J. W., and J. K. Aggarwal. "Computer Tracking of Objects Moving in Space," *IEEE Transactions on Pattern Anal. and Machine Intelligence*, PAMI-1, 1979, pp. 127–135.

[30] Scipio, L. "Principles of Continua with Applications," John Wiley & Sons, Inc., NY, 1967.

[31] Slater, J., and N. Frank. *Mechanics*, New York, McGraw-Hill, 1947.

[32] Tsai, R. Y., and T. S. Huang. "Analysis of Three-Dimensional Time Varying Scene," *Proceedings of the SPIE—The International Society for Optical Engineering*, August 1982, pp. 309–320.

[33] Ullman, S. *The Interpretation of Visual Motion*, Cambridge, MA, MIT Press, 1979.

[34] Webb, J. A., and J. K. Aggarwal. "Shape and Correspondence," *Computer Vision, Graphics and Image Processing*, 21 (1983), pp. 145–160.

INDEX

221

Research Annuals in
COMPUTER SCIENCE AND
RELATED TOPICS